FOOD IN MEDIEVAL TIMES

Recent Titles in
Food through History

Food in Medieval Times

Melitta Weiss Adamson

Food through History

Greenwood Press
Westport, Connecticut • London

Library of Congress Cataloging-in-Publication Data

Adamson, Melitta Weiss.
  Food in medieval times / Melitta Weiss Adamson.
    p. cm.—(Food through history ISSN 1542–8087)
  Includes bibliographical references and index.
  ISBN 0–313–32147–7
  1. Cookery, Medieval. 2. Cookery—Europe—History. I. Title. II. Series.
  TX641.A33 2004
  641.3′0094′0902—dc22   2004014054

British Library Cataloging in Publication Data is available.

Copyright © 2004 by Melitta Weiss Adamson

Library of Congress Catalog Card Number: 2004014054
ISBN: 0–313–32147–7
ISSN: 1542–8087

First published in 2004

Greenwood Press, 88 Post Road West, Westport, CT 06881
An imprint of Greenwood Publishing Group, Inc.
www.greenwood.com

Printed in the United States of America

The paper used in this book complies with the
Permanent Paper Standard issued by the National
Information Standards Organization (Z39.48–1984).

10 9 8 7 6 5 4 3 2

CONTENTS

ACKNOWLEDGMENTS

Any book that covers a topic as broad as this depends on the work of more than just one person. First I must thank the generations of scholars who in endless hours unearthed, catalogued, deciphered, transcribed, edited, translated, and analyzed all the different sources, and brought to light a wealth of information, part of which found its way into the present volume. I must also thank my teachers and colleagues who over the years have supported me in my research on food and nutrition in the Middle Ages, Helmut Birkhan, Gundolf Keil, Constance Hieatt, Terence Scully, Trude Ehlert, Carole Lambert, Gerhard Jaritz, and many others. They patiently answered my many queries, shared with me published and unpublished material, and generously contributed their time and expertise to various collaborative efforts from which this book benefited greatly.

My thanks also go to the University of Western Ontario for fostering cross-disciplinary teaching and research, and for granting me a sabbatical in which to finish the book. Thanks too to all the libraries that helped me in my research and allowed me to work with some of their most prized possessions, the original medieval manuscripts. I am especially grateful to the Österreichische Nationalbibliothek in Vienna for permission to use illustrations from its famous manuscript collection in this book.

My sincere thanks go to Wendi Schnaufer at Greenwood Press for her enthusiasm, constructive feedback, and especially her patience while the work was in progress. It was a time of unexpected challenges in my life, and among those who helped me overcome them were my friends Susan, Cécile, Kathy, Angela, Laurence, Frank, Ina, and Jing. Thank you all.

Finally, I wish to thank my family, who put up with me during all those months when my mind was elsewhere. Special thanks go to my husband Alan, whose moral support and computer expertise were as invaluable as ever.

TIMELINE

541   The Roman-Byzantine world is in the grips of the Great (bubonic) Plague of Justinian that brings farming to a halt and causes famine in Europe, the Middle East, and Asia. It is to last for nearly 70 years.

550–650   A new, lightweight plow equipped with a coulter (knife blade) and pulled by eight oxen is invented by the Slavs. The new agriculture leads to a population explosion in northern and western Europe.

610   A new faith, to be called Islam, is preached secretly by the prophet Muhammad.

629   The sharia, a complex legal system, is recognized by Muslims. Pork, animals of prey, and intoxicating beverages are among the foodstuffs Muslims are forbidden to consume.

687   Venice begins its rise to power in the Mediterranean, and elects its first doge (person holding the chief office in the city-state of Venice).

700–800   Oriental spices are introduced by Arab merchants into Mediterranean markets.

711   Arabs and Berbers from North Africa invade the Iberian Peninsula and defeat the Visigoths. New methods in agriculture introduced by them include intensive irrigation, the use of animal droppings as fertilizers, im-

proved plows, and crop rotation. New foodstuffs introduced by the Arabs include rice, sugar, and saffron.

716   A shipment of cinnamon, cloves, and pepper arrives at the monastery of Corbie in Normandy, France.

732   Christian converts in Hesse, Germany, are forbidden by Pope Gregory II to eat horseflesh.

750   Famine is followed by plague on the Iberian Peninsula.

765   Three-field crop rotation system first mentioned in European sources. Instead of the traditional one in two fields lying fallow in a given year, it is now one in three, which means a substantial increase in agricultural production.

780   Three-field crop rotation is promoted by Charlemagne in his realm.

795   An export ban on grain is imposed by Charlemagne in the Frankish kingdom.

809   Cold weather results in poor harvests and famine in the domain of Charlemagne.

812   Anise, coriander, fennel, flax, fenugreek, and sage are among the plants to be grown on Charlemagne's farms.

827   North-African Arabs invade Sicily, and introduce the Persian plant spinach and many other foodstuffs to the island.

857   Thousands die in the Rhine Valley from ergotism, a disease caused by the consumption of rye bread made from grain infected with the ergot fungus. Symptoms include diarrhea, seizures, headaches, nausea, vomiting, hallucinations, mania, and psychosis.

915, 919   Crop failure causes a famine on the Iberian Peninsula that is ruled in the south by the Arabs, and in the north by Christian princes.

943   Some 40,000 people die of ergotism in Limoges, France.

961   The Arabs begin the production of the spice saffron on the Iberian Peninsula.

1000–1100   Europe suffers recurring famines while food production is gradually being increased thanks to innovations such

	as the iron plow with wheels that replaces the wooden plow in northern Europe.
1066	Among the effects of the Norman Conquest is the introduction of French food terminology into English. (Examples: pork, beef, and mutton, from French *porc, boeuf,* and *mouton.*)
1071	Two-pronged fork reaches Venice from the east via Byzantium.
1110	Les Halles, until the twentieth century the central food market of Paris, is established by Louis VI of France.
1123	Smithfield meat market, later the site of the famous Saint Bartholomew's Fair, is established in London.
1148	Sugar is brought back to Europe by crusaders returning from the Holy Land.
1176	Domestic rabbits are introduced to England from continental Europe.
1189	Crusader pub The Trip to Jerusalem is opened in Nottingham, England.
1191	On the Third Crusade Richard the Lion-Hearted of England defeats the Saracens under Sultan Saladin and is introduced to sorbet (the word derived from Arabic *charbet*).
1200–1300	The Balkans and Baltic Sea region supply much of Europe with cheap grain. Barley malt from the Baltic leads to a booming brewing industry in northern Germany and the Low Countries.
1204	Members of the Fourth Crusade bring damson plum trees from Damascus back to Europe. Citrus fruits, sugar, rice, and other foodstuffs used in Arab cookery are becoming part of European upper-class cuisine.
1241	The northern European trade organization known as the Hanseatic League is established in Germany.
1243	Famine in Germany, rat infestation across Europe.
1258	Germany and Italy suffer crop failures that lead to widespread famine and disease.
1265	Covent Garden Market established in London where monks initially sell surplus fruit and vegetables.

1266	Assize of Bread, a law regulating the quality, weight, and price of bread, and forcing bakers to mark their bread, is instituted in England.
1275–92	The Venetian merchant and explorer, Marco Polo, is in the employ of Kublai Khan, ruler of the Mongol Empire and future Emperor of China.
1280	Marco Polo arrives in the bustling city of Hangchow, China, whose sophisticated food culture he later records.
1284	Ravioli and other pasta dishes are on the menu of many Romans.
	Rats continue to plague Europeans by spreading disease and eating their food supplies.
1296	Marco Polo brings oriental foodstuffs and food ideas back to Venice.
ca. 1300	The first cookbook manuscripts in England are written in Anglo-Norman.
	The Hanseatic League, an alliance of trading cities in northern Europe and the Baltic, is well established; its fisheries improve the production of salt herring.
	The Montpellier, France, professor of medicine and alchemist Arnald de Villanova experiments with distillation and produces brandy.
1305	The Italian Petrus de Crescentiis writes an extensive book on farming, the first manual of this kind since Roman times.
1314	Wheat prices soar as Europe is in the grip of a famine that lasts several years.
1333	Beginnings of the Black Death in China.
1343	Genoese merchants returning from the Far East are attacked by Tartars infected with the plague, and subsequently introduce the disease to Constantinople, Venice, and other ports in the Mediterranean.
1347	The Black Death spreads to Cyprus.
1348	In April, Florence, Italy, falls victim to the plague, to be followed in the summer by much of France and England. Eventually between a third to half of Europe's population succumbs to the disease.

1349	Severe labor shortages and wage hikes across Europe as a result of the Black Death. Much arable land lies fallow or is turned into pastures because they are less labor-intensive.
ca. 1350	The oldest German cookbook, *Daz buoch von guoter spise* (The Book of Good Food), is written in Würzburg.
1364	Crop failure leads to famine and another plague epidemic in France.
1375	The French cookbook *Le Viandier* (The Provisioner) by Guillaume Tirel, called Taillevent, cook of King Charles V of France, is written.
1383	The Bavarian brewery Löwenbräu is founded in Munich.
1390	The English cookbook *The Forme of Cury* (The [Proper] Method of Cookery) with recipes from the kitchen of King Richard II of England is written.
ca. 1393	The French household manual and cookbook *Le Menagier de Paris* (The Householder of Paris) is compiled by a Parisian bourgeois.
1400	Durum wheat pasta is produced commercially in Italy. The population of Paris reaches 200,000, that of London 50,000, Cologne 30,000, and Lübeck and Nuremberg each 20,000.
1403	Near-complete monopoly held by the Hanseatic League on goods from northern Europe.
1418	Sugarcane from Sicily is first planted in Madeira by a Portuguese explorer.
1419	The City of London forbids by decree the blending of different wines.
1420	The cookbook *Du fait de cuisine* (On Cookery) by Chiquart, cook to the duke of Savoy, Amadeus VIII, is written.
	Grapevines from Crete are planted in Madeira. In time sweet Madeira wines will rival Spanish sherries.
1429	The London Pepperers' Guild is allowed by charter to sell spices, drugs, and dyes wholesale, or *en gros*, and is renamed the Grocers' Company.
1430	Sugarcane is refined on the Madeira islands.

1444	Increased efforts by Venice to find new spice routes to the Orient.
1453	End of the Byzantine Empire with the fall of Constantinople to the Ottoman Turks on May 29. The Middle Eastern beverage coffee reaches Constantinople via the Turks.
	End of the Hundred Years' War. The English lose nearly all their holdings in France, including the wine-growing region of Bordeaux.
1454	At a famous banquet given by Philippe le Bon of Burgundy, noblemen take the "vow of the pheasant" and swear to fight the Turks.
1468	Rice is planted in northern Italy.
1473	Venice takes control of Cyprus, an important sugar producer.
1475	The world's first printed cookbook, *De honesta voluptate et valetudine* (On Right Pleasure and Good Health) by Platina (Bartolomeo Sacchi), appears in Italy and is subsequently translated from Latin into Italian, French, and German.
	In Constantinople the first coffeehouse opens its doors.
1485	The first printed German cookbook, *Kuchenmeysterey* (Kitchen Masterey), appears in Nuremberg. It, too, is translated into other European languages, and in the next two centuries is reprinted numerous times.
1492	In an attempt to reach Asia, Spanish navigator Christopher Columbus lands by accident in the Bahamas. His discovery of the New World will lead to the introduction of many new foods to Europe, among them potatoes, peppers, maize, tomatoes, pineapples, allspice, cacao, and turkey.
1495	Growing orange trees in sheltered gardens, known as "orangeries," becomes the rage at European courts.
1497	The Venetian Giovanni Caboto, better known in North America as John Cabot, lands in Labrador, Canada, and reports of an abundance of codfish off the coast of Newfoundland.

1498   Portuguese navigator Vasco da Gama discovers a sea route to India and the Spice Islands of southeast Asia. In cutting out the Arab and Venetian spice dealers, the Portuguese manage to bring down the price of oriental spices such as pepper, cinnamon, and cloves, and control the spice trade for centuries to come.

1500   Headed for India, Portuguese explorer Pedro Álvares Cabral accidentally discovers Brazil and later continues his journey to India past the Cape of Good Hope, which is to become a favorite shipping route in the spice trade.

INTRODUCTION

Going back in time to the Middle Ages to find out what Europeans ate means going back to an age before our modern means of communication and transportation, and before the invention of all those handy appliances, the freezer, refrigerator, stove, and microwave, that make it possible for us today to buy, prepare, and preserve any foods our hearts desire from around the globe at any time. With the New World yet to be discovered then, it means going back to an age when the potato, tomato, corn, cacao, or the turkey were unknown to Europeans, and when the western edge of the world they knew was a place on Spain's Atlantic coast, aptly called *finis terrae,* or end of the earth. The period under investigation in this volume is the millennium between the Fall of Rome and the Renaissance, from approximately A.D. 500 to 1500. To study the food, gastronomy, and nutrition of a whole continent over a thousand years is a formidable task, made even more daunting by the fact that for much of the period and many of the regions of Europe we have relatively few sources.

Looking at medieval cookbooks may seem an obvious place to start such an undertaking, and yet nearly all the cookbooks that have survived are from the tail end of the period, from the fourteenth and fifteenth centuries, and they tell us little or nothing about the way food was prepared in the early Middle Ages. Furthermore, these cookbooks were compiled and copied by members of the educated elite, the clergy, nobility, and rich bourgeoisie, and are generally silent on the food of the lower classes, which made up the vast majority of medieval society. What the recipes do give us is some idea of the kinds of dishes that were prepared and presumably eaten, the names they were given, the ingredients that went into them, and the ways in which these ingredients were processed. But even in these areas they often withhold crucial pieces of information from us, such as quantities, measurements, and exact lists of seasonings, much to the frustration of modern hobby cooks trying to recreate these dishes. Not having the luxury of our medieval forebears, who knew what a dish was supposed to taste like because they had eaten it before, we are left to guess temperatures and cooking times, or how much of a given ingredient to add. When compared with the recipes published today, cookbook writing in the late Middle Ages was truly in its infancy. We must also keep in mind that thermometers were not yet invented, and clocks and scales were few and far between. Unless these old texts have meal plans or menus of regular meals or memorable feasts attached to them, with information on what monks and noblemen ate during the week, on special occasions, or in a particular season, recipe collections also tell us little about the context in which the dishes were consumed.

To paint as complete a picture of the medieval food culture as possible, we must consult a variety of other sources that have the potential of providing further pieces to the puzzle. Among the written sources that sometimes contain valuable information are literary texts, such as the legends surrounding King Arthur and the Knights of the Round Table, for instance, or religious texts, such as those outlining dietary restrictions, or elaborating on the sin of gluttony. Other sources that may hold some clues are historical records, among them chronicles, household, hospital, or municipal accounts, but also legal texts that relate to food in some way, as well as medical texts on nutrition. Together, all of these sources can contribute greatly to our knowledge of food customs during the period, but when studied in isolation each one has its limitations. Courtly literature often seems more concerned with banquets on festive occasions, and the fashion and manners displayed by the nobility, than with actual dishes or the food of the less privileged. Even chronicles should not be trusted completely. Many a chronicler has been shown to exaggerate, or to lift whole passages from another work. Account books, while they may contain fairly realistic lists of foodstuffs and their prices, do not normally tell us about the foodstuffs that were not purchased but instead came from the kitchen garden or were received as gifts, nor do they tell us how these foodstuffs were prepared. Like much of the religious and legal literature that dealt with food in the Middle Ages, medical texts were largely prescriptive, in other words, they gave people dietary or nutritional advice; but can we really be sure that the advice was followed all the time, or even some of the time?

In addition to these written sources and the information they contain, archeology can provide valuable data, especially regarding the type and quantity of food eaten in a certain area. What the remains of plants and bones cannot tell us, however, is when these foods were eaten, by whom, and in what form. Visual representations, such as drawings, paintings, tapestries, stained glass windows, and the like, together with other forms of material culture, such as furniture, kitchen equipment, and dinnerware, allow us to picture what a dish or a meal may have looked like. The present volume will draw on all these sources and more to give as comprehensive an account as possible of the role food played in medieval times.

One thing becomes abundantly clear from even just a cursory glance at these sources: we have substantially more information on the food of the medieval upper crust than the masses at the bottom of society. To be sure, there were some equalizing forces at work that the rich could not entirely escape, try as they might. Among them were limitations imposed by geography and climate, the seasons, natural disasters, diseases such as the bubonic plague, and the fasting laws that religions imposed on their believers. By the Middle Ages, cooked food was already the norm in all segments of society, but what foodstuffs went into a dish, and how it was prepared and eaten, depended to a large degree on one's station in life. More than today, food served as a status symbol then, and dietary transgressions were not just frowned upon, they were punishable by law. In often exact detail, so-called sumptuary laws spelled out what people of a certain class and income level were allowed to consume. Medicine did its share in maintaining social inequality by claiming that the dietary needs of manual laborers and those of the leisure class were completely different. To stay healthy peasants simply had to eat the coarse, rough food that just happened to be of the lowest price and social prestige, while the more delicate, rare, and costly foods were ideal for the dainty stomachs of the rich. And when it came to warding off disease, a two-tier health system also applied, with compound drugs made up of the most expensive spices for the lord, and garlic for the serf.

Serfs were the lowest ranks in the feudal system that by the twelfth century was in effect across western Europe. It was based on the allocation of land in return for service. At the top of this hierarchical system was the king, who gave out grants of land or fiefs to nobles in return for their loyalty and military service. While remaining vassals or servants to the king, the nobles in turn divided their land among lower lords or knights, who then became their vassals. Serfs, the overwhelming majority of the population, were bound to the land, hence the English term "bondsmen," and when the land was sold, they went with it. Living and working on the land of the lord who gave them protection, these peasants had to pay much of what they produced as taxes, in the form of either money or goods. They were also required to do boon work, that is, to work for a certain number of days a year on the land held directly by the lord. In addition, they were charged fees by the lord for anything from using the local flour mill or bread oven to getting married. Not bound to the land were the "free-hold tenants," many of them working in a trade, who paid a fixed rent to the lord, but on the whole were not much better off than the serfs.

When compared to our fast-paced world, where planes make it possible to cross continents in a matter of hours, and computers are sometimes already outdated by the time they arrive on the store shelf, the medieval period may seem rather static. And in some ways it was, but it was also a time when important inventions, and contact with other cultures, notably the Arab world, brought about significant change. Improvements in agriculture, thanks in part to better plows, and the introduction of the horse collar and the horseshoe, led to a growth in the population of Europe in the High Middle Ages, the period between 1000 and 1300. As a consequence, more and more land was cultivated, trade expanded, and towns grew in size and wealth. A new urban middle class of merchants and craftspeople emerged with a sense for the finer things in life that had traditionally been reserved for the aristocracy and high clergy. Many of the new foodstuffs, such as spices, and other luxury goods were introduced to Europe by the Arabs.

By the fourteenth century, however, the rapid population increase and economic boom came to a sudden halt. Already weakened by famine and malnutrition brought about by crop failures in the early 1300s, and often living in cramped conditions with poor sanitation and hygiene, Europeans succumbed in record numbers to the plague that hit the continent in 1348. Coming from Mongolia via the Middle East, the virus, *Yersina pestis,* which is transmitted by fleas living on the blood of infected rats, arrived in the bustling port cities of the Mediterranean first, and from there spread quickly along the trade routes, killing between a third to half of the population of Europe. As tragic as the epidemic was for the millions who lost their lives, for those who survived it, living standards were often much improved afterward. Housing and land, so scarce before 1350, were now plentiful, and since there were fewer mouths to feed, food prices began to drop, too. With labor all of a sudden in high demand, increases in wages followed, but even so, much arable land eventually lay fallow or was used as grazing land. This in turn meant that more meat became available and affordable to the average consumer. The firm grip landlords once had on society began to slip by the end of the Middle Ages, as peasants and wage earners demanded better working conditions and higher pay, and resorted to violence when their demands were not met.

Given the fact that the source material on food that we have is so much more abundant for the upper classes, and for the late medieval period, much of what is written in this book will refer to this particular segment of society and this particular time. However, an effort has been made to include as much information as possible on the earlier centuries and on the diet of the peasants and townspeople. We should also keep in mind that the food of the rich served as a model for the society as a whole. It was what most people tried to emulate, or at least dreamed about, in the Middle Ages. Its relevance therefore must not be underestimated, since it went way beyond the select few who enjoyed it as part of their lifestyle. Aiming to cover a broad range of food-related topics, the book will look at everything from foodstuffs, their preparation and presentation, to regional and international dishes, medical theories on nutrition, and food symbolism.

Chapter 1 offers a representative list of the foodstuffs used in the medieval kitchen, divided into 12 separate categories: grains, legumes, vegetables, herbs, spices, fruits, nuts, condiments, domestic and wild animals, fish, dairy products, and beverages. Information is provided on the origins of the various plants and animals, when they became part of the European diet, how they were prepared and consumed in the Middle Ages and in earlier times, and what their medicinal properties were thought to be. Comments on the hot, cold, wet, and dry nature of a foodstuff refer to the theory of the four humors that underlies all of medieval medicine, including nutrition. Readers who want to learn more about this classification should consult Chapter 6, which provides a detailed description of the theory and its application in the field of dietetics. Chapter 2 deals with the way the foodstuffs were turned into dishes. It begins with a look at the individuals who did the cooking, housewives and professional cooks mostly, as well as other kitchen staff; the chapter continues with cooking facilities, garbage disposal, kitchenware, processing methods, types of cooking, adulteration of food, spicing, coloring, and the use of molds, and ends with imitation food and kitchen humor.

Following a list of dishes that were international favorites, Chapter 3 analyzes the regional cuisines of western Europe starting in England, and moving across the Channel to northern and southern France, Spain, Italy and Sicily, and north to Germany, and the Low Countries. To bring this cookery to life, and perhaps give the more adventurous reader the opportunity to try out one or the other of the dishes, a number of authentic recipes taken from a variety of European cookbooks are provided in modern English translation. In Chapter 4 the focus is on the consumption of food, real and imagined. Mealtimes are discussed, as are dining rooms and their decor, seating arrangements, table- and dinnerware, serving and dining etiquette, dinner entertainment, almsgiving, the food of the poor and famine victims, and the food fantasy known as the Land of Cockaigne. Chapter 5 highlights the connection between food and religion. Topics include food taboos, the Eucharist, asceticism, fasting, gluttony, temperance, the connection between food and sexuality, vegetarianism, extreme fasting by women, as well as the role of food in Judaism, and in the interaction between Jews and Christians in the Middle Ages.

The final chapter, Chapter 6, deals with the medieval theory of nutrition and the importance ascribed to diet in the overall maintenance of health. A brief introduction to humoral theory, the six non-natural causes of sickness and health, and the classification of foodstuffs and drugs is followed by an analysis of the dietary advice contained in medieval books on preventive medicine known as *Regimen sanitatis* (Regimen of Health). Among the recommended diets featured in the chapter are those for healthy adults, pregnant women and wet nurses, children, the elderly, the sick, convalescents, the rich, the poor, and people in times of epidemics.

Aside from Latin, European manuscripts from the Middle Ages come in a multitude of languages and dialects, and usually with no consistent spelling. To give just one small example, *hippocras,* the famous spiced wine drunk at the end of a medieval banquet and named after the Greek physician Hippocrates, may appear as *hipocras, hypocras, hyppocras, ypocras,* and in a variety of other forms. So as not to confuse the audience unnecessarily, efforts have been made to standardize the spelling of such terms in the book. For modern English food terminology whose meaning may not be entirely clear, readers

are advised to consult *The Oxford English Dictionary,* an amazing re-
source that holds many clues for people interested in the history of
food. Not only does it provide the spelling and meaning or meanings
of a given word, but also its first documented uses and changes that
occurred over time.[1] In the chapter notes the reader will find the primary and secondary sources cited. Suggested further readings, most
of them in English, are arranged by chapter at the end of the book.
Geographically, the focus of the study is on Britain and continental
Europe, with the exclusion of eastern Europe and Scandinavia.

The food of medieval Europe has received much attention in recent
years from scholars and nonspecialists alike. Many manuscripts that lay
dormant in libraries for more than half a millennium are finally being
published, translated, and studied. Recreations of medieval banquets
have become a popular pastime in Europe and North America. Web
sites by individual food historians, teams of researchers, and associations of medievalists and hobby medievalists offer bibliographic references, and entire texts in the original and in translations. Book
illustrations from the Middle Ages, too, can be downloaded with the
click of a mouse, and in chat rooms food lovers exchange ideas about
cooking the medieval way. It seems that never before since the end of
the medieval era has there been so much interest in this field. It is
hoped that the present volume will serve as a stepping stone for the
uninitiated to plunge into the exciting world of medieval food and
cookery.

NOTE

1. *The Oxford English Dictionary,* 2nd edition, prepared by J. A. Simpson
and E.S.C. Weiner, 20 vols. (Oxford, U.K.: Clarendon Press, 1989).

CHAPTER 1
FOODSTUFFS

A remarkably wide variety of foodstuffs was available to consumers in the Middle Ages. Besides homegrown and raised products, exotic fruits and spices were brought by Arab merchants into the Mediterranean markets and sold across Europe at premium prices. Although bad harvests resulting in famine and disease occurred periodically, the staple foods—bread, dairy products, cheap cuts of meat, and preserved fish—were usually available to the general population.[1] In richer households the foodstuffs were more exclusive and the dishes more sophisticated and varied. Ingredients that could not be preserved for future use were eaten in season. The following list of foodstuffs, representative of medieval food culture, is divided into 12 different food groups. Information on each item's origin and history, preparation, social significance, and medicinal use is provided, compiled from both primary and secondary sources.[2]

GRAINS

Wheat

Native to western Asia, and domesticated in Anatolia, Iran, and Syria, wheat is the second-oldest cultivated cereal after barley. It was the most highly esteemed grain in the ancient and medieval world. Durum wheat, a harder species of wheat ideal for pasta making, is a more recent cultivar that has been used for cooking since the first century B.C. The Romans were large consumers of wheat, which they grew as far north as Britain. In addition to wheat of the *Triticum aestivum* genus and durum wheat, the Romans and medieval Europeans cultivated several other wheat species whose plants bore only a single or double grain, among them *einkorn,* spelt, and emmer. Although wheat played some role in stuffings, potages, soups, and sausages, most of it was turned into bread. For thousands of years bread has been synonymous with food and has figured prominently in religion and society. The breaking and blessing of bread is a fundamental aspect of orthodox Jewish custom, and Christians believe that in the Eucharist bread is transformed into the body and blood of Jesus. To modern consumers it may seem like a simple foodstuff, and yet much technological progress was needed to turn cultivated grain into leavened bread. Milling, leavening, and baking went through various stages of development over the centuries. In Roman times, waterpower was already used to grind flour, and by A.D. 1000 windmills began to appear. To make a loaf of bread rise requires leaven, and it was the ancient Egyptians who are credited with this improvement in bread making. On their Exodus from Egypt the Israelites left behind their leaven, hence the unleavened Passover bread known as "matzoh." Only gradually did the Romans adopt the custom of leavening bread, for which they eventually used brewer's yeast. Before the invention of the cooking oven, unleavened bread was cooked on flat stones in the fire. Reaching Europe probably via Mesopotamia and Egypt and via the Balkans, the earliest forms of ovens were cone- or beehive-shaped, heated from inside, and had a doorway that was sealed. For economical reasons, milling and bread baking have traditionally been communal activities. As early as 2000 B.C., there were professional bakers in Egypt. In much of medieval Europe ovens were owned by the community, by lords, or professional bakers. Bakers' guilds were among the earliest associations of craftsmen in Europe. Then as now bread was sold in many different varieties. The most expensive white bread from the finest wheat was known as *paindemaigne* or "bread of the Lord" in medieval England and later it was called *manchet*. The cream-colored bread was made from sieved or bolted wholemeal flour that still contained the wheat germ that is normally removed from our modern white bread. The higher the bran content, the coarser, darker, and cheaper the bread. Mixed seed that was ground to flour and used for bread making included *maslin,* a combination of rye and wheat. The poor and victims of famine would mix what little flour they had with barley, oats, beans, chestnuts, vetches, and the like. Many of these crops were normally grown as an-

Plowing in March. From *Losbuch*, ca. 1350. Cod. Vind. Series Nova 2652, fol. 7v. Courtesy of Österreichische Nationalbibliothek, Vienna (Photo: Bildarchiv, ÖNB Wien).

imal fodder. Unable to afford commercially made bread, or even ground flour, many would revert to grinding their own small batch of grains and turning it into unleavened flat bread, or simply into porridge. In upper-class cooking both flour and bread were used in a variety of ways. Pies, tarts, cakes, fritters, and mushes such as frumenty all contained wheat flour. Baked bread, especially barley or rye bread, was served as a disposable and edible plate known as a "trencher," and bread crumbs were used as the thickener of choice for many preparations such as sauces and stuffings. Bread was also a popular coloring agent. Depending on the degree of toasting, it imparted to a dish a color ranging from light brown to black. Physicians regarded leavened bread made from the purest and finest wheat as the best and most nutritious. The coarser and denser rye bread and barley bread were seen as inferior and suitable for manual workers whose stomachs, unlike those of the rich, could handle such coarse foods full of bran. Warm bread fresh from the oven was considered nutritious but difficult to digest. Rye bread was said to digest quickly, produce "weak" blood, and overall provide little energy, while barley bread was criticized for being of a cold and flatulent nature.

Barley

Native to the Middle East and domesticated in the sixth millennium B.C., barley is quite possibly the oldest cultivated cereal in the world. A staple in the eastern Mediterranean, it spread to France and Germany via Spain, and reached Britain around 5000 B.C. In antiquity it was used to make porridge, unleavened bread, and beer. Containing less gluten than wheat, barley produces leavened bread that is coarser, darker, and denser than wheat bread. In medieval Europe, which preferred wheat and rye to barley, barley bread was eaten by the poor and used by the rich as trencher bread instead of plates. Barley water was popular as a potion for the sick. In those parts of Europe where much ale and beer were consumed, barley production sometimes exceeded wheat production. Physicians considered barley an inferior foodstuff that caused wind and that cooled and moistened the body. It was the latter two qualities that made barley water an ideal antidote to fevers.

Rye

Cultivated in the region of eastern Turkey, Armenia, and northwestern Iran around 3000 B.C., rye eventually became the favorite cereal for bread making in northern and eastern Europe. Flourishing in the cold and wet climate of northern Germany, it was brought to England by the Anglo-Saxons. Rye bread is darker and denser than wheat bread. Rye flour mixed with wheat was used for bread making, and for a lower-grade bread rye flour was mixed with barley flour. When attacked by a certain fungus, rye develops a disease called "ergot." The consumption of ergot-infested rye could lead to ergotism, a condition that caused hallucinations, "dancing mania," and even death.

Oats

Oats were first cultivated in central Europe around 1000 B.C. A cereal that thrives in cool, moist climates, oats became a favorite food among the people of northern Europe, especially of Wales, Scotland, Scandinavia, and parts of Germany and Russia, who ate it in the form of oatmeal or porridge. Among southern Europeans and the rich it had the reputation of poor man's food or animal fodder. Physicians, if they listed it at all as a foodstuff fit for human consumption, described it as a coarse food for coarse people that had a cooling and constipating effect on the body.

Millet

Common millet was cultivated in Europe before 2000 B.C. For the Greeks and Romans it was a staple food eaten primarily in the form of porridge or coarse, unleavened bread. In medieval Europe it was eaten by peasants and the poor in soups and porridges, or it was used as animal feed. The upper-class cookbooks rarely mention it. Physicians criticized the cool and dry nature of millet, its constipating effect, and its low nutritional value unless it was prepared with milk, meat, or meat broth, which supposedly made it more easily digestible.

Rice

Rice was first cultivated in Asia, and from India it spread to the Middle East via Afghanistan and Persia sometime between 300 B.C. and A.D. 200. The Greeks and Romans used this expensive import sparingly and for medicinal purposes only. By the seventh century A.D. it was grown in Egypt and was supposedly a favorite food of the Prophet Muhammad. As a result of Arab expansion into Europe, rice came from North Africa to Spain and Sicily in the early Middle Ages. In the thirteenth century it was traded as a luxury foodstuff across Europe, and in the fifteenth century it was grown on a large scale in northern Italy. The four types of rice sold in central Europe and named after their places of origin, were Ostiglia, Mantua, Verona, and Milan rice. In the late-medieval cookbooks rice plays a dominant role. Often in the form of rice flour, it was used for stuffings, sauces, the famous white dish *blanc manger* (a sweet, creamy chicken or fish dish), as a side dish, and for various Lenten dishes. Regarded by the medical community as a fortifying and nutritious foodstuff that increased the blood, especially when cooked with milk, it played an important role as food for the sick and convalescent.

LEGUMES

Beans

Broad beans or fava beans were indigenous to Europe, North Africa, and western Asia. They had been a staple for thousands of years before the discovery of the New World led to the introduction of the haricot bean. Perhaps because the consumption of beans causes flatulence, and, in some people, a disease called "favism," beans have over time been the subject of much superstition. In antiquity they were associated with death and the underworld, the spirits of the dead, decay, and impurity, but also with sex, rebirth, meat eating, and even cannibalism. Pythagoras and his followers, for instance, abstained from eating meat as well as beans. In medieval Europe both green and dry fava beans were eaten, mainly by the poor and by monks. Beans were a popular Lenten fare, and in times of famine bean meal was used in bread making. Most European upper-class cookbooks of the late Middle Ages contain few if any bean recipes. Physicians recommended beans as a remedy for various ailments, but often warned of their consumption as food. It was thought that they caused dizziness, confusion in the head, sighing, a feeling of malaise, and an abundance of bad humors.

Peas

Like the fava bean, the pea was a staple in Europe for thousands of years. It was either eaten green or dried and used as a source of protein, especially during the long winter months and on fast days. Judging from the many recipes using peas in the cookbooks of the wealthy, the pea did not have a reputation as poor man's food, as the bean did. In addition to pea soup and potage, the combination of peas and bacon was popular even then, as were "peas on a spit," a mixture of peas and eggs, seasoned, and fried, and then roasted. Peas also played a role in imitation meat dishes for Lent. Physicians generally approved of cooked peas as food that was easy to digest.

Chickpeas

First cultivated in the Levant and ancient Egypt, the chickpea was a popular legume throughout the Mediterranean region in the Middle Ages. It played an important role in Arab cuisine and in the cuisines of Spain, southern France, southern Italy and Sicily, which were heavily influenced by the Arabs. Like the bean, it causes flatulence and was thought to increase sperm, and provoke urine and menstruation. Physicians also recommended it against kidney and bladder stones.

VEGETABLES

Garlic

From central Asia garlic reached Europe via the Middle East. In ancient Egypt and Greece it was a highly esteemed vegetable thought to give strength, especially to manual laborers and soldiers, and to possess magical powers against evil. Some upper-class Romans, however, rejected it on account of its strong smell. In the Middle Ages, garlic was an important flavoring across Europe, used for many different sauces. One of them, the *aillade,* from southern France was even named after it. Since time immemorial garlic has also been known for its medicinal properties, as a cure for anything from headaches to snake bites. Those who could not afford the dozens of rare and expensive ingredients mixed with honey that formed the compound drug theriac, an ancient antidote for the bite of venomous animals, were advised to eat garlic, the "theriac of the poor." It was also used to ward off the plague, but had little effect. With its extreme heating and drying effect on the body, garlic was believed to incite lust.

Onions

Onions, garlic, and leeks all belong to the same family of vegetables that came to Europe from central Asia via the Middle East. They were documented in Egypt as early as 3200 B.C., and were a popular foodstuff throughout the ancient world. Because of the bad breath they cause, they have traditionally been associated with the lower classes, who ate them both raw and cooked. In medieval upper-class cookbooks they do appear; in fact, the medieval French dish *civet* is named after onions. Eaten in conjunction with the meat of wild and domestic animals, onions were added to a variety of sauces, broths, and stuffings. Some recipes specify particular kinds of onions, such as shallots. Doctors generally praised cooked onions for their heating and diuretic effects on the body. Onions were also thought to increase male sperm, and to incite appetite for food and sex. When consumed raw, onions supposedly caused headache, stomachache, and superfluous humors, especially phlegm.

Leeks

Milder and sweeter in taste than garlic and onions, leeks were highly esteemed in the ancient world. Perhaps because the Roman emperor Nero was so fond of leeks, leek recipes abound in the Roman cookbook of Apicius. Whether or not it was the Romans who introduced leeks to Britain, the fact remains that leeks were cultivated and consumed across Europe in the Middle Ages. The dietetic qualities of leeks, according to medieval physicians, were similar to those of onions. To reduce the amount of wind created in the body by leeks, cooks were advised to boil them twice in different water.

Cabbage, Kale

Of European ancestry, cabbages were originally headless, and were eaten by the ancient Egyptians, Greeks, and Romans. Not until the first century B.C. do we hear of headed cabbages that may have been cultivated in northern Europe first. In the Middle Ages the headless kale, or colewort, was a staple food of the Scots, while headed cabbage was favored by the Dutch and Germans. Other varieties belonging to the cabbage family that were cultivated in medieval Europe, especially in Italy, were cauliflower and broccoli. Headed cabbage was usually boiled or made into sauerkraut, as it still is today. The fact that in Bavaria cabbage was eaten three to four times a day, as one sixteenth-century physician tells us, illustrates how important a foodstuff cabbage was for the common people. In the upper-class cookbooks, however, cabbage is rarely mentioned. Not only did it lack exclusivity, it was also thought to generate melancholy and cause nightmares. Its one redeeming feature was that it was considered an antidote to drunkenness. Cabbage juice with honey was recommended for people who had lost their voice, and cabbage leaves were used to dress wounds.

Lettuce

Lettuce has been used in the kitchen for thousands of years. Hippocrates and other Greek writers discussed it, and the Romans were fond of it. Because of its proven sleep-inducing or soporific qualities, it was originally eaten at the end of a meal, but later also with vinegar at the beginning as an appetite stimulant. In the Middle Ages lettuce appears to have played a minor role in European cookery, at least before 1400. By the sixteenth century, however, it was used for raw salads across the Continent. Part of the resistance to eating raw lettuce came from the medical community, which classified lettuce as so extremely cold and moist in nature that it was believed to be capable of quenching a person's thirst and even extinguishing any feelings of lust.

Turnips

Turnips presumably originated in northern Europe around 2000 B.C. Considered rustic food by the Romans and in medieval Europe, they generally played a minor role in upper-class cookery. German peasants and craftsmen were said to eat turnips boiled with beef or butter, or pickled like sauerkraut. Turnip greens, too, were used and put into potages. Physicians described turnips as hot and moist, flatulent, and an aphrodisiac. They were said to be good for the chest and the lungs, and as an appetite stimulant when combined with vinegar and salt.

Parsnips

Growing wild in Europe and western Asia, the parsnip has been cultivated since antiquity and was an integral part of the Roman diet. Up to the early modern period writers did not always make a distinction between parsnips and carrots. Sweet and starchy, the white parsnip was used in the Middle Ages as a substitute for honey and sugar, which were substantially more expensive. Easily stored for the winter in a cool place, or left in the ground until needed, it was an important vegetable, especially for the peasants.

Carrots

Known in Europe since prehistoric times, the carrot appears to have been cultivated for something other than its root early on, since it is not mentioned as a foodstuff by the Greeks and Romans. The carrot eaten in medieval Europe was introduced by the Arabs probably between the eighth and tenth centuries. Its root came in a tasty purplish red variety, and a coarser, somewhat inferior yellow-to-green variety. From Arab Spain carrots gradually moved north and reached France, the Netherlands, and Germany in the fourteenth century, and Britain in the fifteenth century. The orange carrots we still eat today first appeared in the Netherlands in the seventeenth century. Physicians described the dietetic qualities of carrots and parsnips in much the same way.

Beets

A native of the Mediterranean and Atlantic coasts of Europe and North Africa, the beet was by 300 B.C. already cultivated to yield edible roots. In addition to the red beet, also called "Roman beet," there were several other varieties that had yellow roots. Both the roots and leaves of beets, and of the related chard, the leaves and stalks, were eaten in the Middle Ages. As a staple of the lower classes, beet is rarely mentioned in the cookbooks of the rich. If it does turn up, then as an ingredient in sauces and broths, and as a coloring agent. Beets were considered by medieval medicine as being of a cold and moist nature.

The juice extracted from their leaves was used as a stool softener, and the root, burned and mixed with honey, as a remedy against hair loss.

Radishes

Radishes, which have traditionally come in a variety of shapes, sizes, and colors, were eaten by the ancient Egyptians, Greeks, and Romans but are apparently not mentioned in European sources until the thirteenth century, when the German scholar and monk Albertus Magnus described different kinds, including a giant radish. The medieval literature that does mention radishes classifies them as warm and dry in nature, as a diuretic, and as a foodstuff that generates bad humors, but is beneficial to people with a cold complexion, to weak people, as a winter food, and for those living in the cold north.

Gourds, Melons

Gourds were cultivated in the Old World. Physicians considered them as cold and moist in their effect on the diner, as a thirst quencher, a laxative, and as beneficial to the young and in hot temperatures.

Cucumbers

Thought to have originated in southern India, the cucumber was eaten in the ancient world and in medieval Europe. Because of their presumed cooling effect on the body cucumbers were recommended against fever, for hot climates, and for people with a naturally hot temperament.

Asparagus

Native to the Old World, asparagus was known to the Greeks and cultivated by the Romans. After the fall of the Roman Empire, it was mainly grown in Arab-ruled Syria, Egypt, and Spain. By the end of the Middle Ages it was cultivated in France, and by the early sixteenth century in England as well. It was usually eaten boiled and seasoned, but sometimes also coated in flour and fried. Praised by physicians as a nutritious food, it was also considered an aphrodisiac for men.

Eggplant

Originally from India, eggplants were introduced to medieval Europe by the Arabs, but outside Spain and Italy only found slow acceptance. In the Spanish recipes they are usually peeled, cored, and stuffed, or chopped, fried, seasoned, and cooked. Medieval medicine warned of the melancholic humor they supposedly generated in the body.

Spinach

Cultivated in Persia by the fourth century A.D., spinach became a favorite vegetable of the Arabs, who brought it to Spain in the eleventh century. Eventually it replaced the green vegetables that had traditionally been used in Europe, such as sorrel and orach (also called mountain-spinach, a tall, hardy annual and common potherb). Spinach was frequently boiled together with other green vegetables, or parboiled and fried. Spinach juice was also a favorite coloring agent in the late-medieval kitchen. Regarded as a moderately cold and moist foodstuff, spinach was considered good for the chest, and especially for coughs, but bad for digestion.

Mushrooms

Since prehistoric times fungi of various kinds have been gathered and eaten in Europe. Aside from the common field mushroom, and porcini cep or king bolete, chanterelles and morels appear to have found particular favor with medieval cooks. Truffles were already highly prized by the Romans, judging from the six truffle recipes in the Roman cookbook of Apicius, and they continued to be an exclusive foodstuff in the Middle Ages. Occasionally, dough preparations in the shape of fungi, such as morels, were served and named after the mushrooms they resembled. The German nun Hildegard of Bingen called mushrooms the foam and sweat of the earth. Classical and medieval physicians warned of the mushrooms' harmful moisture and earthiness that were thought to cause melancholy.

HERBS

Parsley

Native to the eastern Mediterranean, possibly Sardinia, parsley was by far the most popular herb in medieval Europe. Both curly-leafed and flat-leafed parsley are already mentioned in classical sources from around 300 B.C., and were later grown in herb gardens across the

Continent. Parsley was a principal ingredient in herb omelets, green sauces, pickles, and many other dishes, and like today it was also used as a garnish. Described as moderately warm and dry in the medical literature, parsley was thought to generate good blood and to provoke urine, stool, and the menstrual flow. It was recommended for old people and those of a cold and moist disposition.

Anise

Anise originated in the Levant, was known to the Greeks, and was used by the Romans in green and dried form for dietary and medicinal purposes. In the Middle Ages, anise appears as a seasoning in a variety of dishes, such as fish and chicken dishes. Sugar-coated anise was one of the *comfits* eaten at the end of a meal in order to sweeten the breath and aid digestion, a bodily function likened to the cooking process. Because of its warm and dry nature anise was prescribed against a cold stomach, wind in the digestive tract, as a diuretic, laxative, and a means to generate milk in women.

Sage

Native to southern Europe and Asia Minor, the perennial herb sage was used by the Greeks and Romans for medicinal purposes only. There is no mention of it in the Roman cookbook of Apicius, for instance. In the Middle Ages sage was grown in most of Europe and appears in cookbooks from the Mediterranean to Germany, France, and all the way to England. The dominant taste of sage was a favorite with fish, fowl, and various sauces. In Germany it also served as a flavoring for mead or honey. Moderately warm and dry in character, sage was said to be good for the stomach and the nerves.

Dill

Originating in western Asia, dill reached southern Russia and the Mediterranean first before coming to western Europe. In the Middle Ages it became especially popular with the Germanic peoples. Both leaves and seeds were used, the latter in sausages, for example. Dill was thought to be a remedy against gas in the stomach. Being moderately warm and dry, it was recommended for people of a cold and moist disposition.

Fennel

Like anise a member of the parsley family, fennel was cultivated in Europe throughout antiquity and the Middle Ages. The fennel whose stalk and seed were eaten by the Greeks and Romans was the original wild form indigenous to southern Europe, and is known as "bitter fennel." Its seeds were used in spice mixtures and its stalks in stews and pickles. As early as the ninth century A.D. a distinction was made between bitter and sweet fennel, with the latter being the one especially favored in medieval cookery. The stalk was frequently added to vegetable and meat dishes, and the seed dried, sugar-coated, and eaten as a breath-freshener or *comfit* at the end of a meal. Physicians classified fennel as dry and warm, and described it as good for the eyes, for the movement of the bladder and bowels, and for the flow of milk. It was recommended for cold complexions and climates.

Mint

Mint was known to the Greeks and Romans, and played an important role in classical mythology. In the Middle Ages the plant that was native to the Mediterranean and introduced to England by the Romans was grown across Europe. It was used as a seasoning in dishes ranging from boiled beef to mint sauce, and it was rubbed on teeth to fight bad breath. In medieval medicine mint, classified as extremely warm and dry in nature, was thought to warm the stomach and aid digestion.

Caraway

Native to western Asia and the Mediterranean, caraway is among the oldest plants cultivated in Europe. In the Middle Ages caraway was grown for the seed, which was added to meat and fish dishes. In Germany, where it was especially popular, it was put in stuffings and cheese as well. It was eaten candied at the end of a feast, along with anise, coriander, and fennel seed. Physicians considered its supposed heat and dryness as an aid to digestion.

Mustard

Both the white or yellow and the black mustard belong to the cabbage family native to Europe. It is said that the Teutonic tribes, who used the leaves and the seed, taught the Romans how to prepare the condiment. In the Roman cookbook of Apicius mustard is one of the most popular flavorings, described as a preparation made from mustard seed, vinegar, salt, and honey. It was the Romans who are said to have introduced white and black mustard to Britain. Like caraway, mustard grew in abundance in medieval Europe, and hence was readily available and much cheaper than the highly sought-after exotic spices. To the eleventh-century German nun Hildegard of Bingen it was poor man's food. Then as now the condiment was frequently eaten together with meat and sausages. In the fourteenth century the first commercial mustard production developed around Dijon, France, a place still famous today for its mustard. Classified by physicians as extremely hot and dry in nature, mustard was prescribed against excessive phlegm in the body, especially in the head and the stomach.

Elder-Flowers

The flowers and fruits of the elderberry tree have a long tradition in European cookery. While the berries were usually turned into deep red fruit mousses, with the addition of milk and flour for instance, the flowers were used in fritters that were especially popular in medieval Britain.

Hawthorn-Flowers

The flowers of the hawthorn, a member of the rose family, were sometimes used in salads in the past, or in a dish called *spinée* (a type of porridge prepared with almond milk) in the *Forme of Cury* (The [Proper] Method of Cookery), the English medieval cookbook compiled for King Richard II. The hawthorn, also known as "May tree," has traditionally played an important role in European literature as a sign of the arrival of spring.

Roses

Cultivated in ancient Persia thousands of years ago, the rose was highly esteemed by the Greeks as a symbol of love, beauty, and happiness. Our word "rose" goes back to the Greek word for red, *rodos*. The Romans, who scented their wine with rose petals, connected the flower with Venus, the goddess of love. Fresh and dried rose petals were used in Persia and later in Europe to make jams and to perfume and flavor sweet and savory dishes. The distillation of rose water was a technique that first became popular in the Middle East in the early Middle Ages, and was brought to Europe by the crusaders. The fruits of the rosebush, known as "rose hips," were harvested, too, and boiled down to make a fragrant syrup. At medieval banquets roses were used to perfume the water for hand washing at table. Physicians praised roses for their supposed power to heal eye diseases.

Violets

Native to Europe and North Africa, the violet was a garden flower whose petals served various purposes in the medieval kitchen. They were added to potages of potherbs, to salads and omelets, for instance, or used to color creamy dishes such as *blanc manger* and various puddings. They were also put on dining tables as a decoration. Medieval medicine prescribed violets for cleansing the gall, and violet oil for the eyes.

SPICES

Saffron

Saffron is the stigma of the crocus flower, which is harvested by hand, dried, and sold either in strands or ground to powder. Indigenous to Persia, the saffron crocus has been known in Europe since antiquity. The Roman cookbook of Apicius contains three references to saffron. In the tenth century the Arabs cultivated it in Spain, and in the thirteenth century crusaders returning from Asia Minor introduced it to other parts of Europe. Eventually it was grown across the Continent, from Italy and France to Austria, Germany, and even Saffron Walden in England. Of all the medieval spices, saffron was the most expensive, which is not surprising given that 70,000 flowers only yield one pound of dried stigmas. In the European cookbooks of the late Middle Ages, nearly all of which reflect refined upper-class dining, saffron is ubiquitous. On average a third of the dishes contain saffron, which is used as much for the golden yellow hue it imparts to a dish as for its characteristic taste, and of course its exclusivity. Fish and fowl, legumes and dough preparations were all made with saffron. Medieval medicine classified saffron as hot and dry, and praised it for comforting the heart and liver and for aiding digestion. It was also thought to cause pain in the head, induce sleep, and accelerate childbirth.

Pepper

If saffron was the most exclusive spice, pepper was the most common in medieval Europe. It was consumed by the rich and those of more modest means, albeit in smaller quantities. Indigenous to southern India, pepper is the unripe fruit of the pepper tree, a climber usually grown on other trees for support. Black pepper is the seed surrounded by the outer layer that turns black when dry. White pepper is the seed with the outer layer removed. Known to the Greeks since the fourth century B.C., pepper was in antiquity a commodity paid for in gold, and at times regarded as a currency in its own right. No fewer than three out of four recipes in the Roman cookbook of Apicius contain pepper. The pepper sauce *piperatum* is even named after the spice. In the Middle Ages pepper continued to be regarded as a prized possession, distributed, for instance, by the eighth-century English cleric Bede among his brethren when he was on his deathbed. The Guild of Pepperers is one of the oldest in the City of London, first mentioned in sources from the late twelfth century. In the early thirteenth century the Pepperers, wholesalers selling "in gross," bore the name *grossarii* (from Latin *grossus,* meaning "great"), the ancestor of the modern word "grocer." In medieval cookery, pepper was added to a wide variety of dishes that sometimes amounted to half the recipes in a given collection. A spicy pepper broth traditionally accompanied game and venison. Medieval medicine classified pepper as extremely hot and dry in nature, and praised it for stimulating the appetite and aiding digestion. It was also thought to dissolve wind in the stomach and intestines, and to remove phlegm from the chest.

Long Pepper

Native to northeast India, long pepper is more pungent than black or white pepper, and predates the latter in its use by humans. It is named after the long catkinlike spike that contains the small seeds. In medieval Europe long pepper played an important role as a foodstuff and drug.

Cubeb

The climbing cubeb plant is related to the black pepper tree. Indigenous to Java, it produces seeds with stalks attached to them. The seeds were harvested and dried in the sun. Other names for the cubeb are "Java pepper" or "tailed pepper." The cubeb was used in medieval

Arab cookery, especially in hot spice mixes, in Arab-inspired medieval European cookery, and in medicine. However, it never reached the popularity of black pepper.

Grains of Paradise

Related to cardamom, this hot spice, also known as *melegueta pepper*, is the fruit of a reedlike herb. It was unknown in antiquity but became the rage in European, specifically French, cookery of the late Middle Ages, where for a while it almost completely replaced black pepper as the spice of choice. Described as hot and moist in nature, grains of paradise were transported in great quantity, either by ship from the Melegueta Coast of Liberia or by camel caravan across the Sahara.

Galingale

Galingale is a spice native to China and Indonesia, and a member of the ginger family. It looks similar to ginger, and has the pungent taste of ginger and pepper combined. In antiquity it was used for medicinal purposes, but in the Middle Ages it was added to dishes across the Continent, from Italy to Germany, and all the way to England. It may also have played a role in the adulteration of pepper. Classified by physicians as extremely warm and dry, galingale was recommended for a cold stomach, as a digestive aid, a breath freshener, and an aphrodisiac.

Ginger

Ginger probably originated in India, and early on was also cultivated in East Africa. It was among the first spices to be imported to Europe. The Romans used it extensively as a drug and a foodstuff, as did the Arabs, and Europeans throughout the medieval period. Among the various kinds mentioned in the sources were green, white, and columbine ginger. Green may refer to the young and juicy root, which was pickled in Roman times, and white to the partially dried root; columbine ginger is named after the place Kollam on the west coast of India. We can assume that most ginger traded in Europe was likely dried and whole or ground. Occurring frequently in medieval cookbooks, ginger was added to fish, chicken, and a variety of other dishes, including gingerbread. Physicians described ginger as extremely hot and moderately humid. It was thought to heat the body more slowly than the hot and dry pepper, but to otherwise share most of its medicinal properties.

Cinnamon, Cassia

Cinnamon is native to Sri Lanka, and the related species cassia to southern China, Indonesia, and some parts of southeast Asia. Both types are harvested and traded in the same way, as sticks of dried bark that is curled inward. True cinnamon is of a lighter brown color and a more delicate taste than cassia, and has traditionally been the more highly prized, but both are often sold under the name cinnamon. The confusion between cinnamon and cassia already existed in antiquity. Known in the Mediterranean as early as the seventh century B.C., cinnamon was one of the oldest exotic spices to be imported to Europe. Its place of origin was for a long time shrouded in mystery. Cinnamon was used as embalming powder in ancient Egypt, as an aromatic by the Greeks and Romans, and it is mentioned in the Bible. It played an important role in Arab cookery, and it was Arab spice traders that supplied a hungry European market with cinnamon before the Portuguese, Dutch, and English took control of what is now Sri Lanka in the early modern period. Used across the Continent in medieval upper-class cooking, cinnamon was added to sauces, one of which, the *sauce cameline,* even bears its name, and along with other exotic spices it served as a seasoning for fish. Since fish was classified as cold and moist, and cinnamon as hot and dry by physicians, medical considerations may have played a role in the combination of fish and cinnamon, a spice that was esteemed as a digestive.

Cloves

Indigenous to the Moluccas, or Spice Islands, of eastern Indonesia, cloves are the unopened flower buds of a tree related to myrtle. Their name in many languages means "nail," which is the shape the dry spice resembles. Cloves were known to the Romans as early as the first century A.D., and by the end of the Roman Empire they were used as a foodstuff and drug. In medieval Europe cloves were a highly sought-after spice appearing in countless upper-class preparations ranging from meat and fish dishes to fruit mousses and gingerbread. In the thirteenth century the Italian explorer Marco Polo claimed to have seen clove plantations in the East Indies. The Portuguese gained control over the Moluccas and the trade in cloves in 1514, but a century later lost it to the Dutch, who ruthlessly defended their monopoly. A hot and dry spice, cloves were recommended by medieval physicians as a digestive and a breath freshener.

Nutmeg, Mace

Nutmeg is the seed and mace the netting around the seed of the nutmeg tree, which is native to the Moluccas. The flesh of the nutmeg fruit is also eaten, usually in candied form. There is no evidence that the Greeks and Romans knew nutmeg or mace, which may have been brought to the West by Arab spice traders in the sixth century, but by the ninth century monks in Constantinople were allowed to sprinkle it on their pease pudding, a thick porridge made from peas. Three hundred years later it was used across Europe. Along with cloves, the Portuguese held the monopoly on nutmeg for nearly a century before losing it to the Dutch in the early 1700s. Occurring less frequently in the medieval cookbooks than pepper, cinnamon, and cloves, nutmeg was added, for example, to boiled fish, or to gingerbread. The medical literature of the time distinguishes between nutmeg and mace, and classifies both as hot and dry in nature. Freshening the breath and comforting the stomach are two of the many qualities attributed to the two spices.

FRUITS

Apples

Native to the Caucasus and a member of the rose family, apples were known to the Greeks and Romans, and are mentioned in the Bible. As early as the second century B.C. the art of grafting cuttings of a good tree to another rootstock is described in a Latin text. While enjoying the status of a luxury fruit in classical times, apples were a staple food in medieval Europe. Of the many different kinds, Pearmain, Costard, Pippin and the Pippin-variety Blaunderelle were popular in England, and Faro and Reinette in France. Apples that were not eaten fresh or cooked right away were usually stored in a dry and cool place for the winter or peeled, cored, and dried, either whole or sliced and put on a string. Generally smaller and not as perfectly shaped as the ones we buy in the supermarket today, apples were often processed or cooked. They were turned into cider, especially in Normandy and parts of England, or added to verjuice, the tart liquid food additive that was a characteristic feature of medieval cookery. As early as Roman times, apples were an ingredient in meat dishes. Cored and diced, sliced, or mashed, apples appear in a wide variety of fillings, and pies, fritters, rissoles, apple sauce, and almond-based Lenten dishes. The consumption of raw apples, and most other raw fruit, was frowned upon by the medical community. Describing sour apples as cold and dry in nature, and sweet ones as moist, physicians considered all apples as good for the heart, but bad for the nerves.

Pears

Related to the apple and the quince, the pear, too, goes back to a wild ancestor from the Caucasus. In Greece and Rome the pear was an esteemed fruit that came in many different varieties, and was ranked higher than the apple. Pears were cultivated in most of medieval Europe, but were especially popular in Italy and France. The best known British pear was the Warden pear, a cooking pear cultivated by Cistercian monks in Bedfordshire. Since fresh pears spoiled very quickly, they were often halved and dried. Cooks used pears in much the same way as apples, for stuffings, sauces, meat dishes, and the like. In the opinion of medieval physicians pears were a cold and moist fruit, somewhat more temperate when fully ripened, that fortified the stomach and were best eaten cooked at the end rather than the beginning of a meal. Unripe pears were thought to cause colic.

Quinces

Still growing in the Caucasus in its wild form, this lumpy, yellow fruit that is hard and sour was usually eaten cooked and sweetened. Reaching the Levant and southeastern Europe earlier than the apple, namely in the first millennium B.C., the quince came to play an important role in Greek mythology and the Greek diet. The Romans preserved it in honey and called it, appropriately, *melimelum* (honey apple). This word is at the root of Portuguese *marmelada* from which the English word "marmalade" is derived. The Persians and Arabs frequently combined meat and quinces, in stews for instance, and made quince preserves with honey. In medieval Europe quinces were used for stuffings, sauces, and a quince sweetmeat known as *codignac*. Classified as cold and dry, quinces were praised by physicians for stimulating the appetite, aiding digestion, and as a cure for heartache.

Plums

Plums are related to apricots, peaches, and cherries, and appear to be native to central Europe. They are not mentioned in ancient sources until the first century A.D., when a number of different kinds were already in existence. Medieval Europeans cultivated the plum proper in their gardens, and differentiated it from bullaces and the small, oval, sour damsons named after the city of Damascus in Syria. Plums make occasional appearances in upper-class cookbooks, in the form of fruit mousses, for instance. To physicians the plum was a cold and moist fruit that hindered digestion and was taken as a laxative.

Peaches

Indigenous to China, peaches moved west to Persia and from there were supposedly brought to Europe by Alexander the Great. Their Latin name *persica* reflects their Persian provenance. From the Mediterranean, peaches spread to northern and western Europe in Roman times, and by the thirteenth century peach trees were growing in England. Physicians generally took a dim view of peaches, which they thought caused putrid humors in the body. Eaten at the beginning of a meal they stimulated the appetite, but at the end of a meal they corrupted the other food consumed, and acted as a laxative, it was argued.

Cherries

Both the sweet and sour cherry are native to western Asia. The two kinds reached the Mediterranean sometime before 300 B.C. and were highly prized by the Romans, who introduced cherries to Britain. In the Roman cookbook of Apicius instructions are given how to preserve them in honey. In the Middle Ages cherries were grown commercially, but also in many a monastic or lay garden for private consumption. In the cookbooks cherries appear in fruit mousses and preserves, tarts, and a cherry beverage that, in Germany at least, was reserved for high-ranking officials. Because of their cold and moist nature, cherries were considered bad for the stomach by the medical community. Cooking the fruit and adding wine were two ways suggested to reduce their harmful effects on the body.

Strawberries

Among the berries eaten in medieval Europe were blackberries, raspberries, and strawberries. A member of the rose family, the strawberry was indigenous to Europe. Wild strawberries were a delicacy, and by the fourteenth century cultivated strawberries began to appear. The fruit had positive connotations, being associated with summer and with the Virgin Mary.

Grapes

Since antiquity grapes have played an important role in the European diet. They were eaten fresh, especially in the grape-growing areas, added to dishes dried or in the form of grape juice, or they were made into wine, the drink of choice for anybody who could afford it. The wild grapevine, a climbing plant like the later cultivars, was indigenous to the area between the Black Sea and Afghanistan. The Phoenicians introduced the vine to Greece sometime after 1000 B.C.; from there it spread throughout the Mediterranean. The ancient Egyptians grew grapes, as did the Romans, who were especially fond of various grape syrups in their cuisine. Among them were *defrutum,* or boiled-down unfermented grape juice, *passum,* a cooking wine that was even sweeter, and *mulsum,* a mixture of white wine and honey. As the Roman Empire expanded across Europe, so did the cultivation of grapes, and the art of wine making. In the Middle Ages, great quantities of wine were produced, traded, and consumed in Europe. And in the kitchen, sour wine or vinegar, and the juice of unripe grapes known as "verjuice," were used extensively, often in sauces, to give dishes their characteristic sweet and sour taste. Physicians had much to say about grapes, which they described as moderately warm and moist in nature. Mature white grapes with a thin skin were to be preferred. Sweet grapes were thought to cleanse the belly, nourish the body, and cause wind as well as an erection in the penis. Sour grapes were said to have a cooling effect on the body, and raisins were supposedly good for the stomach, lungs, chest, liver, and spleen.

Pomegranates

Native to Persia, the pomegranate has been eaten in the Middle East for thousands of years. The ancient Egyptians and Greeks knew it, and the Romans got acquainted with it via Carthage in North Africa. The pomegranate is a fruit the size of an apple, hence the English name meaning "grained apple." Its many seeds are surrounded by pulp and retained in a membrane. In antiquity and the Middle Ages it was a symbol of fertility. A characteristic feature of Middle Eastern cuisine, the pomegranate also gained a certain popularity in Europe, especially in the Mediterranean, which was strongly influenced by Arab culture, and in England. Seeds were used as a garnish, and the juice was added to some dishes. Considered warm and moist in nature, sweet pomegranates were prescribed by medieval physicians for coughs and as an aphrodisiac. When eaten before a meal pomegranates supposedly stimulated the appetite.

Citrons, Lemons, and Limes

These citrus fruits originated in northeast India and gradually spread westward to the Middle East and eventually Europe. The citron was imported to ancient Greece from Persia, and initially used as a perfume and for medicinal purposes. From the first century A.D. on it was cultivated in southern Europe. The Romans added the rind of the citron soaked in condiments in their cooking, and the Arabs candied it. There was much confusion over the centuries between citrons, lemons, and limes, the latter two being much later arrivals in the Mediterranean. Citrus fruits were an integral part of Arab cookery, and through Arab mediation also played a role in medieval European cookery, although for northern Europeans they remained an expensive import, one that only the rich could afford, well into the early modern period. Physicians described these fruits as cold and dry and recommended the rind as a digestive and as an antidote to melancholy, the juice boiled down and turned to syrup as a remedy against too much choleric humor, and the seeds against poison.

Oranges

Oranges were native to northwest India and southwest China. Of the two kinds, bitter and sweet, it was the bitter oranges that reached Europe first, some five hundred years before the sweet oranges. Bitter oranges came to Sicily in the eleventh century and to Spain in the twelfth. They were eaten as an appetizer at the beginning of a meal, the juice was sometimes added to dishes, and candied orange peel was a favorite treat at the conclusion of a banquet. Ascribed cold and wet properties by the medical community, oranges supposedly helped counteract an overheated stomach, the heat of youth, and of summer.

Figs

The fig tree, indigenous to western Asia, reached the Mediterranean in prehistoric times. In Egypt it may have been cultivated as early as 4000 B.C., and by 800 B.C. it was grown in mainland Greece. Homer mentions figs, and so does the Bible. Fresh and dried figs were a staple in ancient Rome, where they were eaten raw or added to sweet and savory dishes. In medieval Europe, especially the Mediterranean, they were used in much the same way. Dried figs were the norm in northern Europe where they were an expensive import, associated especially with Lent. Medieval Arab physicians considered figs and grapes the best fruits. Classified as warm and moist, figs were thought to cleanse the stomach, and give strength to the body, dried ones in particular. Fresh figs were said to be less nutritious and to create gas and bad humors.

Dates

Dates are the fruit of the date palm, a tree native to the desert regions of the Middle East, and going back to prehistoric times. Rome imported dates from the East and used them as a sweetmeat or in sauces that accompanied meat or fish. Dried dates were to be had in medieval Europe, albeit at a price. They served as a sweetener, or as a special treat during Lent. Medieval Arab physicians classified them as cold and dry, warm and dry, or warm and moist, depending on the kind. Some were believed to harm the intestines, others the teeth and mouth, or the voice.

NUTS

Almonds

Native to southwest Asia, and related to the peach, apricot, and cherry, the almond was in ancient times cultivated throughout southern Europe, from Greece to Rome, Provence, and Spain. Roman cooks frequently used almonds in sauces that accompanied fowl and venison, and in Arab and European upper-class cuisine of the Middle Ages they were a staple food. Sometimes a quarter or more of a given recipe collection contained almonds. They were the basic ingredient in almond milk, a more durable, nondairy milk substitute that was used for the creamy white dish *blanc manger* and a variety of other sweet and savory dishes, many of them eaten during Lent. The confections marzipan and nougat were almond-based, and almond oil makes an occasional appearance. Both bitter and sweet almonds are mentioned in medieval medical sources, sweet ones being described as moderately warm and moist, and bitter ones as somewhat hotter. Almonds were thought to be nutritious food, good for the brain, especially students' brains, and for people awake at night, but hard to digest. When eaten with sugar they supposedly increased the production of sperm, and when taken before a night of drinking, a handful of almonds was said to keep a person from getting drunk.

Walnuts

Wild walnuts have been eaten by humans for thousands of years. A small and dry wild variety was native to Greece, but more highly prized was one of the earliest cultivated varieties from Persia. It was of superior taste, and suitable for pressing oil. Walnuts were not just a symbol of fertility to the Romans, they also used them as an ingredient in sauces and other dishes. In the Middle Ages, walnuts were especially popular in France, and from the fifteenth century on they were cultivated in England. Pounded in a mortar, they were turned into hearty sauces, such as a nut and garlic sauce, and whole they were sometimes added to meat dishes. Medieval medicine classified nuts as warm and dry, and recommended fresh green ones as a laxative. An excess of dry walnuts, however, was considered bad for the mouth. Together with figs, nuts were a popular food for Lent, and the main ingredient in an antidote to poison called "theriac."

Hazelnuts, Filberts

Wild hazelnuts were common in Europe and southwest Asia, and by the fourth century B.C. they were cultivated in the Mediterranean. Like walnuts they were used to prepare theriac, along with figs, rue, and salt. Warm and moist in nature, they were thought to be more easily digested when peeled, to cause wind in the intestines, to increase the size of the brain, and to act as an aphrodisiac. Hazelnuts and honey were a remedy against cough.

Pine Nuts

The edible seeds of the pine tree, pine nuts have been used in Middle Eastern cookery for thousands of years, and in the Middle Ages also played a role in Spanish, southern French, and Italian cuisine, all of which were influenced by the Arabs. Pine nuts were either ground and added to sweet and savory dishes or used as a garnish. Warm and dry in nature, pine nuts were prescribed by physicians against cough, roughness of the chest and lungs, excess moisture in the body, and as a diuretic.

Pistachios

Pistachio nuts are native to western Asia, and were eaten in Turkey and the Middle East as early as 7000 B.C. In the first century A.D. the Romans introduced pistachios to Europe. In medieval European cookbooks pistachios play a minor role, appearing in a handful of recipes, usually of Arab provenance.

Chestnuts

The sweet chestnut, commonly known as the "European chest-nut," is native to western Asia. The Greeks encountered it in Persia and introduced it to southern Europe, and the Romans brought it to Gaul and Britain. Cooks ground the starchy nut to flour, and mixed it with wheat flour from which they made bread, a practice still found in medieval Europe, especially in times of famine. Boiled or roasted, chestnuts, classified as warm and dry by physicians, were considered nutritious but hard to digest, causing wind and constipation. Then as now chestnuts were recommended for stuffing chickens, ducks, and geese.

CONDIMENTS

Salt

Since time immemorial salt has been the most important seasoning for food, and prior to the invention of canning and refrigeration, salt-ing was the most important way of preserving food, aside from drying and smoking. The two types of salt available to medieval consumers were rock salt and sea salt, also known as "bay salt." Rock salt was mined either in solid form, or by dissolving it in water that was then evaporated aboveground, leaving behind the salt crystals. Sea salt was produced in shallow coastal salt pans of the Atlantic and the Mediter-ranean. France was and still is one of the major producers of sea salt in Europe. Since this type of salt contained many impurities, it was either used for curing, or purified by redissolving, filtering, and evaporating it a second time. Dry salting or curing in brine were the preferred ways of preserving meat, fish, and some vegetables in the Middle Ages. The high salt content of many preserved foods meant that cooks had to be extra careful not to oversalt dishes, and in fact many a medieval recipe concludes with the phrase "do not oversalt." In some cases it was even recommended to remove excess salt from a foodstuff by soaking it in water prior to cooking. With salt being present in every type of dish, including sweets, the medical literature of the time is full of warnings against too much salt in the diet. Classified as a warm and extremely dry foodstuff, salt was recognized as an appetite stimulant and an aid to digestion, but when consumed in high quantities it was thought to dry out the body, burn the blood, darken the face, harm the eyes and the brain, consume the sperm, hurt the limbs, remove necessary moisture from the stomach, and make the whole body itch.

Honey

Since prehistoric times honey has been a foodstuff much enjoyed by humans and animals, notably bears. In ancient Egypt honey was an expensive commodity. The Romans treasured it too, using it for a variety of purposes, among them as an ingredient in mustard and as a medium for preserving fruit and meat. Originally gathered from wild bee colonies, honey was in time harvested from human-made hives. The fact that honey darkens prepared dishes made many upper-class cooks in the Middle Ages reach for the more exclusive sweetener sugar when a pure white appearance was desired. For thousands of years honey had also been used for the preparation of an alcoholic drink known as "mead." It, too, fell out of favor in medieval times when wine became the most prestigious drink. Honey continued to play a certain role in sauces and purees, in gingerbread, in the preservation of food, and in various confections, many of them medicinal. Physicians described honey as moderately warm and dry in nature, and considered it a mild diuretic and laxative. It was recommended for old people and those suffering from a cold temperament. Some believed that inebriation could be avoided by consuming honey after wine.

Sugar

Sugarcane, a plant that resembles bamboo, is probably native to New Guinea. It was first cultivated in Asia, and by the fifth century B.C.

the Greeks knew of its existence. In the fourth century B.C. Alexander the Great encountered it in India. The Roman cookbook of Apicius makes no mention of it, however. The first near-white cone or loaf sugar that was exported to the West came from Persia, where the refining of sugar was substantially improved in the seventh century A.D. The Arabs grew some sugarcane in Spain and Sicily in the Middle Ages, but the most prized sugar came from Cyprus. Despite efforts to produce sugar locally and thus bring down the price, most sugar was imported, and Venetian merchants played a pivotal role in the trade. For the medieval consumer sugar was an expensive luxury, classified as a spice even, and sold in apothecary shops. Often it was sprinkled sparingly on dishes, sweet or savory, or it was combined with other expensive imports, first and foremost almonds and rice, to produce luxurious Lenten food and dishes for the sick and convalescent. Described as moderately warm and moist, sugar was regarded as superior to honey because it did not cause thirst or itching and was easier on the stomach. Sugar was thought to be especially beneficial for the chest, lungs, kidneys, and bladder.

Vinegar

Used for thousands of years for medicinal purposes and to flavor and preserve food through pickling, vinegar is the result of a natural process, the invasion of an alcoholic drink with air-breathing bacteria that turn it to acetic acid. In fact, the English word "vinegar" is derived from French *vin aigre,* meaning "sour wine." There was no shortage of sour wine in the Middle Ages, when most wine was drunk young because it did not keep well. The same was true with beer, which also served as the basis for vinegar. Medieval cookbooks sometimes ask for wine or vinegar, beer or vinegar, and watered vinegar. For the lower classes vinegar was the universal seasoning that was widely available and cheap, but aristocratic cooks also used it for sauces, stuffings, and fish, for instance. As a cool and dry foodstuff it was recommended to be eaten in the summer and in warm regions. It was good for fighting toothache, for cooling the body, quenching the thirst, stopping the flow of blood, treating burns and infected wounds, including bites of rabid dogs, and for stimulating the appetite. Consumed in excess, however, it emaciated the body, led to weakened eyesight, and harmed the nerves, physicians warned.

Verjuice

Also referred to as *agrestum* or *agraz* in the medieval cookbooks, verjuice was the tart juice of crab apples, unripe grapes, or other unripe fruit that was frequently added to medieval dishes. Classified as extremely cold and moderately dry by physicians, verjuice was used in much the same way as vinegar, especially in cooling sauces that were designed to counteract the heat of roasted meat. Produced commercially and for individual use when the fruits were in season, verjuice was normally kept for a whole year.

Rose Water

Rose petals were already used in Persian cookery to perfume and flavor dishes long before the technique of distilling rose water was developed. The person commonly credited with the discovery of rose water was the tenth-century Persian physician Avicenna. Rose water soon became the rage in medieval Arab cookery, and through the Crusades the damask rose and distilled rose water were introduced to Europe. Rose petals and rose water appear in a variety of Arab or Arab-inspired dishes from southern Europe, and as far north as England. Because of its pleasant fragrance, rose water was also used for hand washing at luxurious feasts in the Middle Ages. Physicians described rose water as a fortifying substance that was good for the sense organs, for the heart, and to prevent and cure fainting.

Olives, Olive Oil

The olive tree is native to the Mediterranean, where it has been cultivated for some five thousand years. In ancient Greece and Rome olives were an important part of the diet, eaten whole or in the form of olive oil. Table olives were usually salted or brine cured, in order to remove their bitter taste. Olives that were destined for oil pressing were harvested when they were fully ripe. The Roman cookbook of Apicius differentiates between Italian and Spanish olive oil. To this day Andalusia, the southern part of Spain that in the Middle Ages was ruled by the Arabs, is the most important region for the production of olive oil. In northern Europe, olive oil was an expensive import, initially used by the Christian church for its sacraments, and for medicinal purposes only. As an alternative grease for cooking on fast days, olive oil remained too costly for the average northern consumer, who sometimes tried to substitute animal fats with locally produced seed oils. Physicians considered olive oil a moderately warm and moist foodstuff that gained in heat as it aged. The Italian custom of eating raw salad with olive oil and vinegar only reached Germany by the end of the Middle Ages. Black olives were thought to stimulate the appetite.

DOMESTIC AND WILD ANIMALS

Pig, Suckling Pig

The domestication of wild pigs took place in southwest Asia more than nine thousand years ago. Unlike cattle and sheep, pigs are omnivores that eat anything from household waste to grass, which makes them relatively easy to raise. In antiquity and the Middle Ages wild and domestic pigs were found across Europe and eaten by most people except for Jews and Muslims, who considered them unclean animals. The two main types were the short-legged pig kept in sties, and a longer-legged variety that foraged in the woods and was looked after by a swineherd. The Romans were especially fond of pork and suckling pigs, judging from the great number of recipes in the cookbook of Apicius. There are dishes featuring pork belly, pork hocks, ham, liver, and stomach, and in fact sow's womb was considered a delicacy. Suckling pigs were frequently stuffed or served with sauces. In medieval Europe pigs were one of the most important sources of meat and fat. Pigs not only roamed the forests or were kept in sties in the countryside, but city folk, too, usually had a few pigs that more often than not ran free and lived on the garbage in the streets. Pigs were normally slaughtered at the end of the year to provide the much needed ham, bacon, sausages, and lard for the winter. Practically all parts of the animal were eaten, from ears, snout, and tail to tongue, liver, spleen, and stomach. The head was often served on a platter as a festive dish, and ears and feet were turned into jellies. Bladder, stomach, and intestines were popular casings for sausages, headcheese, or imitation dishes, such as giant eggs for example. Physicians classified pork as a fairly moist and moderately cold foodstuff that was better when it came from castrated or well-exercised animals, presumably because it was then warmer and drier. Pork was seen as extremely nutritious and was described by physicians as similar in taste to human flesh. With the central role the pig played in the medieval diet, it is not surprising that physicians used various parts, such as feet, gall, and lard, for a variety of remedies.

Beef, Veal

The wild ancestor of European cattle is the auroch of the last ice age that prehistoric hunters depicted in early cave paintings found in France and Spain. By 3000 B.C. domestication had already resulted in several distinct breeds. In addition to being a source of food, cattle have always also been used as draft and plow animals; in fact, their strength may have been the initial reason for their domestication. In Britain cattle were raised early on, and in Roman times they were already exported to the Continent. In Anglo-Saxon England cattle continued to play an important role, but it is to the conquering Normans that modern English owes the word "beef" (from Anglo-Norman *boeuf*). Feeding on grass and hey, cattle were kept by peasants in the Middle Ages in smaller numbers than pigs, often just one per household. With a cow a family had a steady supply of milk from which to make butter and cheese, and meat when the animal was eventually slaughtered. As with pigs, nearly all parts of cattle were used as food, including all inner organs, and even the cow's udder. Calves, too, were slaughtered for food, but their meat, veal, never reached the popularity of beef. Veal recipes are found in French, English, German, and especially Italian cookbooks of the time. Beef was frequently boiled, sometimes roasted, but on the whole it played a minor role in medieval upper-class cuisine. Being the cheapest and coarsest meat available, it was not regarded luxurious enough for the aristocratic palate. Furthermore, physicians did not consider it healthy food, especially for the leisure class. Described as a warm and dry foodstuff, beef was thought to generate thick blood that in turn could lead to melancholy or worsen a preexisting melancholic temperament. Both beef and veal, the latter classified as somewhat warmer, were recommended for people engaged in heavy physical labor.

Mutton, Lamb

Domesticated in southwest Asia in the eighth millennium B.C., sheep have long been an important source of milk, cheese, meat, and wool in Europe. The Roman cookbook of Apicius contains 10 recipes for lamb, among them stews, and lamb roasted on an open fire or in an oven. When a sheep is older than a year, preferably three to five years of age, its meat is called "mutton." The best mutton was thought to come from castrated male sheep, or "wether." Mutton played an important role in Arab, southern European, and English cookery in the Middle Ages. It was sometimes the most expensive

Preparing tripe. From *Tacuinum sanitatis in medicina,* 14th century. Cod. Vind. Series Nova 2644, fol. 81r. Courtesy of Österreichische Nationalbibliothek, Vienna (Photo: Bildarchiv, ÖNB Wien).

fresh meat on the market, more expensive even than lamb or veal. The season for lamb was the spring, but older sheep were usually slaughtered in the fall. Roast leg of mutton seasoned with garlic was popular, and so were lamb casseroles with ingredients ranging from cinnamon and saffron to lemon juice, vinegar, and quince. According to medieval medicine, lamb was a warm and moist meat that was especially hard to digest when coming from a very young animal. The fact that the meat of older animals was considered drier and more easily digestible may account, at least in part, for the popularity of mutton. However, this trend began to wane at the end of the Middle Ages.

Goat, Kid

Goats are related to sheep and both were domesticated around the same time. Part of the European diet for thousands of years, goats played a secondary role to pigs, cattle, and sheep in the Middle Ages. The meat of older castrated goats was considered best by one fourteenth-century French writer. Kid, the young animal under half a year whose meat is more tender and has a milder flavor, was also eaten. Like cows and sheep, goats yielded milk that was turned into cheese. Described by the medical community as moderately warm and moist, goat meat was recommended for diners of all temperaments, and especially for those with weak stomachs because it was quickly and easily digested. The meat of white goats was said to be inferior to that of colored goats.

Chicken, Capon

The chicken is originally from India and southeast Asia, and was probably domesticated over three thousand years ago. It reached Greece via Persia in the sixth century B.C., and Britain together with the Celts in the first century B.C. The Greco-Roman world was fond of chicken. Chicken was on the menu at the famous Greek symposia (after-dinner drinking parties), and in the Roman cookbook of Apicius a great number of dishes are included that contain not just the meat, but also the inner organs of the bird. As suppliers of eggs, and of meat that was regarded as especially healthy and nutritious by the medical community, chickens were ubiquitous in the medieval kitchens of the well-to-do, and on holidays and special occasions those of more modest means also partook of chicken. Sometimes as much as a quarter of the dishes in a late-medieval cookbook consisted of chicken recipes. With its white meat chicken was ideal for white dishes, above all the feast-day version of *blanc manger*. The meat was frequently shredded or pounded into a paste, and used in pie fillings, or as a topping on flat dough preparations not unlike our modern pizza. Chicken liver and stomach are also mentioned as ingredients in a variety of dishes. Chicken soup was prescribed even then for convalescents as a restorative. Capon, the castrated domesticated cock, was a luxury usually reserved for the tables of the rich. Physicians classified chicken as moderately warm, and capon as somewhat cooler. Both were considered easily digestible, nourishing, and overall ideal for the dainty stomachs of the leisure class and those recovering from illness. Young hens and cocks that had not reached sexual maturity were considered the best. Plump chickens were said to provide a healthy complexion and blood that was neither too thick nor too thin. Chicken brain supposedly led to an increase in human brain and male sperm.

Goose

The goose is native to Europe, North Africa, and central Asia. In ancient Egypt geese were already domesticated and perhaps even then already force-fed to enlarge their liver, a practice that later became popular with the Romans and with the French, who coined the term *foie gras*. In addition to the meat, liver, and grease used in the kitchen, goose feathers were an important commodity in the Middle Ages. In England goose was the traditional meal on the church holidays Whitsuntide and Michaelmas, and in Germany at the Feast of Saint Martin. Goose was also frequently served at Christmas in Europe. The bird was often roasted or boiled and served with a sauce or condiment, or the meat was minced and put in pies. Medieval physicians warned of the hard and coarse meat of geese and other water birds that in their opinion was difficult to digest. Dripped into the ears, goose fat was a popular remedy against earache.

Duck

The wild duck was domesticated in China more than two thousand years ago. Ducks were also raised in classical Rome, and in medieval Europe they were eaten but play a rather minor role in the cookbooks that have come down to us. This may be due to the fact that physicians did not consider them healthy food on account of the bad humors they were thought to generate.

Peacock

The peacock is native to India and came to ancient Greece and Rome via Persia. Already in Roman times the decorative bird was served at banquets, a tradition that continued throughout the Middle Ages in Europe. Skinning the usually domesticated bird, returning it to its plumage and mounting it on a platter with its tail feathers fully fanned out required great skill on the part of the kitchen staff. When it came to the taste of peacock meat, however, it in no way matched the bird's exquisite appearance. It was tough and coarse, and was criticized by physicians for being difficult to digest and for generating bad humors. To make the meat more easily digestible, it was recommended to hang the slaughtered bird overnight by its neck and weight down the legs with stones.

Wild Boar

Found in Europe, Asia, and North Africa, the wild boar is frequently mentioned in classical mythology. The Roman cookbook of Apicius dedicates a whole chapter to the animal and lists recipes for roasting and boiling it as well as several different sauces with which to accompany it. Wild boar was also highly regarded by the Teutonic tribes and the Celts. In the Christian Middle Ages wild boar's head was the crowning of Christmas feasts and other festive dinners of the nobility. Aside from the head and the meat, the liver, lungs, stomach, and even blood of wild boar appear in the recipes of the time. How prized an animal wild boar was can be seen from the fact that some of the medieval recipes promise to make beef liver taste like wild boar liver. According to the physicians of the time, the meat of wild boar was healthier than that of the domestic pig. It was thought to be not quite as moist, but as nutritious and easy to digest as pork.

Venison

"Venison" is the term used for meat from roe deer, fallow deer, and red deer, the three kinds of deer common in Europe. Among them the male, called "stag" or "hart," has traditionally been the most sought after by hunters. In addition to being killed in the wild, often as an aristocratic sport, deer were kept in enclosed tracts of land, perhaps as early as antiquity and certainly in the Middle Ages, when extensive deer parks were a part of many noble estates. They helped ensure a steady supply of venison, especially when a big banquet was planned. The stag, popular in Roman times, judging from the chapter devoted to it in the cookbook of Apicius, also appears in many medieval recipe collections. Venison was usually roasted, or chopped up and surrounded with pastry to form venison pasties. In the Tyrolean Alps roe deer head seems to have been a local delicacy. The liver of deer was prepared in a similar fashion as that of wild boar, and for it, too, beef liver served as a less-expensive alternative. Hartshorn (deer horn) was used both in the medieval kitchen and apothecary. It was thought that a drink containing hartshorn strengthened the heart and drove away worms. Although the meat of roe deer was considered preferable to that of other deer by medieval physicians, all venison was said to generate bad melancholic blood.

Hare, Rabbit

The hare is native to Europe and has been part of the human diet for some 20,000 years. It is larger than the rabbit, has darker, more strongly flavored meat, and has never been domesticated. It was eaten by the Greeks and Romans, and in medieval Europe was frequently prepared in a sauce thickened with bread and the blood of the animal, and seasoned with pepper, or made into an onion-based stew known as a "civet of hare." The rabbit, whose flesh is lighter and milder in flavor, is native to Morocco and the Iberian Peninsula. In Roman times the animal, which can be domesticated, was brought to Italy, but not until after A.D. 1066 was it introduced to Britain by the Normans. An expensive novelty, rabbits, especially those older than a year and known as "coneys," are frequently mentioned in late-medieval English cookbooks. Along with beaver tail and barnacle goose, unborn and newly born rabbits were apparently not considered meat and hence could be eaten on meatless days. Rabbits were often roasted, stewed, or their meat was put in pies. Rabbits and hares are small game animals belonging to the same family. Physicians classified them as moderately warm and dry in nature, and warned of the melancholic humors they supposedly generated in the human body. Eaten by the aristocracy and wealthy bourgeoisie, the animals were recommended against obesity, a condition that in the Middle Ages was practically unknown among the lower classes.

Pheasant

Legend has it that the pheasant, a bird native to the Caucasus, was brought from Colchis to Greece by the Argonauts along with the Golden Fleece. By the early Middle Ages the bird had been introduced to Europe. Thanks to the colorful plumage of the cock, redressed pheasants, like peacocks, were a popular *sotelty,* or surprise dish, at aristocratic banquets. When the cooked birds were not served on a platter in a lifelike pose, they were sometimes boiled, or wrapped in dough, then pressed in a mold and cooked. This highly prized game bird, described as warm and moist in nature, was not only eaten but also hunted by the nobility with the help of even more highly prized falcons trained for the purpose. It was the ideal food for the dainty stomachs of the leisure class, convalescents, and the young and the old, physicians claimed, but it was thought to be harmful to manual laborers whose digestive tracts needed coarser foods.

Partridge

The partridge is native to Europe and central Asia. It was eaten by the Romans, judging from the three recipes contained in the cookbook of Apicius, and in the Middle Ages it was regarded as the healthiest of all the game birds. Like the pheasant it was hunted and consumed by the aristocracy, roasted or encased in dough, for instance. Mousier in appearance than the pheasant, to which it is related, the partridge does not figure as prominently as a medieval surprise dish. Physicians raved about the moderately warm and moist bird that according to them was easy to digest and generated good blood, especially when the bird was not cooked immediately after it had been killed but several days later.

Pigeon, Dove

Pigeons and the smaller doves can be found around the globe. The best-known European species include the wood pigeon, the turtledove, and the ancestor of domesticated pigeons, the rock dove. The raising of pigeons for use in the kitchen was first practiced in Egypt. The Roman cookbook of Apicius mentions one recipe for a sauce to accompany cooked turtledove. In the Middle Ages the birds were upper-class fare, often served roasted or in the form of pies. Physicians praised the birds as excellent food, and in their descriptions of the dietetic qualities, they frequently differentiated between young and old birds. Classified as warm and moist in nature, young birds were thought to heat the body, while old male birds were supposedly beneficial to people suffering from nervous disorders. The meat of turtledoves was said to sharpen the mind and improve a person's memory.

Quail

Smaller than the partridge, to which it is related, the quail was common in classical and medieval Europe. It was generally considered less wholesome than the other game birds because it fed on poisonous plants such as hellebore. This may explain why quails are hardly mentioned in medieval cookbooks and dietetic texts. The Arab health book *Tacuinum sanitatis* (Tables of Health) is one manual that does list quails. It describes them as a warm and moist foodstuff similar to the other small game birds. According to this text, quails generate good blood and provide good nutrition, especially for skinny people. Pomegranates, nuts, and cinnamon supposedly help prevent any negative side effects the consumption of quails may have.

Crane

A long-legged migratory bird, the crane was eaten in classical Rome and medieval Europe. While the Romans preferred braising it in sauce, late-medieval cooks usually roasted the bird and served it at banquets with such standard sauces as the cinnamon-based *sauce cameline*. Cranes were hunted by falcons and hawks, a method physicians approved of. Classified as warm and dry, cranes, like peacocks, were supposed to be hung by the neck and weighted down to make the dry meat more tender. When prepared with aromatic substances and thoroughly cooked, cranes were thought to be easier to digest than peacocks.

Herons

Like the crane, the heron is a long-legged waterbird. It is not mentioned in the Roman cookbook of Apicius, but figures prominently in some late-medieval European recipe collections, including the oldest German one from the mid-fourteenth century. The bird was hunted by the aristocracy with falcons, and in some places, notably the Low Countries, herons were also bred. In the Alpine region, heron appeared on the tables of the rich as heron puree, heron roast, in a spicy broth, or roasted and larded, for instance. Alternatively, it was stuffed and mounted on a platter to be served with great fanfare at luxurious banquets.

Swan

Throughout the Middle Ages the swan was not just admired for its majestic appearance but also eaten. Especially in Britain and France it was considered a delicacy. Although the meat of the young cygnets is of superior taste, it was the fully grown bird that was usually served in a lifelike pose at medieval banquets. With the skin and head carefully removed, the swan was roasted and then returned to its full plumage. To add drama, parts of the bird were sometimes gilded, or the head was made to breathe fire. Easily domesticated, and generally less tasty than most other fowl prepared in the medieval aristocratic kitchen, the swan nevertheless fetched the highest price in the market.

FISH

Saltwater fish and freshwater fish have been a staple food in Europe for thousands of years. The Roman cookbook of Apicius contains an abundance of recipes for fish and seafood, and so do many medieval cookbooks, but for different reasons. While Apicius reflects Mediterranean cookery that has traditionally been rich in fish dishes, the medieval recipe collections show the strong influence of the Christian church on the diet of the believers. Not allowed to eat meat on the 40 days of Lent, on Wednesdays, Fridays, Saturdays, and on the eve of major feast days, many Christians, especially those who could afford it, chose fish as an alternative. Fish recipes in the late-medieval cookbooks often do not specify the type of fish to be used, or they list a number of different species as suitable for a given dish. Fish appeared on the medieval table prepared in a variety of ways: it was roasted, fried, boiled, baked, encased in a pie shell, or in jelly, to name just some of the methods of preparation. Medical texts, too, frequently did not differentiate between individual species of fish, but offered instead a number of general guidelines regarding the consumption of fish and its effects on the human body. Fresh fish were described as cold and moist, hard to digest, causing thirst, generating phlegmatic humors, and increasing sperm. The best fish were thought to come from clear, rocky currents, to be scaly and of medium size, not too skinny, and not foul smelling or tasting. Most fish in the Middle Ages that were not eaten fresh were preserved in salt or dried, and some were also pickled in vinegar. To make them less harmful, physicians frequently recommended boiling the fish in wine.

Herring

This fatty fish of the North Atlantic was one of the most important foodstuffs of medieval Europe. Swimming in big shoals, herrings were caught in large numbers by fishing fleets in the Baltic and the North Sea. Only some of the catch was eaten fresh; the vast majority was pickled, packed several hundred to a barrel, and shipped to consumers across the Continent. Soaking in brine, drying, and smoking were the most common ways of making this highly perishable foodstuff more durable. Red herring were fish that were first gutted, then cured in brine, hung up to dry, and heavily smoked, which changed their color. White herrings were cured fish that retained their silver appearance and kept better than red herring. Other popular ways of preserving herring were to hot-smoke the gutted or ungutted fish to the point of cooking the meat, or to pickle herring in wine and vinegar or just vinegar. The amounts of herring consumed in medieval households were sometimes staggering. In one year in the early 1300s, an English priory feeding some three hundred people reportedly bought close to 250,000 herring. And in Lent even the lay household of a countess would consume up to a thousand herrings a day.[3] Eaten primarily by the poorer segments of society in the Middle Ages, herrings play less of a role in the cookbooks of the nobility and high clergy than the enormous size of the herring trade might suggest. In social prestige a herring was simply no match for a pike, for instance.

Cod, Stockfish

Like the herring, the larger North Atlantic cod was of eminent importance in the European diet of the Middle Ages. Much of it was caught off the coast of Iceland and traded in salted or dried form. Less oily than the herring, dried cod kept well, and it was the penitential food par excellence for medieval Christians. Also eaten and considered delicacies were the roe, tongue, cheeks, and liver of the fish. The type of cod most frequently mentioned in late-medieval cookbooks and household accounts is stockfish. Produced by splitting the fish in two halves and air-drying the meat, stockfish seems to have been a staple across Europe, from England and Scandinavia to Germany and Italy. The exact origin of the term "stockfish" is not known. According to some, the fish got its name from the sticks or poles on which it was dried, while others claimed that it was named after the sticks with which the stiff dried fish was beaten to soften up the meat. The Hanseatic League, an alliance of trading cities in northern Europe and the Baltic, which dealt in dried cod and called it "stockfish," may have played a role in the spread of both the product and the term. Medieval instructions for treating stockfish included beating it for hours with a mallet, and then soaking it in water for days before cooking it in sauce, baking it, or turning it into paste.

Salmon

This big fish of the Northern Hemisphere, which spawns inland and spends the rest of its life in the open sea, was quite common in medieval Europe. It is said that in northern England it was so common that apprentices objected to being served salmon more than three times a week. In continental Europe the salmon caught in the Rhine and other major rivers that was not sold fresh was usually dried, salted, or smoked, and shipped via Hamburg, Lübeck, Bremen, and other Hanseatic towns to all parts of Germany and beyond. A very decorative dish was salmon in jelly, served at festive banquets. Salmon meat was also sometimes surrounded with dough and fried or put in a mold and boiled in water. During Lent its pink meat could be used to simulate ham or bacon. Physicians considered salmon caught in May best to eat.

Sturgeon, Caviar

The sturgeon is another big fish that, like the salmon, spawns in rivers and lives in the ocean, although there are some species that remain in freshwater all their lives. In medieval Europe sturgeon was caught in the Danube and other major rivers flowing into the Atlantic and the Mediterranean. Among the species of sturgeon found in the Black Sea and the Caspian Sea is the famous great sturgeon that yields the highly prized beluga caviar. By the twelfth century caviar from the Black Sea was imported to Constantinople, where it was regarded as a new delicacy.

Bream

A member of the carp family, the freshwater bream is found across central and northern Europe, where its preferred habitat is the bottom of stagnant and muddy waters. This made it an ideal fish for medieval fish ponds, where it multiplied quickly. Introducing pike, a predatory fish, to these ponds helped prevent overcrowding. In Germany, bream caught in February, March, and June were considered the best. As a fish living in slow-flowing or stagnant waters, the bream was not highly esteemed by the medical community.

Carp

This large freshwater fish is native to the Danube and other European rivers flowing east to the Black Sea. In the Middle Ages it was also bred in fish ponds, and was a popular food fish among Christians and Jews alike, often served on festive occasions. Carp were only introduced to England toward the end of the medieval period.

Perch

Perch, native to the lakes and rivers of Europe and Asia, is a predatory fish that was eaten by the Romans and medieval Europeans alike. In the cookbook of Apicius it is prepared with seasoning, and in late-medieval cookbooks it figures prominently in dishes for fast days. It is combined with vinegar, or mashed and mixed with almond milk, and also appears as a topping on pizzalike dough preparations. Preferring clean rocky waters as a habitat, perch was more highly esteemed by physicians than fish living in muddy waters.

Pike

The carnivorous pike is a big freshwater fish of the Northern Hemisphere whose favorite habitat are the lakes and rivers of low-lying areas. In the medieval kitchen of the nobility the pike, which by then was also raised in fish ponds, was one of the most favored fish. It was frequently stuffed, encased in dough or aspic, or the meat was mashed and put in fast-day versions of *blanc manger*. Both meat and roe were used for imitation dishes during Lent, among them fake ham, eggs, or cheese. Cookbooks from France to southern Germany also list pike prepared simultaneously in three different ways as a *sotely*, or surprise dish, at festive banquets. According to the recipe, one-third of the fish was to be baked, one-third fried, and one-third boiled or steamed while leaving the whole animal intact. To physicians pike was a fish that was healthier than most others. Some considered the bigger female pike superior to the male.

Trout

A freshwater fish related to salmon, trout was not just caught in the wild but also reared in medieval Europe. Considered best to eat from late spring to the end of the summer, trout was sometimes listed as an alternative to other fish, notably salmon, in the cookbooks. Physicians maintained that trout was best when boiled in wine until all the liquid had evaporated. Baking it in dough was another alternative.

Crayfish

The crayfish is a freshwater crustacean whose marine equivalent is the lobster. In medieval Europe the crayfish that was caught in rivers was a highly esteemed alternative to meat on the many fast days of the year. Among the many recipes are crayfish pureed with milk, crayfish in spicy sauce, crayfish in jelly, and crayfish meat wrapped in dough, pressed in a mold, and boiled in water. According to some physicians, crayfish was best in March. Others maintained that the cold and wet crustacean induced sleep, and recommended it for hectic people and those suffering from consumption, especially when prepared with milk. The shell, turned to ash and mixed with gentian, was prescribed against the bites of rabid dogs.

Eel

The eels found in Europe, North Africa, and the Mediterranean are spawned in the Sargasso Sea, from where they travel east, and spend most of their lives in fresh water. In the Middle Ages, eels were eaten in great quantities in Europe, especially during Lent. Eel traps were set in many rivers and streams, such as the Severn and Avon in England, and often near mills. Eels were eaten fresh, salted, or smoked. Their fatty meat appears in a variety of pies, pastes, and jellies. Sometimes their skin was carefully removed, the meat seasoned and prepared, and returned to the skin. The eels were then roasted on a grill, or wrapped in dough and fried. Many physicians rejected the snakelike eel as a food fish, along with all other fish that lack scales.

Lamprey

This slimy parasitic fish that sucks the blood of larger fish lives in the sea, but like the salmon it spawns in rivers. The Romans not only considered lampreys a delicacy, those who could afford it also kept them in ponds as pets. In medieval Europe, lampreys continued to be eaten by the wealthy, especially on meatless days. Along with other sea fish they were sold by fishmongers in the big cities. Judging from the surviving recipes, eel and lamprey were at times used interchangeably. One way of preparing lamprey was to cut it in pieces and roast them on a grill, another was to pickle the pieces in vinegar. Classified by physicians as cold but less moist than eel, lampreys were generally considered nutritious food. However, unless prepared with salt and pepper, they were thought to be harmful to people with weak and moist stomachs, and to generate blood of a phlegmatic nature.

Porpoise, Whale

Both of these mammals were classified as fish in the Middle Ages, and hence were considered suitable for consumption on fast days. Together with sturgeon they were listed as royal fish in England, not to be eaten by members of the lower classes unless special permission was granted. Aside from the meat, which was often preserved with salt, the tongue was also eaten, in fact it was considered a delicacy.

Oysters, Mussels, Cockles, and Scallops

All these marine mollusks were eaten in medieval Europe, especially by people living directly along the Mediterranean and Atlantic coasts. Not being as closely regulated as certain fish, game, and venison, shellfish were also part of the diet of the lower classes. Oysters were consumed in great quantities, followed by mussels, which by the thirteenth century were already cultivated on poles erected off the French coast. Scallops were especially common in northern Spain, and many pilgrims from across Europe who flocked to Santiago de Compostela, believed to be the burial place of Saint James, returned home with a scallop shell as a souvenir.

Frogs and Snails

Snails have been part of the human diet for thousands of years. They were eaten in ancient Mesopotamia and later by the Romans, who also bred them. In the Middle Ages snails were consumed in some parts of Europe, notably France and Italy, but not in central and northern Europe. The cookbook *Menagier de Paris* (Householder of Paris), from circa 1393, contains a recipe for frogs followed by a recipe for snails. Both animals were classified as fish by the Christian church, and as such were acceptable food on meatless days. In a fifteenth-century chronicle of the Church Council of Constance, Germany, frogs and snails are among the foodstuffs sold at the market, but the text makes clear that they were eaten by visiting dignitaries from Italy and not by the local Germans.

DAIRY PRODUCTS

Milk

All mammals raise their young on milk, which has long been recognized as a special foodstuff capable of providing complete nourishment. But milk does not keep well, and so from the time that humans started domesticating animals and milking them, there was a need to find ways to prevent it from spoiling. Before refrigeration and pasteurization, the most common methods in Europe of extending the shelf life of this highly perishable foodstuff was to turn it into butter or cheese. In the Middle Ages, infants were fed the breast milk of mothers and wet nurses, and animal milk after they were weaned. Cow's milk was the most common milk, but milk from sheep and goats was also available to many people in Europe. Wealthy adults usually did not drink milk but the poor did, along with buttermilk, whey, and curds. Animal milk was sometimes used for cooking in noble households but many recipes call for almond milk, a nondairy liquid made from ground almonds that were suffused in water or stock and then filtered. It had several advantages over animal milk; for instance, it could be produced quickly as the need arose, and it could be used for cooking on fast days when animal milk was not allowed. Medieval physicians recognized the value of breast milk for small children. Animal milk, especially cow's milk, they recommended for the young and the old, but healthy individuals in their prime were generally dissuaded from drinking milk. If they did drink it, they were advised not to drink wine right after. It was maintained that milk was more easily digestible when combined with honey, sugar, or salt.

Butter

The method of turning cream into butter through churning has been known since antiquity, but the main use of butter was not always culinary. In ancient Greece, for instance, butter figured more prominently as an ointment than a foodstuff, and there is no mention of butter in the Roman cookbook of Apicius. In medieval Europe butter was usually made from cow's milk, and it was a staple food in areas that were rich in cattle, such as northern Germany, the Low Countries, and Scandinavia. Occasionally there are also references to butter made from sheep's milk. Bread with butter was said to be a Flemish invention. Butter is sometimes mentioned as a cooking medium, or it was dripped on roast meat and fish, but more often that not cooks in Europe turned to lard or olive oil as their preferred fats. Classified by physicians as a warm and moist foodstuff that is nourishing and generates good blood, butter was considered beneficial to the lungs and the chest, and especially good against coughs. Tart, acidic foods such as quinces were thought to remedy the supposed loss of appetite caused by butter. Fresh butter was put on the gums of teething children to alleviate any pain and irritation.

Cheese

A more durable foodstuff than either milk or butter, cheese has been made by humans since prehistoric times. The ancient Egyptians ate cheese, and so did the Greeks at the time of Homer. The Romans produced a great variety of different cheeses, and cheese is also mentioned several times in the cookbook of Apicius. To make cheese, ripened or sour cow's, goat's, or sheep's milk was first curdled by adding rennet, an enzyme taken from a calf or other young ruminant. The curd was then separated from the whey, heated, formed into the cheese, salted (if it had not been salted earlier), and aged. The remaining whey was either drunk by the lower classes, or cooked again to make ricotta cheese, or fed to farm animals. In the Middle Ages, cheeses ranging from fresh and soft to well aged and hard were popular across Europe, and cheese soup made from cheese, eggs, and pepper, was standard fare in German monasteries. Then as now, French Brie, Dutch Edam, German Limburger, and Italian Parmesan were well-known cheeses. During Lent almond milk, too, was turned into a cheese substitute called "almond cheese." Doctors described freshly made cheese as cold and moist in nature. It was thought to increase in heat and dryness as it aged. Cheese that was fatty, moderately salted, and of medium age was considered best. All cheese was slow to digest, and excessive consumption of cheese could lead to bladder stones, it was claimed. At the conclusion of a meal, however, cheese and pears were recommended, to "close" the mouth of the stomach and ensure proper digestion of all foods consumed. One of the dairy products sometimes referred to as "white meats" of the poor, cheese was thought of as a coarse food suitable for people engaged in heavy labor.

Eggs

One of the most versatile foodstuffs, eggs have been part of the European diet for thousands of years. The Romans used eggs in their cookery, but if the cookbook of Apicius is any guide, eggs were not yet as ubiquitous as they were to become in medieval Europe. In a fourteenth- or fifteenth-century cookbook it is not uncommon that 50 percent of the recipes list eggs as a primary or secondary ingredient. Usually the eggs in question were chicken eggs, but eggs of other birds such as geese, ducks, or partridges are also occasionally mentioned in the culinary and dietetic literature. Along with meat and dairy products, eggs were subject to the fasting laws of the Christian church. They were eaten on feast days throughout the year, and perhaps as a symbol of spring, or perhaps because they were most plentiful at that time, eggs were consumed in great quantities at Easter. Then as now, eggs were frequently hard boiled, soft boiled, poached, fried, or scrambled and made into omelets. As a secondary ingredient, eggs were used raw or cooked; sometimes just the yolks or whites were required for a given recipe. Eggs were a popular thickener for soups and sauces, and they were added to many different dough preparations. There is also evidence that sophisticated cooks at the end of the Middle Ages employed egg whites to clarify jelly. Physicians classified egg whites as cold and moist, and yolks as warm and moist. Chicken eggs were thought to provide quick nourishment and increase virility. The yolk was considered less harmful than the white. When eaten whole, eggs could cause freckles, was another claim. Like the meat of chicken and partridge, their eggs were recommended for the dainty stomachs of the leisure class and convalescents, while goose and duck eggs were at best suitable for the coarse stomachs of the common man, it was argued.

BEVERAGES

Water

Water is fundamental to human survival, yet in the Middle Ages most people's water intake came from foodstuffs other than water itself. Concerns over purity and its lack of prestige made water a drink that was shunned by the upper classes, and even those of more modest means opted for fruit juices, beer, or wine whenever possible. A custom medieval Europe inherited from the ancients, however, was to mix wine with water. Although as a beverage water was drunk only by the poor, it nevertheless played an important role in medieval food production and consumption. Water was the principle ingredient in ale, beer, and mead, and also in brine, a salt solution used extensively for the preservation of foodstuffs. As a liquid ingredient water also figured prominently in countless recipes. In addition, water was the primary cleaning agent for foodstuffs and kitchen- and tableware. Physicians advised against drinking water with a meal because of its cold and wet qualities that were thought to hinder digestion. Of the various types of water such as rainwater, springwater, well water, river water, lake water, snow, and ice, pure springwater was considered the best, and stagnant water, snow, and ice were considered the worst.

Ale, Beer

For thousands of years cereals have been used not only for bread making but also for beer brewing. Alcoholic drinks from grains were known in ancient Egypt and the Middle East, as well as northern Europe. Usually made from barley malt, water, and yeast, ale was typically produced in small batches by individual households in the Middle Ages, or by brewers, many of them women known in England as "alewives." It was sold to the public in alehouses, or peddled by hucksters in the streets. Not until the sixth or seventh century A.D. did monks in northern Italy begin to add hops as an ingredient in the brewing process. The natural preservatives and bitter taste of hops resulted in a drink that kept better than ale and was bitter rather than sweet. It became known as "beer," a word presumably derived from Latin *bibere,* meaning "to drink." The practice of brewing hopped beer spread northward and became especially popular in the Low Countries, that is, the area of today's Belgium and the Netherlands, where by the fourteenth century there were towns with a hundred or more breweries. Although beer of the type brewed in Flanders was known across the Channel in England before 1300, it took another two hundred years until beer brewing became accepted in England. Opposition to the new drink came not only from the authorities but also from the ale brewers, who felt their livelihood threatened by this cheaper and more durable beverage. Even as late as the mid-sixteenth century, voices were heard that touted ale as the drink of the English. Ale and beer were drunk in great quantities in the Middle Ages; in fact, for the majority of the population in England and the Germanic countries, they were the main beverages consumed on a daily basis. Wine was often just reserved for Sundays, holidays, and special occasions, or the tables of the rich in places where the vine did not flourish. Aside from being drunk pure, ale was sometimes mixed with other ingredients such as milk, spices, or brandy. As an ingredient in medieval aristocratic cookery, ale and beer played only a minor role, in part perhaps because ale and beer were associated with peasants and manual laborers, and in part because many of the cookbooks and nutritional texts that have survived were written in places like southern Europe where wine drinking was the norm. Ancient and medieval physicians, many of them from the Mediterranean, had a relatively low opinion of beer as a foodstuff, inasmuch as they discussed it at all in their treatises. It was thought to be cold in nature, more intoxicating than wine, and bad for the head, breath, stomach, and nerves. A sixteenth-century German physician, in an attempt to rehabilitate the favorite drink of his countrymen, praised it as a thirst quencher, appetite stimulant, laxative, and diuretic that was also considered good for the bile.

Wine

As early as 3500 B.C. the ancient Egyptians already turned cultivated grapes into wine. The Greeks spread the technique of wine making throughout the Mediterranean region, and the Romans northward to Burgundy, Britain, and Germany. In Roman times wine was not just drunk as a beverage, but also boiled down and added to food as a sweetener. Because of wine's central importance in the Mass, the Christianization of Europe went hand in hand with the spread of vineyards from southern Europe all the way to Scandinavia and the Baltic. Monasteries, especially those of the Benedictine order, were instrumental in improving the quality of wine. Any excess amounts of wine they produced they traded for cash. To maximize the yield, grapes were pressed several times in the Middle Ages. The best wine was that made from the grape juice of the first pressing. For the third pressing water was added to the crushed grapes, which made the resulting wine less strong, and also less expensive. Unlike the Romans, who stored their wine in jars, medieval Europeans generally used wooden barrels. Since wine did not age well, it was usually drunk young, white wine in particular. Red wine containing not just the juice but also the skin of the grapes aged better and was higher priced. With glass being a luxury material in the Middle Ages, and the technique of corking still unknown, wine bottles did not yet exist then. Wine was drawn from barrels as needed. Much is written in medieval cookbooks and household manuals about salvaging wine that has turned to vinegar or otherwise gone bad, which suggests that the storage of wine was far from ideal. Regions where wine was the common drink for both the elite and the masses (albeit of a lower quality) were the Iberian Peninsula, France, and Italy. Despite the fact that in England ale played such a dominant role, vast quantities of wine were also imported, mostly from Gascony, in southwestern France; some wine was produced locally as well. Among the towns that rose to prominence in the medieval wine trade were La Rochelle on the French Atlantic coast, Bruges and Antwerp in the Low Countries, and Malvasia on the Mediterranean island of Crete, after which the famous wine malmsey was named. Especially sought after by discerning European consumers were French wines from Beaune, near Dijon, and the Bordeaux region, German wines from the Rhine and Moselle, and from Alsace, Italian wines from Rivoglio and Sicily, and a variety of sweet Spanish and Greek wines.

In the Middle Ages wine was drunk either pure or mixed with water, the latter form being recommended by physicians. Spiced or mulled wines were also consumed at luxurious meals, but usually in small quantities and for medicinal purposes, namely at the beginning to "open" the stomach, or at the end as an aid to digestion. There were wines infused with sage, roses, or cloves, but the most famous, *hippocras* and *claret,* contained complex blends of powdered spices that merchants even sold ready-made. Selections of the spices ginger, cinnamon, grains of paradise, pepper, galingale, nutmeg, cloves, mace, spikenard, and sugar all figure in the different medieval recipes for *hippocras.* The *claret* of the Middle Ages, unlike its modern namesake, which is simply a type of red wine, was a heavily spiced red or white wine whose characteristic flavor was achieved by pouring the wine over a bag containing powdered spices, some of which were identical with the *hippocras* spices. Others added just to *claret* were fennel, anise, caraway, and cardamom.[4] Considered by the medical community as eminently healthy, wine was not only drunk but also included in many different dishes. For those who had the means or lived in a region where wine was plentiful and cheap, pieces of bread, or "sops," soaked in wine were a popular breakfast. Cooks, too, made extensive use of wine in the kitchen, judging from the many late-medieval recipes that ask for the liquid. It figures prominently in soups and potages, especially in Germany, and in a variety of sour sauces, for instance. As an accompaniment to food, clear, fragrant, and good-tasting wine was recommended in the health books. Diners were also advised to drink wine in more concentrated form at the beginning of the meal, the reason being that the food consumed later would prevent the wine from going to the person's head. It was generally held that children under five should not be given any wine, and those under fourteen only small amounts that were well diluted. Described as warm and dry in nature, wine was thought to be the ideal drink for convalescents, pregnant and lactating women, and the elderly. Many were the virtues ascribed to wine, such as fortifying the body, acting as a digestive and a diuretic, correcting humoral imbalances, and brightening the mood. Thick red wine was especially praised as a foodstuff easily converted into healthy blood, from which, of course, it was not dissimilar in appearance to begin with. In conjunction with other food, wine supposedly acted as a kind of "vaporizer," carrying even the smallest food particles to all regions of the body. Excessive wine consumption, however, was blamed for a variety of ills, ranging from damage to the brain to trembling and the loss of motor skills.

Mead

Mead, with its principal ingredients water and honey, is the oldest known alcoholic drink of the Teutonic tribes; it was later adopted by the Romans and still drunk in Europe in medieval times. After the invention of beer brewing, and wine making, however, the importance of mead slowly waned, and by the end of the Middle Ages it appears only occasionally in the culinary literature. The relatively few dishes that ask for mead usually mention it as an alternative to wine or beer. A detailed recipe for mead is contained in the oldest German cookbook from the mid-fourteenth century. In addition to two parts water and one part honey, hops, sage, and yeast are listed as ingredients. A similar recipe from Paris circa 1390 suggests the infusion of the ground spices ginger, long pepper, grains of paradise, and cloves as a further refinement. The inclusion of this recipe in a section on beverages for the sick suggests that the once-revered social drink of the Germanic tribes was later administered as a medicinal potion before it disappeared altogether.

Cider, Perry

Fermented and unfermented fruit juices of various kinds were consumed in medieval Europe. Most of them were homemade and drunk mainly by the lower classes. Among the best known, especially popular in parts of England and France, were cider and perry, two drinks prepared from apples and pears respectively. Other fruits used by Europeans to prepare juices and wines were medlars, quinces, pomegranates, sorb-apples, wild plums, mulberries, cornel berries, and blackberries.

Aqua Vitae and Other Distillates

Distillation is a process that around 800 B.C. was already known to the Chinese, who refined rice beer with it. The Greeks, Egyptians, and Romans also distilled various mostly nonalcoholic substances, among them seawater, in order to desalinate it, and resin, which they turned into turpentine. Some distilled alcohol may already have been used in the ancient world for medicinal purposes. The technique of distillation came to Europe in the late Middle Ages through Arab mediation, as can be seen from such words as "alcohol," and "alembic," the term for the apparatus necessary for distillation, both of them Arabic in origin. Since Islam did not allow the consumption of alcoholic beverages, the Arabs used distillation mainly to produce a variety of essences such as rose water, which served as perfume, medicine, and culinary ingredient. In medieval Europe distillation initially captured the imagination of alchemists, for whom the alembic was a way to produce the "quintessence," that is, the fifth essence after air, water, earth, and fire. The pure spirit created through distillation was thought to be able to prolong life, and was fittingly called "aqua vitae," the water or elixir of life. Prescribed by physicians and sold in apothecaries, or produced in monasteries, often with the addition of various herbs, the distilled drinks of the late Middle Ages were first and foremost medicinal potions. Only occasionally was distilled alcohol used for nonmedicinal purposes then, as in the case of English spiced ale, or to make boars, swans, and other stately animals breathe fire with the help of a cotton swab soaked in alcohol and lit as the presentation dish was served at a luxurious banquet.

NOTES

1. Some information on famines and epidemics between A.D. 500 and 1500 is contained in the timeline. For more detailed information on these and other food-related events during the period from Europe and around the world, see James Trager, *The Food Chronology: A Food Lover's Compendium of Events and Anecdotes, from Prehistory to the Present* (New York: Henry Holt and Company, 1995), 39–82.

2. The sources used for this chapter include Alan Davidson, *The Oxford Companion to Food* (Oxford, U.K.: Oxford University Press, 1999); Melitta Weiss-Amer [Adamson], "Zur Entstehung, Tradierung und Lexik deutscher Kochbücher und Rezepte des Spätmittelalters" (master's thesis, University of Waterloo, 1983); Terence Scully, *The Art of Cookery in the Middle Ages* (Woodbridge, U.K.: Boydell Press, 1995); P.W. Hammond, *Food and Feast in Medieval England* (Stroud, U.K.: Alan Sutton, 1998); Barbara Flower and Elisabeth Rosenbaum, trans., *The Roman Cookery Book: A Critical Translation of "The Art of Cooking" by Apicius for Use in the Study and the Kitchen* (London: George G. Harrap, 1958); Lorna J. Sass, *To the King's Taste: Richard II's Book of Feasts and Recipes Adapted for Modern Cooking* (New York: Metropolitan Museum of Art, 1975); Barbara Santich, *The Original Mediterranean Cuisine: Medieval Recipes for Today* (Kent Town, Australia: Wakefield Press, 1997); Franz Unterkircher, ed. and trans., *Das Hausbuch der Cerruti: Nach der Österreichischen Nationalbibliothek* (Dortmund, Germany: Harenberg Kommunikation, 1979); Luisa Cogliati Arano, ed., *The Medieval Health Handbook (Tacuinum Sanitatis)*, translated and adapted by Oscar Ratti and Adele Westbrook (New York: George Braziller, 1976); Priscilla Throop, trans., *Hildegard von Bingen's Physica: The Complete English Translation of Her Classic Work on Health and Healing* (Rochester, Vt.: Healing Arts Press, 1998); Christa Hagenmeyer, *Das Regimen Sanitatis Konrads von Eichstätt: Quellen-Texte-Wirkungsgeschichte* (Stuttgart: Franz Steiner Verlag, 1995); Guualterus H. Rivius [Walther Ryff], *Kurtze aber vast eigentliche nutzliche vnd in pflegung der gesundheyt notwendige beschreibung der natur/eigenschafft/Krafft/Tugent/Wirckung/rechten Bereyttung vnd gebrauch/inn speyß vnd drancks von noeten/vnd bey vns Teutschen inn teglichem Gebrauch sind/etc.* (Würzburg: Johan Myller, 1549); for herbs, also Claire Kowalchik and William H. Hylton, *Rodale's Illustrated Encyclopedia of Herbs* (Emmaus, Pa.: Rodale Press, 1987); and for spices, Maggie Stuckey, *The Complete Spice Book* (New York: St. Martin's Griffin, 1999), and Andrew Dalby, *Dangerous Tastes: The Story of Spices* (Berkeley and Los Angeles: University of California Press, 2000).

3. Hammond, *Food and Feast*, 20f.

4. Scully, *The Art of Cookery*, 150.

CHAPTER 2
FOOD PREPARATION

Where in the social hierarchy people found themselves in the Middle Ages determined not only what foodstuffs they could afford, but also how their food was prepared. The most basic form of cooking food was on an open fire. Eggs in their shells, for instance, could easily be cooked this way. When their contents were broken directly on the embers, such eggs were called "lost eggs" (*oeufs perdus* in French, or *verlorene eier* in German). Before eating these eggs it was advisable to clean off the ash.[1] Most members of the lower classes, when they had a roof over their heads, lived in one-room dwellings with a fireplace in the center that served as a source of heat, a source of light, and a cooking facility. Stones were used to contain the fire. If the walls of the building were not of wood but of stone, the fireplace was often moved away from the center and against one of the walls.[2]

A basic piece of equipment for any medieval cook was the cast iron cauldron that either had legs already molded to its body or was placed on a ring, usually with three legs, that was set in the coals. Alternatively, the cauldron could be hung from an adjustable hook attached to a beam or to a chimney crane, an iron arm swinging horizontally. This had the advantage that the heat could be better regulated to avoid burning the food. When earthenware pots were used by the housewife, she would either place them in the hot ashes beside the fire or put them on a hot stone in the coals. Since boiling and stewing were the most economical ways of preparing food because no valuable juices were lost, and because only the most basic of cooking facilities were needed, the typical dish of the lower classes was the potage or

Food preparation. From *Losbuch*, ca. 1350. Cod. Vind. Series Nova 2652, fol. 4v. Courtesy of Österreichische Nationalbibliothek, Vienna (Photo: Bildarchiv, ÖNB Wien).

stew. In fact, from the French word for cauldron, *chaudière*, comes the modern English word "chowder."[3]

Bread was a foodstuff much more difficult, if not impossible, for a housewife of modest means to bake in her own home. If she had the necessary grain, she needed to have it ground to flour first, and lords of the manor usually insisted that she pay a licensed miller to do that rather than do it in small batches in her own mortar or quern, a primitive hand mill. And even if she had the bread dough kneaded and the loaf ready to go in the oven, she had to find an oven. In medieval villages and towns ovens were few and far between, and their construction and operation closely regulated. Only the baker and some of the wealthier households would be granted permission to have such a cooking facility that used up a lot of valuable firewood. As substitutes for a full-sized baker's oven, households would sometimes use covered pots that they buried in the coals, or small portable ovens. The latter were especially popular in southern France.[4]

The richer the household in the Middle Ages, the better equipped its kitchen was, the more refined its cuisine, and the greater the likelihood that the food was not prepared by a lone housewife, but by one or more professional cooks with an army of helpers. Monasteries, manor houses, castles, and the houses of the wealthy bourgeoisie were the places where cooks exercised their craft, if they did not run their own business. Like many other professions at the time, cooks were organized in guilds. To become a master cook in Paris, for instance, one had to first work as an apprentice for two years, and then as a journeyman for another master.[5] Having attained the title of master, a cook had several options: he could open his own cookshop, work for another master, or seek employment in a wealthy household. The relatively low pay cooks received compared to members of other professions suggests that their status in society was not particularly high. There were exceptions, of course, such as the famous Taillevent, chief cook of the king of France, who was handsomely rewarded for his services and was even given a coat of arms. Judging from the literary sources, however, it would appear that on the whole cooks suffered from an image problem in the Middle Ages, a time in which the spirit was held in much higher esteem than the body, at least by the educated elite. Hence the work of a scribe copying a religious text was regarded as vastly superior to that of a cook who catered to the needs of the flesh.[6] Aside from their perceived lack of education, cooks and their staff were often looked down upon because their job was a messy and smelly one that made them reek of kitchen odors. Furthermore, they were accused of drinking on the job, of being hot-tempered and crotchety, and of possessing a rough sense of humor. In their defense it must be pointed out that their job was not always easy, besieged as they were by boarders, nibblers, and tasters, who were not only of the human kind, but included dogs, cats, foxes, rats, mice, and flies, to name a few. Little wonder, then, that cooks were known to use their trademark ladle, with which they were usually depicted, not just to taste the food but also to discipline and chase away the various interlopers.[7]

But how did cooks themselves view their profession? The little evidence we have suggests that at least when it came to aristocratic cooks, they regarded their work as much more than just a craft. Master Chiquart, chief cook to the duke of Savoy, for instance, saw himself as an artist and a scientist.[8] Entrusted with the health and well-being of their employers and families, not to speak of the many high-ranking guests they had to feed in the course of the year, cooks worked closely with court physicians, and even if cooks could not read Latin, they must have had some basic knowledge of the medieval theory of nutrition. Food was regarded as the primary means to keep the four humors in the human body in balance, and to rein in any excessive humor with a diet that was appropriate for the particular humoral imbalance.[9] In addition to this scientific knowledge, and mastery of the various cooking methods, a good cook was also expected to possess artistic talent. With appearance playing such an important role in the medieval dining experience, it was up to the cook to devise dishes in ever more intricate shapes and colors, and to entertain the dinner guests with illusion food that would do any modern magician proud.

But if the invention of a memorable dish was the crowning of a cook's career, immortalized perhaps in the chronicle describing the banquet at which it was served, most of the work the cook and his kitchen staff had to perform day in and day out was unglamorous, tedious, and tiring. Being in charge of supplies from firewood to foodstuffs and kitchenware, cooks usually had to report their expenses daily to their superiors, the kitchen clerks or the steward.[10] The household of the duke of Burgundy employed three cooks, of whom one was the chief cook or master. Taking orders from the cooks were 25 specialists and their helpers, among them a roaster, a pottager, and a larderer, who was in charge of the larder where the food was stored. Given the real and perceived danger of poison in medieval upper-class households, the office of the cook was one of trust. In his absence the cook was to be replaced by the roaster, with the pottager being next in line.[11] Other specialists at court who did not perform their tasks directly in the kitchen but whose work was nevertheless essential for the preparation of a meal, were the saucers and their helpers, who supplied the standard sauces and made sure that enough salt, vinegar, and verjuice, the sour juice of unripe fruit, was in store, and the fruiters, whose responsibilities extended to candles and tapers as well. Working either from within or outside of noble households were the bakers, pastry cooks, waferers and confectioners, butchers, and poulterers.[12] The general rule in wealthy households was, however, to process foodstuffs as much as possible in house, since buying prepared dishes from outside castle walls carried the danger of serving food made from inferior, tainted, or outright poisonous ingredients.

In every medieval kitchen there were also a number of menial jobs that had to be performed. They ranged from hauling firewood and tending the fire to drawing water, scrubbing, and guarding the food-stuffs from theft. At the court of the duke of Burgundy fuellers, fire tenders, potters, and doorkeepers carried out these tasks. But by far the biggest contingent of workers in a big medieval kitchen were the scullions. They were the unpaid apprentices who turned the spits, cleaned the fish, scoured the pots and pans, and usually also slept in the kitchen. Some scullions managed to climb in the hierarchy of the kitchen and end up as cooks or master cooks. The already mentioned Taillevent, chief cook of King Charles V of France, too, began as a kitchen boy in the early fourteenth century.[13]

The primary workplace where cooks and their staff prepared most of the food was the kitchen. In the early Middle Ages the hearth was still centrally located, even in the wealthier households, with the kitchen and dining hall forming one big room. Gradually the kitchen became a separate room, or in some cases a separate building connected with the main building through a walkway that was usually covered to protect the servitors and their precious cargo from the elements.[14] There were several reasons why those who could afford it tried to separate cooking from dining, first and foremost to minimize the danger of fire, but also the noise and the smells emanating from the kitchen area. The big aristocratic and monastic kitchens of the later Middle Ages usually had stone walls and a stone floor, and more than one fireplace built against the walls. The kitchens of the dukes of Burgundy in Dijon, France, for instance, had six stone-hooded hearths built in pairs against three of the four walls. A big window and sinks occupied the fourth wall.[15] Windows and louvers in the roof made sure that medieval kitchens were properly ventilated. Derived from the French word *l'ouvert*, meaning "the open one," the louver was a lantern-like structure on the roof that allowed the smoke to escape through openings on the sides. Slatted louvers were closed in bad weather by pulling on a string. More durable and entertaining than these wooden louvers were the ones made of pottery, often in the shape of a head with the smoke escaping through the eyes and mouth.[16] Windows and the glow from the fireplaces were the main sources of light in medieval kitchens, complemented at times with candles and torches.

Kitchen waste was either dumped into the river, if the castle or monastery was situated on one, or dumped down a chute into the moat that surrounded the castle walls and was periodically cleaned. In medieval towns householders frequently dumped their garbage directly in the street below, judging from the various laws that tried to curb the practice. City dumps did exist, but they were normally located a distance away, outside city walls.

When one thinks of the logistics of a medieval feast, the first things that usually come to mind are the vast amounts of ingredients necessary to prepare all those fabulous dishes the cookbooks and chronicles tell us about. And yet, any cook, even the best one, would have failed miserably without an adequate supply of firewood to fuel the hearths and ensure that all the food was cooked to perfection. Ordered by the cartloads, dense dry wood was continuously hauled into the kitchen, either through the wide doors or perhaps even some big windows. Toward the end of the Middle Ages coal became more and more popular as a fuel because it produced a more even and longer lasting heat.[17] Fire irons were used to spark a fire, which with the help of kindling was gradually turned into the desired blaze. Air from the mouth of a kitchen boy or from bellows also helped in drawing up the flames. Instead of putting out the fire in the evening and starting a new one the next day, householders often chose to leave the embers dormant overnight. Since unattended embers were a fire hazard, a pottery cover with ventilation holes was put over the fire. In towns a special bell was rung in the evening reminding people to put out or cover up their fires. The modern English word "curfew" is derived from the name for this bell, *couvre-feu*, which in turn was named after the above-mentioned pottery cover.[18]

To make the most of the fire for cooking took a lot of skill, and medieval cooks were true masters in exploiting the heat for a variety of tasks simultaneously. Big cooking pots were hung above the fire on adjustable hooks that, when attached to swinging chimney cranes, allowed for heat regulation by moving the pot vertically and horizontally to or from the fire. The burning logs were placed in andirons under the pot, and if necessary could be removed to reduce the heat. Sometimes small metal baskets were attached to the upright posts of andirons. Filled with hot coals, they were an extra heat source for a pan or pot placed over them.[19] Bigger pots and cauldrons would be placed on tripods or the somewhat lower trivets set over or in the coals.

To make fritters, pots with cooking oil were placed directly in the coals.[20] For roasting meat and fish, or for toasting bread, spits and grills were used that were either made of wrought iron or of wood. Varying in length and thickness depending on the size and weight of the food to be roasted—ranging from a small bird to a whole ox— spits were placed either right over the fire or to the side, often resting on the andirons or a similar contraption, and turned by one of the scullions. So as not to be directly exposed to the heat of the fire, these spit turners would frequently do their work behind metal shields.[21] To catch the juices and basting liquids dripping from the roasts, a special pan, called *lechefrite* in French, was put under the spit. This pan was also used for gently heating delicate foods.[22] Frying pans came in various depths and sizes, and looked quite similar to the frying pans we still use today. When frying food, cooks either held them directly over the fire or placed them on a tripod above the fire.

In addition to boiling, stewing, roasting, and frying, which could all be done on the hearth, some dishes required baking. Pies, if they were not simply put in a covered pot and embedded in coals, or placed in portable ovens, were baked in bakers' ovens, and so, of course, was bread. Built either into the masonry of the fireplace where the other cooking took place, or as a separate structure in the bakehouse, the medieval oven was normally heated by lighting a fire within. Once the oven walls were sufficiently hot, the coals and ashes were removed, and the pies, tarts, pastries, and bread were lifted into the oven on a flat hardwood peel.[23] If a household employed a cook and a baker or pie maker, the cook would prepare the meat, fish, fruit, or vegetable fillings for the pies and then send them over to the bakery, where they were encased in the pie shells and baked.

Another place where food was handled was the dairy. From the dairymaid's pails the milk was poured into wide, shallow containers. Due to the lack of refrigeration and pasteurization, most of it was turned into cheese with the help of a cheese press, or into butter in a tall churn.[24] Specialized rooms or separate buildings that often supplemented the kitchen were pens for livestock, a brewery, a scullery for washing up, the larder, the cellar, and other storerooms.[25] Since the freshness of food was a major concern, larder shelves were constantly monitored for rotting food or the presence of rodents, such as mice and rats. To keep the flies away, meat was put in safes that allowed some airflow.[26]

To make a medieval kitchen run smoothly, more equipment was needed than the heat source, cauldrons, pots, pans, and the contraptions to place them on or hang them from. Cooks and their staff, all wearing long aprons, did most of the cutting on a solid table that was their main work surface. For meat they used a chopping block. Utensils and containers frequently mentioned or depicted in medieval sources included flesh hooks, long-handled basting spoons, big stirring spoons, ladles, graters, rasps, sieves, tongs, cleavers, knives, whetstones, mallets, whisks and brooms made of twigs, oven shovels, an assortment of hampers, basins, ewers, flasks, platters, trenchers, saltboxes and saltshakers, and mortars and pestles. Cloth was used both for cooking and, along with scouring sand or ashes and tubs, for cleaning the kitchenware.

One of the most basic tasks in the kitchen was to chop the meat and vegetables with a sharp knife. Often the ingredients were cut up, mixed, and seasoned, and the resulting forcemeat or farce (from Latin *farcio* meaning "to cram") was used as a pie filling or stuffing, was formed into meatballs, or re-formed around the animal bones from which the meat had previously been removed.[27] In some extreme cases the food had to be treated with a hammer first before it could be further processed. This was the case with the Lenten staple dried cod, known as "stockfish," which was to be beaten with a hammer, then soaked in warm water prior to cooking.[28] In the absence of modern food processors, the mortar and sieve cloth were the most important utensils for preparing the smooth sauces and pastes that were the hallmark of medieval upper-class cuisine. Rooted in the medical-dietetic idea that a foodstuff in granular or powder form "will exert the fullest possible influence when in contact with another substance," medieval cooks would frequently pound ingredients first in the mortar, then moisten them and filter them through a sieve cloth for the desired fine consistency.[29]

Every foodstuff in the Middle Ages was assigned a combination of two humoral qualities (warm-dry, warm-moist, cool-dry, or cool-moist). (See Chapter 6.) The humoral composition already predetermined, to some degree, what form of cooking to use. This was especially important for the preparation of meat. A good cook knew that pork was cool and moist, and that these qualities would be counteracted by the warming and drying effect of roasting; or that a hare, like most other wild animals, was warm and dry in nature, hence boiling was the recommended way to prepare it. Frying or baking was used for meats of moderate humors.[30] One of the characteristic features of medieval food preparation was multiple cooking. Meat, in particular, was often precooked before it was larded and roasted. This was done to cleanse and firm the flesh, perhaps also to make sure the meat was well done by the time it left the roasting spit.[31] The recipe for suckling pig from the oldest German cookbook goes even further. It calls for the animal to be skinned first, the meat to be cooked and returned to the skin, the piglet to be boiled, and later grilled over low heat.[32] Fish, too, was subjected to multiple cooking. The same Ger man cookbook contains several recipes for stuffing the prepared meat back into the raw skin and then grilling the fish. In some cases the roasted fish was subjected to an additional cooking process by encasing it in dough and baking it.[33]

A different kind of multiple cooking is found in a popular entertainment dish served in-between courses at medieval banquets across Europe: the fish prepared in three ways. Keeping the fish in one piece, the tail end is boiled, the middle part roasted, and the front part fried. With each part the appropriate sauce is to be served: green sauce for the boiled part, orange juice for the roasted part, and *sauce cameline,* a cinnamon-based sauce, for the fried part.[34] This suggests that multiple cooking was not just done for reasons of health or taste, but also for fun.

The average housewife or neophyte cook in the Middle Ages, however, was concerned about more fundamental issues than how to prepare a three-way fish. Then as now, temperature and timing were the two most important factors that often meant the difference between success and failure in the preparation of a dish. And both were extremely hard to communicate in a recipe, given that the instruments to measure them were either nonexistent (thermometers), or very crude, if available at all (clocks). Not surprisingly, then, medieval cookbooks are full of helpful hints on how to stop food from boiling over, or burning to the pot, and how to avoid the taste of smoke in a dish.[35] With directions as vague as "cook it on a gentle fire," or "make a tiny fire," in the culinary literature, a cook had to know from experience—or intuition—what temperature was appropriate for a certain dish, or for a certain step in the preparation of a dish.

The same is true with cooking times. Even if a recipe provides information on the quantities of ingredients, which is rare enough, it almost never provides cooking times in hours or minutes. The best the reader can hope for is a comment referring to a generally known activity like saying a prayer or walking a certain distance. Hence a sauce is to be stirred for as long as it takes to say three Paternosters, nuts are to be boiled for as long as it takes to say a Miserere, some ingredients for mead are to be boiled for as long as it takes to walk around a field, and others for as long as it takes to walk half a mile.[36] The weights and measurements used in trade were known to medieval cookbook authors but are seldom mentioned in the recipes. In addition to the occasional gallons, quarts, pints, pounds, ounces, inches and the like, quantities and sizes are often expressed with the help of other foodstuffs, such as eggs, or nuts, or parts of the body, such as the length and width of a finger.[37] And then, of course, there are the relative measurements "twice as much as," "a quarter of the amount of," or simply "not too much of."

When it comes to food-related fraud in the Middle Ages, most of it was connected with the weight and quality of foodstuffs. Much of the adulteration that occurred concerned the basic foodstuffs wine, beer, bread, meat, fish, and salt, of which great quantities were traded. Of the high-end products, spices in particular were subject to adulteration. Although they were sold in much smaller quantities than the other foodstuffs, the profit margin was much higher which made them a prime target of fraud. To protect medieval consumers from unfair pricing or food of dubious quality that had the potential of endangering public health, governments passed a variety of laws and also appointed food inspectors. One such law was the *Assisa Panis et Cervisae* (Assize of Bread and Ale) passed in England in 1266. It regulated the weight and price of bread and ale in relation to corn.[38] With weights and measures being far from standardized in medieval Europe, legislation was needed for both wholesalers and retailers of food products.

Wine, for instance, had to be imported in barrels of a certain size. Prior to sale, their contents were measured by the king's own wine gaugers. Endless confusion was caused when the barrels did not conform to the standard size but a foreign one customary in the wine's land of origin. On the retail side, too, standard measures regulated the sale of wine and ale in taverns. The adulteration of wine in the Middle Ages took many different forms. Good wine was sometimes mixed with bad, Spanish with French or German wine, or sweet wine from the Mediterranean was counterfeited. There is even evidence of an artificial wine made from pure alcohol and spices with no grape content whatsoever. To ensure that the wine sold in London taverns was in good condition, inspectors known as "searchers" made the rounds and ordered any dubious draughts to be condemned or destroyed. One of the punishments for selling bad wine was to have the taverner drink part of it and pour the rest over his head.

Ale and beer were subject to similar kinds of quality control by officials called *Alkonneres* in England. Adding water, salt, or resin were some of the ways ale was adulterated, and, of course, consumers would get shortchanged if a measure smaller than the one prescribed by law was used. When in the late Middle Ages Europe gradually switched from ale made with malt and yeast to beer brewed with hops, the once small-scale operations dominated by women known as "alewives" were slowly being replaced by larger breweries run by men.[39] Their product tended to be cheaper than the traditional ale. To ensure that only beer of good quality was sold, surveyors inspected the breweries, paying special attention to the purity of the ingredients used.

One group of professionals with an especially bad image in the Middle Ages were bakers. Justified or not, bakers were constantly accused of selling bread of less than the prescribed weight or bread made with inferior dough, or dough contaminated with sand, dirt, cobwebs, ashes, and the like. Since bakers' ovens were not just used for baking bread but also pies, bakers were at times accused of selling tainted pies, too. According to one such scheme that was uncovered in the City of London, cooks sold kitchen waste to the bakers who in turn filled pies with it and sold them at a handsome profit.[40] The standard punishment for a fraudulent baker, as depicted in a medieval manuscript, was to draw him through the street on a sled with the lightweight loaf bound around his neck.[41]

To prevent the sale of bad meat or fish, a number of measures were taken by authorities that included laws against selling meat by candlelight, reheating cooked meat, inflating meat with air to make it look larger, or stuffing rags into inner organs to add weight. Fresh fish was especially problematic because it had a very short shelf life. Hence it was only supposed to be put on sale for two days, and freshened with water only twice.[42]

Spices, first and foremost among them pepper, ginger, cloves, nutmeg, cinnamon, and saffron, were the ultimate in luxury food in the Middle Ages. According to estimates, western Europe annually imported approximately 1,000 tons of pepper and 1,000 tons of ginger, cloves, nutmeg, and cinnamon combined. The value of these imports was the equivalent of 1.5 million people's bread supply for a whole year.[43] The abundance of spices in medieval cookbooks clearly marks them as an upper-class commodity because an average household in the High Middle Ages could barely afford 20 to 25 grams of pepper, and about the same amount of the other imported spices a year.[44] Poor people's substitutes for imported spices were the garden herbs dill, fennel, chives, leeks, onions, garlic, and parsley. If these were in short supply, the German physician Hieronymus Bock recommended the use of vinegar as a universal seasoning for sauces, fish, crayfish, meat, and cabbage.[45] The high price of spices made them attractive for adulteration by spice merchants intent on increasing their profit margin even more. Ground spices especially were frequently mixed with a variety of foreign substances. The officials appointed to examine imported spices were known as "garblers" in England. The term, derived from the verb "to garble" meaning "sifting impurities from," adequately describes their job, which was primarily to clean spices and dried fruit by sieving them and removing any foreign matter such as leaves or dirt, before grocers were allowed to sell them.[46]

According to one source, a London apothecary filled the order for ginger, wormwood, and frankincense made by a Gloucestershire merchant by substituting the items with rapeseed and radish, tansy seed, and resin.[47] According to Hieronymus Bock, white bread or wheat flour were often mixed in with ground ginger, dried wood with cloves, tanner's bark or the bark of oak trees with cinnamon powder, and ground nutmeg was frequently nothing more than dry and wrinkled nuts. Saffron was stretched with sandalwood, and sometimes even gold dust was mixed in with the spices to bring them up to the right weight.[48] This is an impressive demonstration of the fact that some spices were considered more precious even than gold. Another, more mundane way of increasing the weight of spices was to wet them.[49] Peppercorns were adulterated with a whole range of different substances, ranging from unripe juniper berries to vetch (climbing vines of the bean family) to mouse droppings.[50]

Throughout antiquity and the Middle Ages physicians, too, put together lists of substitute foodstuffs and drugs known as "quid pro quo." In them ginger is suggested as a substitute for pepper, figs for dates, and hyssop for thyme, for instance. Cheap substitutes that could be grown in one's garden were savory for pepper, and the root of myrtle flag for ginger. High-priced saffron could be replaced by safflower as a coloring agent. The fact that adulteration of spices was such a widespread problem in the Middle Ages shows what a lucrative business the spice trade was. The quid pro quo lists, on the other hand, are an indication that the poorer segments of medieval society also wanted to emulate the tastes of the upper-class dishes that were laced with expensive imported foodstuffs. This raises the question, what exactly was the taste so sought after by medieval diners?

Spices were used extensively, and in a much wider variety of dishes and drinks than today. They were usually added in powdered form, but sometimes also whole. Ready-made spice mixtures with names such as *powdour douce* or mild powder, and *powdour fort* or strong powder, were commercially available. The former often contained sugar and cinnamon, while the latter consisted of more pungent spices such as pepper.[51] Judging from the medieval recipes that have come down to us, spices must have played a leading role, and yet we do not really know how dominant their taste was in a given dish. Spices surely lost some of their strength between the time they were harvested in Africa and Asia and the time they finally reached the European consumer, which could be months. Being sold and stored in powder form rather than whole also likely diminished their potency. And, of course, adulteration reduced the quality and strength of spices, if not changing their taste altogether. On top of that, medieval cookbooks hardly ever give amounts for the ingredients to be added.

Aside from spices, acidic liquids were a medieval predilection, one that the lower classes also could afford. Wine, vinegar, and verjuice, or the fermented or unfermented juice of unripe grapes or other unripe fruit, formed the basis for a wide variety of dishes. In the fifteenth century citrus fruits such as lemons, limes, citrons, and bitter oranges, together with pomegranates became part of the repertoire of acidic food substances. Unlike vinegar and verjuice, however, these fruits were exclusive foodstuffs only the upper class could afford. To produce the many sauces that accompanied roast meat, these tart liquids were usually combined with powdered spices and thickened by way of reduction or concentration, bread crumbs, eggs, the liver and breast meat of fowl, ground almonds, or rice flour. Starch was used only rarely as a thickener, and flour, dairy products, or roux, the combination of fat and flour, not at all.[52]

To counterbalance the tart flavor of the various acidic liquids, sugar, honey, must (unfermented grape juice), dried fruit, and other sweeteners were frequently added giving the dishes the desired sweet-and-sour or bittersweet taste that was the hallmark of medieval European cookery. When it comes to fat, pork fat was the undisputed king in the Middle Ages. Olive oil and nut and seed oils were used in salads—inasmuch as salads were eaten at all in a given region—and these oils were used as substitutes for pork fat on fast days. Butter played a comparatively minor role in the medieval cookbooks. Much more prevalent than the taste of cow's milk and butter was the taste of almonds. Like the ubiquitous grape juice, almonds were a durable if somewhat pricier foodstuff that was immensely versatile. Not as distinct in flavor as vinegar or verjuice, in fact rather bland, almonds were used in various ways, whole, slivered, or ground, or turned into almond oil, almond milk, or almond butter. The almond's flavor would either disappear completely, blend in with the other flavors, or be the main flavor, albeit a dainty one, as in the case of marzipan, the famous sweetmeat.[53]

For those who could not afford the luxury of expensive spices, garden herbs and bulbs were a way to add flavor to their dishes. Leeks, onion, and garlic were popular all over Europe and were often associated with the lower classes. Due in no small part to its odor, garlic especially was considered as peasant food.[54] Sometimes as much as the taste, it was the appearance of a dish that mattered. Color and shape were important factors for cooks to consider, especially when they prepared the myriad of dishes that made up a medieval banquet.

Already in Roman times cooks cared about the color of the dishes they prepared. From the third-century cookbook *De re coquinaria* (The Art of Cooking) attributed to the first-century Roman gourmet Apicius, we learn that a boiled-down wine called *defrutum* was used to give the gravy of meat dishes a deeper color.[55] Adding soda to green vegetables was known even then to brighten the natural color of vegetables. There are also examples of white and green sauces in the cookbook, and saffron already played a role as an additive to wine. And yet, these Roman examples of enhancing and manipulating the color of food were nothing compared to the color craze that swept Europe in the wake of the Crusades to the Holy Land and other contacts by European Christians with the Arabs, notably in Sicily and southern Spain. Gold, red, white, and silver are the colors that abound in the few Arabic cookbooks we have from the Middle Ages. These colors were of enormous significance to Arab alchemists, whose goal was to turn the mercury extracted from cinnabar into gold with the help of sulfur. To create white dishes medieval cooks did not usually color the ingredients but combined those that were by nature white, such as almonds, the white meat of poultry, sugar, rice, and ginger.[56] Dramatic effects could be achieved by preparing a dish in batches of different colors and arranging them on a platter with one half white and the other yellow, for instance, or creating the pattern of a checkerboard. Golden yellow, the result of using saffron and/or egg yolk, was the absolute favorite in Arab and European kitchens of the time. Saffron was added ground if an even coloring of the dish was desired, or sprinkled on top of a dish to cover the surface with golden dots or lines.[57] A cheaper way of gilding or "endoring" food was to cover it with egg yolk before the final cooking. Meatballs were covered this way in Arabic recipes that eventually made their way into European cookbooks of the fourteenth and fifteenth centuries.

Green was a color that had long appealed to Europeans, as the Roman attempts at enhancing its appearance in vegetable dishes has shown. When yellow and green were mixed, it resulted in a bright green that was called *gawdy grene* in English, and *vert gay* in French.[58] For darker greens, chard, spinach, parsley, mint, basil, and other herbs were used.[59] To color a dish, either the pounded leaves or the juice extracted from them was added. Much effort went into creating the various shades of red, from light pink to deep purple, with which cooks delighted the discerning diner. Sandalwood was frequently used and yielded an old-rose color, and *draco,* or dragon's blood, was a plant-based dye that resulted in bright reds. The root of the plant alkanet, or dyer's bugloss, also appears as a food dye in the medieval sources, as do rose petals, blood, and red grape juice. *Tournesoc* or *tournesol,* an orchil lichen, gave medieval cooks the option of dying alkali-based dishes blue, which was the plant's natural color, or red when combined with acids.[60] Other ways of creating blues were adding columbine blossoms or blackberry pulp. For the many shades of brown cooks utilized sandalwood, which gave them a pinkish brown, cinnamon for a camel's hair color, blood for dark brown, or toasted bread or gingerbread, which, depending on the degree of toasting, would produce any shade from light brown to black. Cooked chicken liver, dark raisins, and prunes were other ingredients that could be used to color a dish black. An especially dramatic effect was achieved by covering a dish or part of a dish, such as boar's head, with gold or silver leaf that was ingested along with the meat and was regarded as having medicinal qualities. (See Chapter 3 and Chapter 6.)

Some types of dishes lent themselves especially well to coloring. Processed foods ranging from liquids to creams and pastes were habitually colored. Roast meat was usually accompanied by sauces that came in all the colors of the rainbow. Some of them were actually known by their color, such as green sauce, white sauce, or the famous camel- or cinnamon-colored sauce known as *sauce cameline.* Saffron gave many rice and almond dishes a radiant golden hue, and also added sparkle to jellies. A medieval cook could show his mastery of the craft by creating multicolored jellies in the pattern of a checkerboard, for instance, or a round center in one color and an outer ring in a different color.

But color was not the only means to enhance food in the Middle Ages. Another way was to give the processed food a distinctive shape through the use of molds. They seem to have been especially popular in Germany, as, in fact, they still are today. A pan known as a "Turk's head pan," presumably named after the shape of a turban it gives to the cake baked in it, continues to be used for making *Gugelhupf,* a favorite coffee cake.[61] But the Turk's head pan was not a medieval invention. As early as A.D. 200 the Romans used similar molds made of bronze. In the opinion of one scholar, the swirls symbolized to the

Romans not a turban, but the rotating sun. Prior to the Romans, the Egyptians were known to prepare sacrificial food in a pan of this type.[62]

In addition to bronze, clay was used in antiquity for the production of molds. Stone was another durable material for such cooking vessels, but most of them were probably made of wood. Due to the rapid decay of wood, examples of wooden molds from earlier centuries are rare, however. Molds are already mentioned in the oldest German cookbook, as the following recipe illustrates:

Diz ist ein guot spise von eime lahs [This Is a Good Salmon Dish]

Take a salmon, scale it, split and cut the two halves in pieces. Chop parsley, sage, take ground ginger, pepper, anise, and salt to taste. Make a coarse dough according to the size of the pieces, sprinkle the pieces with the spices, and cover them completely with the dough. If you can fit them into a mould, then do so. In this way you can prepare pike, trout, bream, and bake each one in its own dough. If it is a meat-day, however, you can prepare chickens, partridges, pigeons, and pheasants, provided that you have the moulds, and fry them in lard or cook them in their moulds. Take chicken breast or other good meat. This will improve your art of cooking even more, and don't oversalt.[63]

When these molds were used for baking in an oven, they were covered on the inside with butter and on the outside with clay. Molds also played an important role in the preparation of gingerbread and confections. To create fully formed shapes, two corresponding molds were used, held in place by aligned holes through which sticks were pushed. At the end of the Middle Ages, molds made of wax are mentioned in the preparation of sugar figurines. Jellies and confections were poured into molds in the shape of boxes. Molds consisting of dough were filled with jelly, according to the fifteenth-century German cook Meister Hannsen.[64]

Pie shells, too, were cooked in special containers or molds that were first sprinkled with flour, and then boiled in a water bath before being filled with the farce. Some molds had the shape of stamps whose relief was pressed into the marzipan or dough preparation; alternatively, the mixture could also be pressed onto the stamp and then baked. This was a favorite technique of gingerbread makers.

The popularity of waffles and wafers in the Middle Ages, especially at the conclusion of a multicourse meal, meant that waffle irons were part of the standard kitchenware in upper- and middle-class households. They usually consisted of two flat planes with interlocking handles. Decorations found on the planes could include images or inscriptions. Waffle irons made of cast iron were used less often. A variation of the waffle iron for oven use was the stove-top waffle iron, which was equipped with a mechanism to turn the iron 180 degrees. Waffles were either eaten flat, or rolled up into little sticks.

With so much attention being paid to the color and shape of food in the Middle Ages, it should not surprise us to find that over the centuries cooks came up with an ever increasing number of dishes that pretended to be something else, dishes that are sometimes referred to as "pretend-foods" or "imitation food."[65] One of the possible reasons why such foods evolved may have been the periodic unavailability of foodstuffs. For consumers of the twenty-first century accustomed to buying anything their hearts desire at any time of the year, it may be hard to imagine that for most of human history seasonal cooking was the norm. If a foodstuff was not in season or could not be stored or preserved for future use, the next-best thing diners could do was to make believe they were eating it, by substituting it with something else that was made to look like the real thing. In addition to the "natural" unavailability of food in the Middle Ages, when frozen food did not yet exist, transportation was slow and cumbersome, and trade not nearly as global as it is today, there were the food restrictions imposed by the Christian church for parts of the year. After a long winter with little or no fresh food, the subsequent 40 days of Lent must have left many a believer yearning for a succulent roast. If the cook was able to conjure up a dish that at least visually resembled a roast, even if the taste of the meat substitute was not quite the same, it nevertheless meant that the burden of fasting was alleviated somewhat. Not only was the craving for meat partially met, but since no forbidden foodstuffs were used and no fasting laws broken, the pleasure derived from indulging in imitation meat was a guilt-free one.

Aside from compensating for the lack of a given foodstuff, the imitation food of the period always also displayed a strong sense of playfulness. It is fair to say that in the kitchens of late-medieval Europe the idea of playing with food was elevated to an art form. It was in the creation of a new dish whose composition and presentation contained an element of surprise that the cook could prove the mastery of his craft and demonstrate his artistic talent. As in many other professions of the time, skill, technical know-how, and virtuosity were valued highly in a cook. With an audience that was both well informed and alert, the pressures on the cook to come up with more and more complicated and dazzling creations must have been considerable, especially when the occasion was a festive dinner, or even worse, a festive dinner during Lent.[66]

Medieval cookbooks, which for the most part reflect wealthy upper-class cooking, are full of imitation dishes for Lent, a time when the consumption of warm-blooded animals, dairy products, and eggs was forbidden to Christians. Sometimes it is just a single sentence at the end of a recipe that contains the fast-day variation of a meat dish. This is the case, for instance, with the medieval favorite known as *blanc manger*, or white dish, which on fast days was to be prepared with pike meat instead of chicken meat.[67] At other times the recipes for imitation dishes are quite elaborate. A fifteenth-century cookbook from northern Germany, written in Low German, provides two detailed recipes for imitation eggs. One uses the shells of chicken eggs to trick the diner into thinking she or he is breaking the fast. The empty shells are to be stuffed with a filling made from ground pike roe (a type of egg acceptable for Lent, one might say), parsley, pepper, saffron, and figs or raisins. The eggs are then put on skewers and grilled.[68] The other recipe is the fast-day version of a medieval crowd-pleaser, the giant egg designed to make dinner guests wonder what fabulous animal could have produced such a marvel. Normally an animal bladder filled with a great number of egg yolks was inserted in a larger bladder filled with egg whites, and then cooked. In the case of the giant egg for lean days, the egg yolk consists of ground pike roe mixed with saffron and chopped figs, and the egg white of pike roe and almonds. Once cooked, the giant Lenten egg is cut in two and sprinkled with sugar and ginger.[69] In these two examples, fish roe and almonds figure prominently, but fish meat, various other nuts and seeds besides almonds, peas, and bread were also popular ingredients in imitation dishes. Ground almonds, however, were by far the most versatile of ingredients used to prepare a whole range of Lenten foods, from substitutes to cow's milk, butter, and curds, to cheese, cottage cheese, hedgehogs in different colors, eggs, and egg dishes. Fish meat is shaped into fake roasts, ham, and game birds such as partridges, and fish roe into sausages or bacon. Mincemeat is simulated with chopped almonds and grapes, and cracklings or greaves (the sediment of melted tallow) are made from diced bread.[70]

As the Middle Ages drew to a close, the church began to allow the consumption of eggs and dairy products on the lesser fast days of the year. This relaxing of the rules is reflected in various recipes for imitation roasts that required eggs and butter as ingredients. To give a meat substitute the appearance of roasted meat, the cook had several options. The most popular was to cover the fake roast with ground gingerbread that had first been fried or roasted. Egg white was sometimes used to simulate the barding (interlarding; inserting of fat in lean meat) of a roast that was otherwise made from fish. French cooks came up with the idea of combining salmon and pike meat for imitation ham and bacon by using salmon to represent the pink meat, and pike the fat.[71] At times the diners were fooled by more than just the imitation meat itself. A number of recipes from the period suggest that cooks were also skilled in employing markers to make the illusion even more complete. They would use sauces and broths normally reserved for meat, and not just any meat but the most highly prized of all: venison. There are examples of fake roasts made from fish or crayfish meat, or of sausages made from dolphin meat—which along with barnacle goose and beaver tail was regarded as Lenten food in the Middle Ages—all of them served in a dark and spicy pepper broth that was the hallmark of venison dishes.[72]

Aside from the obvious desire on the part of the diner to have his meat and eat it, too—in other words, to be a good Christian and still forego the rigors of fasting—what we observe here is a game of make-believe that cooks and dinner guests engaged in. But the Middle Ages did not invent this game, nor were they the last to play it. From ancient Rome several examples of pretend foods have come down to us that were clearly designed to fool the diner. At Trimalchio's Feast in Petronius's *Satyricon* a boar is served that looks ungutted from the outside but when cut open turns out to be filled with delicious sausages. The fact that a number of recipes for this kind of surprise dish can be found in a Roman cookbook from the third century A.D., Apicius's *De re coquinaria* (The Art of Cooking), is a strong indication that the boar in the *Satyricon* was not just the product of a writer's fertile imagination, but a dish actually prepared by gourmet cooks.[73] And if Trimalchio's wonder dish consisting of a well full of fat fowl, sow's bellies, a hare sporting Pegasus's wings, and four figures of flute-playing satyrs pouring a spiced sauce over fishes bears any resemblance to reality, then Roman cooks could easily hold their own against the best royal cooks late-medieval Europe had to offer.[74]

But important impulses for the evolution of pretend foods may have come from outside Europe as well. Medieval Arab cookery, which subscribed to the heavy processing, coloring, and shaping of food much earlier than European cookery, was full of sophisticated dishes that were designed to look like something else.[75] What medieval Europe did was to make such dishes an integral part of lavish banquets. In England these entertaining dishes were known as *sotelties,* literally "subtleties," and in France as *entremets.* The latter word, meaning "between courses," points to the position such dishes occupied within a multicourse meal. Initially just simple dishes sent to the hall for guests to nibble on as they waited for the next course to arrive, the *sotelties* or *entremets* soon became substantially more elaborate and more playful, as cooks began to experiment with unusual colors and color combinations, edible building structures, making cooked food look raw and vice versa, live animals look dead and vice versa, making animals look and act like humans, inventing fabulous creatures, and assembling entire allegorical scenes.[76]

If the medieval French cookbook known as *Le Viandier* (The Provisioner) by Taillevent is any indication, then the earliest *entremets* were nothing more than millet porridge, frumenty or wheat porridge, rice, or such lowly ingredients as the livers, gizzards, and feet of poultry cooked and garnished or served in a sauce.[77] All these recipes have one thing in common, however: they contain saffron to give the dishes a golden hue. More sophisticated than these monochrome dishes was the *blanc manger* that was no longer only a "white" dish, as the name suggests, but was served in two contrasting colors on a plate.[78] Jellies, too, soon became the subject of much experimentation by cooks. With jelly squares in different colors the desired checkerboard effect could be achieved.[79] And, of course, encasing fish, crayfish, and the like in clear jelly made these animals look as if they were still immersed in water, their natural element.

It has been noted that English cooks, in particular, liked to make towers and castles out of dough.[80] Given the strong Italian and Sicilian influence on Anglo-Norman and English cookery, this predilection for edible structures made from dough may have had Italian roots. (See Chapter 3.) Cases in point are the famous Parmesan Pies or Parma Pies that were covered in gold or silver leaf and shaped like towers, complete with crenelations and banners at the top.[81] But more than buildings, it was animals that inspired imitation dishes in the Middle Ages. Ground almonds were the basis for hedgehogs that had almond slivers for quills and came in different colors. Alternatively, the meat of fish, fowl, or seafood was often heavily processed and pressed in molds, or stuffed back into the raw skin of the animal.[82] Carrying the theme of "the raw versus the cooked" or "nature versus culture" even further was the idea of returning the prepared meat into the full plumage of a decorative bird such as a peacock or a swan, and mounting the animal on a platter in a lifelike pose.[83] That even cows or deer were mounted in such a fashion shows that in the Middle Ages there were no limits to what an aristocratic cook and his kitchen staff would be willing to tackle in order to impress a dinner party.[84]

When cooks no longer saw the need to return the meat of a cooked animal solely to its own skin, this opened the door for a whole new range of culinary tricks. The plumage of a peacock could be stuffed with a goose, that of a dove with some other farce, and the roasted and coated carcass of the dove placed beside it to miraculously make two doves out of one.[85] Even entirely new animals were invented by imaginative cooks, such as the *Cokagrys*, a creature half cock, half piglet, found in the English cookbook known as the *Forme of Cury* (The [Proper] Method of Cookery).[86] And one wonders how medieval diners felt when the *sotelties* appearing at the table were animals that parodied such human endeavors as going on pilgrimage or riding into battle. The edible pilgrim was either a capon or a pike that was given a roast lamprey as a pilgrim staff, and the knight a cock equipped with paper lance and paper helmet and riding on a piglet.[87]

An even more dramatic special effect was achieved when the animal served on a platter was not only mounted and dressed in a lifelike manner, but also made noises, or breathed fire. In a fifteenth-century French recipe collection, the *Vivendier* (The Provisioner), we find a recipe for making a dead and roasted chicken sing as if it were alive. This is done by filling the tied neck of the bird with quicksilver and ground sulfur, and then reheating the animal.[88] More common was the practice of having a boar's head, swan, piglet, or fish breathe fire by combining cotton with camphor or fire-water, that is alcohol, and lighting it.[89] For really grand occasions cooks would assemble a whole range of such edible wonders to form a complete allegorical scene, such as a "Castle of Love," for instance.[90] In the fifteenth century the edible *sotelties* and *entremets* were replaced more and more by inedible decorations that no longer required the skill and imagination of cooks but of artists and craftsmen such as painters, carpenters, and metal-workers. They were now the ones producing the tableaux of mythical and religious figures and scenes, among them the "Lady with the Unicorn," the "Knight of the Swan," or the "Lamb of God," *Agnus Dei*.[91]

Hand in hand with the development of dishes that made animals appear lifelike, went the development of dishes that made them look dead and cooked while in reality they were still alive. Their inclusion in a meal, like that of the inedible figures made of wood or metal, was purely for the purpose of entertainment. One such creation that would have animal rights activists up in arms if served today was the live chicken that was made to look roasted. First the bird was to be plucked alive in hot water, then covered with a glaze that gave it the appearance of roast meat, and subsequently it was put to sleep by tucking its head under one wing, and twirling the animal. Then it was to be put on a platter together with other roast meat. What was going to happen next, the cookbook describes as follows, "When it [the chicken] is about to be carved it will wake up and make off down the table upsetting jugs, goblets and whatnot."[92] Another practical joke of this kind was to color live lobsters red by covering them with extra-strong brandy, and mixing them in with the cooked lobsters. An easier way of grossing out especially the women at table, was to serve live cocks and other birds, or live eels in bowls, which when uncovered would have their contents flutter about or slide all over the dining table.[93] To this category of dishes also belong the "four-and-twenty blackbirds baked in a pie." The live birds were to be inserted in a baked pie immediately before serving, and when the top of the pie was cut open, the birds would escape to the amazement of the assembled dinner party. To avoid any of the guests feeling cheated, the Italian cook Maestro Martino suggested filling the pie not just with live birds but with another smaller pie that was edible.[94]

Sometimes prepared dishes were made to look disgusting just prior to serving. This is the case with two recipes in a Middle English cookbook called the *Liber cure cocorum* (Book of Cookery). One of them gives instructions for making a meat or fish dish appear raw and bloody by sprinkling the powder of dried hare's or kid's blood on it; the other suggests covering meat or fish dishes with "harp-strings made of bowel" to make the food look as if it were full of worms.[95] In both cases it is conceivable that the dubious garnish was put on after the dishes had left the kitchen, perhaps by somebody intent on discrediting the cook. This is not as far-fetched as it may seem, since the same cookbook does in fact contain a recipe describing how to get back at a cook. This is to be done by casting soap in his potage, which will make the pot boil over incessantly.[96] As this example shows, kitchen humor when carried too far could easily turn into all-out war. In medieval cookbooks recipes for punishing the cook by spoiling or manipulating his food are quite rare. But this is to be expected, given that it was neither in the interest of cooks to give readers any ideas for pranks, nor in the interest of upper-class households to admit to a diners' revolt. It is in books on magic and, yes, books on warfare, that we find such recipes listed, and the picture they paint of a cook under attack is not a pretty one: He was faced with chickens, pieces of meat, peas or beans made to jump out of the pot with the help of such unsavory additives as quicksilver, vitriol, and saltpeter, or with the pieces of meat in his pot sticking together in one big lump because somebody had poured in comfrey powder.[97] It would appear as if the games cooks played with their dinner guests in the form of *sotelties* and *entremets* at times came back to haunt them.

NOTES

1. Barbara Ketcham Wheaton, *Savoring the Past: The French Kitchen and Table from 1300 to 1789* (Philadelphia: University of Pennsylvania Press, 1983), 23.

2. For this and the following see Bridget Ann Henisch, *Fast and Feast: Food in Medieval Society* (University Park: Pennsylvania State University Press, 1976), 109.

3. *The Oxford English Dictionary*, 2nd edition, prepared by J. A. Simpson and E.S.C. Weiner, 20 vols. (Oxford, U.K.: Clarendon Press, 1989), "chowder."

4. See chapter 3, esp. the cuisine of southern France.

5. Terence Scully, *The Art of Cookery in the Middle Ages* (Woodbridge, U.K.: Boydell Press, 1995), 236f.; see also Alan S. Weber, "Queu du Roi, Roi des Queux: Taillevent and the Profession of Medieval Cooking," in *Food and Eating in Medieval Europe*, eds. Martha Carlin and Joel T. Rosenthal (London: Hambledon Press, 1998), 145–58.

6. Henisch, *Food and Fast*, 67.

7. Ibid., 59–65.

8. Scully, *The Art of Cookery*, 40.

9. See chapter 6; and also Melitta Weiss Adamson, "*Gula, Temperantia*, and the *Ars Culinaria* in Medieval Germany," in *Nu lôn ich iu der gâbe: Festschrift for Francis G. Gentry*, ed. Ernst Ralf Hintz (Göppingen, Germany: Kümmerle, 2003), 112f.

10. Scully, *The Art of Cookery*, 243.

11. Ibid., 246.

12. See ibid., 243–45; Henisch, *Fast and Feast*, 75–82; and Stefan Weiss, *Die Versorgung des päpstlichen Hofes in Avignon mit Lebensmitteln (1316–1378): Studien zur Sozial- und Wirtschaftsgeschichte eines mittelalterlichen Hofes* (Berlin: Akademie-Verlag, 2002).

13. Wheaton, *Savoring the Past*, 18.

14. Cf. Henisch, *Fast and Feast*, 97.

15. Scully, *The Art of Cookery*, 86f.

16. Henisch, *Fast and Feast*, 96.

17. Scully, *The Art of Cookery*, 92.

18. Henisch, *Fast and Feast*, 89.

19. Scully, *The Art of Cookery*, 94.

20. Wheaton, *Savoring the Past*, 23.

21. Scully, *The Art of Cookery*, 94.

22. Wheaton, *Savoring the Past*, 24.

23. Maggie Black, "Medieval Britain," in *A Taste of History: 10,000 Years of Food in Britain*, eds. Peter Brears, Maggie Black, Gill Corbishley, Jane Renfrew, and Jennifer Stead (London: English Heritage in association with British Museum Press, 1993), 110.

24. Ibid.

25. Henisch, *Fast and Feast*, 97.

26. Ibid., 92.

27. Odile Redon, Françoise Sabban, and Silvano Serventi, *The Medieval Kitchen: Recipes from France and Italy*, trans. Edward Schneider (Chicago: University of Chicago Press, 1998), 19f.

28. Henisch, *Fast and Feast*, 87.

29. Scully, *The Art of Cookery*, 99f.; see also Redon et al., *The Medieval Kitchen*, 20.

30. Scully, *The Art of Cookery*, 95.

31. Redon et al., *The Medieval Kitchen*, 21.

32. Melitta Weiss Adamson, *Daz buoch von guoter spise (The Book of Good Food): A Study, Edition, and English Translation of the Oldest German Cookbook* (Sonderband 9) (Krems, Austria: *Medium Aevum Quotidianum*, 2000), 30 and 93 ("A stuffed roasted suckling pig").

33. Ibid., 96 ("The following tells about stockfish").

34. Terence Scully, *The Vivendier, A Fifteenth-Century French Cookery Manuscript: A Critical Edition with English Translation* (Totnes, U.K.: Prospect Books, 1997), 44f. ("To cook a fish in three ways and styles").

35. See Wheaton, *Savoring the Past*, 23f.; Scully, *The Art of Cookery*, 98; and Henisch, *Fast and Feast*, 41f.

36. See Scully, *The Art of Cookery*, 92; Henisch, *Fast and Feast*, 144; and Adamson, *The Book of Good Food*, 22 and 93 ("A stuffed roasted suckling pig").

37. Adamson, *The Book of Good Food*, 22.

38. For the following on food adulteration and quality control see P.W. Hammond, *Food and Feast in Medieval England* (Stroud, U.K.: Alan Sutton, 1993), 80–87.

39. See Judith Bennett, *Ale, Beer, and Brewsters in England: A Woman's Work in a Changing World, 1300–1600* (New York: Oxford University Press, 1996).

40. Henisch, *Fast and Feast*, 78.

41. For a depiction see Hammond, *Food and Feast*, 85; and Henisch, *Fast and Feast*, 85.

42. Hammond, *Food and Feast*, 87f.

43. Wilhelm Abel, *Strukturen und Krisen der spätmittelalterlichen Wirtschaft* (Stuttgart: Gustav Fischer, 1980), 31.

44. Ibid., 32.

45. Hieronymus Bock, *Teutsche Speißkammer: Inn welcher du findest / was gesunden vnnd kranncken menschen zur Leibsnarung von desselben gepresten von noeten/Auch wie alle speis vnd dranck Gesunden vnd Krancken jeder zeit zur Kost vnd artznei gereichet werden sollen* (Strasbourg: Wendel Rihel, 1550), fol. 54r-v.

46. Hammond, *Food and Feast*, 88f.

47. Henisch, *Fast and Feast*, 81.

48. Bock, *Teutsche Speißkammer*, fol. 107r.

49. Hammond, *Food and Feast*, 89.

50. For this and the following on substitute foodstuffs see Hans Wiswe, *Kulturgeschichte der Kochkunst: Kochbücher und Rezepte aus zwei Jahrtausenden mit einem lexikalischen Anhang zur Fachsprache von Eva Hepp* (Munich: Moos, 1970), 82f.

51. Hammond, *Food and Feast*, 130.

52. Redon et al., *The Medieval Kitchen*, 23f.

53. Scully, *The Art of Cookery*, 112.

54. Redon et al., *The Medieval Kitchen*, 29.

55. For this and the following on food coloring see C. Anne Wilson, "Ritual, Form, and Colour in the Medieval Food Tradition," in *'The Appetite and the Eye': Visual Aspects of Food and Its Presentation within Their Historic Context*, ed. C. Anne Wilson (Edinburgh: Edinburgh University Press, 1991), 17f.

56. Redon et al., *The Medieval Kitchen*, 26.

57. Wilson, "Ritual, Form, and Colour," 19.

58. Scully, *The Art of Cookery*, 114.

59. Redon et al., *The Medieval Kitchen*, 26.

60. Scully, *The Art of Cookery*, 115.

61. See Constance B. Hieatt, "Medieval Britain," in *Regional Cuisines of Medieval Europe: A Book of Essays*, ed. Melitta Weiss Adamson (New York: Routledge, 2002), 28.

62. Wiswe, *Kulturgeschichte der Kochkunst*, 101.

63. Adamson, *The Book of Good Food*, 96 ("This is a good salmon dish").

64. For the different molds and waffle irons see Wiswe, *Kulturgeschichte der Kochkunst*, 102.

65. Scully, *The Art of Cookery*, 104; and esp. Melitta Weiss Adamson, "Imitation Food Then and Now," *Petits Propos Culinaires* 72 (2003): 83–102.

66. Cf. Henisch, *Fast and Feast*, 101f.

67. Adamson, *The Book of Good Food*, 92 ("If you want to make *blanc manger*").

68. Hans Wiswe, "Ein mittelniederdeutsches Kochbuch des 15. Jahrhunderts," *Braunschweigisches Jahrbuch* 37 (1956): 39 ("If you want to make eggs in Lent").

69. Ibid., 39 ("If you want to make a big egg in Lent").

70. See esp. Adamson, "Imitation Food," 91.

71. Wheaton, *Savoring the Past,* 12.

72. Adamson, "Imitation Food," 91.

73. Melitta Weiss Adamson, "The Greco-Roman World," in *Regional Cuisines of Medieval Europe: A Book of Essays,* ed. Melitta Weiss Adamson (New York: Routledge, 2002), 6.

74. See *Satyricon,* in Petronius, with an English translation by Michael Heseltine; Seneca *Apocolocyntosis,* with an English translation by W.H.D. Rouse (Cambridge: Harvard University Press, 1939), 55.

75. Wilson, "Ritual, Form, and Colour," 18.

76. For the evolution of the *sotelty* or *entremets* see esp. Scully, *The Art of Cookery,* 104–10.

77. Terence Scully, ed., *The Viandier of Taillevent: An Edition of All Extant Manuscripts* (Ottawa: University of Ottawa Press, 1988), 286 ("Faulxgrenon," "Pettitoes: feet, livers and gizzards," "Frumenty," "Taillis," and "Millet") and 288 ("Fancy rice for meat-days").

78. Ibid., 301 ("A particoloured white dish").

79. Terence Scully, ed., *The Neapolitan Recipe Collection: Cuoco Napoletano* (Ann Arbor: University of Michigan Press, 2000), 191 ("Jelly like a checkerboard").

80. Scully, *The Art of Cookery,* 106.

81. Scully, *Viandier,* 300f. ("Parmesan pies"). Crenelations are a "notched battlement made up of alternate crenels (openings), and merlons (square saw teeth)"; see Joseph and Francis Gies, *Life in a Medieval Castle* (New York: Harper & Row, 1979), 225.

82. Scully, *Viandier,* 286f. ("Stuffed poultry").

83. Ibid., 304 ("Peacocks [redressed in their skin]").

84. Scully, *The Art of Cookery,* 106.

85. Ibid., 107.

86. Constance B. Hieatt and Sharon Butler, eds., *Curye on Inglysch: English Culinary Manuscripts of the Fourteenth Century (Including the Forme of Cury)* (Early English Text Society SS.8) (London: Oxford University Press, 1985), 139 ("Cokagrys").

87. Scully, *The Art of Cookery,* 107; for a depiction of this peculiar knight, see the book cover of Jean-Louis Flandrin and Carole Lambert, *Fêtes gourmandes au Moyen Âge* (Paris: Imprimerie nationale Éditions, 1998).

88. Scully, *Vivendier,* 82f. ("To make that chicken sing when it is dead and roasted").

89. Ibid., 44f.

90. See Scully, *The Art of Cookery*, 108.

91. Ibid., 108f.

92. Scully, *Vivendier*, 81 ("To make a chicken be served roasted").

93. For the above examples see Wiswe, *Kulturgeschichte der Kochkunst*, 97.

94. Redon et al., *The Medieval Kitchen*, 32.

95. Melitta Weiss Adamson, "The Games Cooks Play: Nonsense Recipes and Practical Jokes in Medieval Literature," in *Food in the Middle Ages: A Book of Essays*, ed. Melitta Weiss Adamson (New York: Garland, 1995), 178 and 183.

96. Ibid., 184.

97. Ibid., 185–88.

CHAPTER 3
CUISINES BY REGION

Although people in the Middle Ages were not nearly as mobile as people have been since the beginning of the modern age, they did travel and in the process experienced different cultures and different cuisines. They went to war, on Crusades, on pilgrimages, to fairs, or to market. There were other factors, too, that favored cultural exchange: Nearly all the cookbooks from medieval Europe originated in the aristocracy and the clergy, and both these groups had a strongly international outlook. The dietary rules of the Order of Saint Benedict, for instance, applied to Benedictine monks across Europe. Even more general were the fasting laws of the Christian church that applied equally to clerics and believers everywhere. European aristocrats, for their part, frequently intermarried, waged war, participated in tournaments, paid formal and informal visits to their counterparts in faraway lands, exchanged cooks and cookbooks, and overall tried to emulate each other's court culture. Food, as the most immediate human need, was a favorite way for the nobility to show their wealth and their exquisite taste, and thereby affirm their status.

Despite the regional differences found in the various European cuisines in the Middle Ages, some foodstuffs, modes of preparation, and dish names seem universal. Typical of upper-class cookery were the use of spices, almonds, eggs, chickens, and pork.[1] Among the spices, pepper, cinnamon, ginger, and saffron were the favorites, often complemented with salt and sugar. Whole spices were pulverized in a mortar, and sometimes used in ready-made combinations. According to one scholar, *whyte pouder* (white powder) may have referred to ground ginger or a combination of ginger or mace with confectioner's sugar, *pouder fort* (strong powder) to ginger or a blend of cinnamon and mace, and *pouder douce* (mild powder) to a combination of one or more of the spices anise, fennel, and nutmeg.[2] Almonds, cultivated in southern Europe, were popular across the Continent, especially in the form of almond milk, a tasty and instantly available alternative to cow's milk. Chickens and eggs were versatile foodstuffs that played a dominant role in all European cuisines, as did the pig. Various kinds of cheeses, fish, bread, and wine were also staples in the medieval kitchen.[3]

With color being an important aspect of medieval cookery, a predilection Europe may have inherited from the Arabs, it is not surprising that dishes were often named for their color. Dish names such as "white sauce," "green sauce," "black pepper broth," or "yellow potage" in the various European vernacular languages are not uncommon. If there is one standard dish that is found in nearly every cookbook of the time from Portugal to Germany, from England to Italy, it is the white dish known as *blanc manger.* In its basic form it was composed of the white ingredients chicken meat, rice, and almond milk. In many cases sugar was also added. The variations of the dish name, such as French *blanc mengier,* English *blank maunger,* Catalan *manjar blanch,* Portuguese *manjar braquo,* Italian *bianco mangiare,* Flemish and Dutch *blanc mengier,* and Latin *albus cibus* all point to white as the dish's distinguishing feature. And yet it has recently been suggested that it may not have started off as a white dish at all, but as a "bland dish" suitable for sick people, and that the French word *blant* may in time have been (mis-)understood as *blanc.*[4] What lends this theory some credence is the fact that *blanc manger* recipes are also included in collections of dishes for invalids, which is the case in the two most famous French cookbooks of the Middle Ages, the *Menagier de Paris* (Householder of Paris) and the *Viandier* (The Provisioner) of Taillevent. The dual function as a dish for the sick and an upper-class dish is not as far off as it may seem, since the aristocracy was believed to be of a delicate constitution not dissimilar to that of a convalescent. The ubiquitous nature of *blanc manger* tempted one French food historian to try and identify regional preferences. What he concluded was that using whole rice and less sugar was typically French, rice flour and more spices typically Italian, and decorating plates with almonds typically English.[5] An English recipe for *blanc manger* from the fourteenth-century court of Richard II, spelled *Blank-Mang* in the source, runs as follows:

Butchering pigs. From *Tacuinum sanitatis in medicina*, 14th century. Cod. Vind. Series Nova 2644, fol. 74v. Courtesy of Österreichische Nationalbibliothek, Vienna (Photo: Bildarchiv, ÖNB Wien).

Blank-Mang [White Dish]

Take capons and cook them. Then remove them from the pot. Take blanched almonds. Grind them and mix them with the capon broth. Cast the [almond] milk in a pot. Wash rice and add it and let it cook. Then take flesh of capons, tear it small, and add it. Take white grease, sugar, and salt, and cast them in. Let it cook. Then divide it into portions and garnish it with red or white confectioned anise and with almonds fried in oil, and serve it forth.[6]

But *blanc manger* was not always white; in fact, it sometimes came in bright colors. One recipe from fourteenth-century Germany asks for pounded violets as an ingredient, for instance. What is also remarkable about this recipe is that it provides a fast-day variant of the dish, and gives information on quantities, something not normally found in medieval cookbooks. The instructions are to take goat's milk and to prepare half a pound of almonds. A quarter pound of rice is to be ground to flour and put into the milk. Then the breast of one chicken is chopped and added. The mixture is simmered in pure lard, and finally pounded violets and a quarter pound of sugar are added before the dish is served. During Lent the recipe recommends pike as an alternative to chicken breast.[7]

Somewhat more varied in name and preparation than the "white dish" but nevertheless standard fare on medieval dining tables were the many egg dishes found in the various cookbooks. As every novice in the kitchen knows, an omelet is one of the quickest ways to prepare a meal and satisfy one's hunger. An elaborate example of *arboulastres,* or herb omelets, is the "green omelet" by the Italian cook Maestro Martino. To color this cheese omelet green, either the juice of chard, parsley, borage, mint, marjoram, and sage or the finely chopped and lightly fried herbs are added.[8]

Brewets and *civets* are variations of another type of medieval dish, the potage.[9] As the most economical means of preparing a cooked meal, the stewing pot was especially popular among the lower classes, for whom roasting or baking in an oven were luxuries they could not afford. But broths, or *brewets,* are also included in aristocratic cookbooks, sometimes with names that point to foreign lands, such as the *Brouet sarrasinois,* or "Saracen brewet," and the *Brouet d'Alemagne d'oeufs* found in the *Viandier* of Taillevent. For this "German egg brewet," eggs poached in oil, almond milk, and sliced onions fried in oil are boiled together. Then ground ginger, cinnamon, cloves, grains of paradise, and a little saffron infused in verjuice (the tart juice of unripe fruits) are added to the other ingredients, and the broth is brought to a boil. The broth, which should be quite thick but not too yellow, can be eaten with Mustard Sops (pieces of toasted bread).[10] A *civet* was a potage that started with fried onions, to which a liquid, spices, and pieces of meat were usually added. Popular in France and Italy were *civets* of hare, rabbit, and venison.[11]

Pies and *tortes* (pies with edible crust) are found in recipe collections from across Europe. The foodstuffs enclosed in pastry could be manifold, from meat, cheese, and vegetables to fruits and nuts. These pies often reflected local preferences, but some managed to rise to international stardom, as was the case with the "Parma Pie," a truly luxurious dish that was, no doubt, the crowning of many a medieval banquet. It was an unusually tall pie filled with layers upon layers of meat and fowl. On fast days these layers would consist of fish and eel, fruits, nuts, herbs, and spices. Below is the meat-day version of a "Parma Pie" contained in the *Viandier* of Taillevent:

Tourtes parmeriennes [Parmesan (Parma) Pies]

Take mutton, veal or pork and chop it up sufficiently small; then boil poultry and quarter it—and the other meat must be cooked before being chopped up; then get fine powder and sprinkle it on the meat very sensibly, and fry your meat in bacon grease. Then get large open pastry shells—which should have higher sides than usual and should be of the size of small plates—and shape them with crenelations (square, saw-toothed indentations at the top); they should be of a strong dough in order to hold the meat. If you wish, you can mix pine-nut paste and currants among the meat, with granulated sugar on top; into each pasty put three or four chicken quarters in which to plant the banners of France and of the lords who will be present, and glaze them with moistened saffron to give them a better appearance. For anyone who does not want to go to such expense for poultry, all he has to do is make flat pieces of pork or mutton, either roasted or boiled. When the pies are filled with their meat, the meat on top should be glazed with a little beaten egg, both yolks and whites, so that this meat will hold together solidly enough to set the banners in it. And you should have gold-leaf or silver-leaf or tin-leaf to glaze the pies before setting the banners in them.[12]

Much more modest than this "Parma Pie" but nevertheless found in many medieval cookbooks from across Europe, was the *mortarolum*. Named after the mortar in which the main ingredient, ground meat, was turned into a paste, it appears, for instance, as *morterol* in Catalan, *mortereul* in French, *mortrewes* in English, and *mortroel* in Dutch.[13] A fifteenth-century English manuscript contains an example of this recipe. For the *Mortrel de le chare*, or "Mortrews of Meat," chicken meat and pork are cooked together, then taken out of the pot and the bones removed. The meat is to be chopped small, ground well, and returned to the broth. Fine white bread is added, as well as saffron to give it color. When it is boiled, the dish is taken off the fire, mixed with egg yolks, and sprinkled with (spice) powder.[14]

Another group of dishes that adorned many a medieval banquet table were the various kinds of aspics and jellies. The word frequently used for jelly in the Middle Ages was *galentine*. It was derived from the Latin word *gelâta*, which meant "something frozen." Meat, fish, or other foodstuffs were "frozen" in a gel that was extracted from animal hooves or from the skin of certain animals and fish.[15] Perfectly transparent jellies were especially sought after. They were achieved by repeatedly boiling and straining the gelatine broth. Maestro Martino, however, refined this method further by using lightly beaten egg white that trapped the tiniest impurities as it coagulated in the hot liquid.[16] He also gives recipes for multicolored jelly dishes, including one in the shape of a woven basket. Many jellies were probably humbler creations, especially those that used bread crumbs as a binding agent, which must have made them opaque rather than transparent. But gelatin lent itself to more than making fancy dishes. It also helped to preserve the food that was encased in it for longer. On fast days jellies were made from fish. For the *gelatina di pesce* from Italy, for instance, the fish is cooked in wine and a little vinegar, then removed, the liquid reduced to one-third, seasoned with saffron and other spices, as well as bay leaves, and then strained. Lavender is added and the liquid left to cool before it is poured over the fish.[17]

Roast meats served at medieval banquets were usually accompanied with sauces that were designed to counteract the presumed hot and dry qualities of the meat by providing coolness and moisture (see Chapter 6). Of the various sauces named after their appearance as white, pink, blue, green, yellow, black, and camel- (or cinnamon-) colored, the last two were among the most widespread in Europe. King Richard II of England in all likelihood dipped his meat in an unboiled sauce from the *Forme of Cury* (The [Proper] Method of Cookery) called *Sawse Camelyne,* or "Cameline Sauce." It consists of currants, nuts, the crusts of bread, powdered cloves, and cinnamon, all mixed together. Then salt and vinegar are added and the sauce is ready to serve.[18] However, for veal, wildfowl, and venison, the aristocratic meats par excellence, a boiled pepper sauce was the sauce of choice. According to a recipe for black pepper sauce found in the *Viandier* of Taillevent, ground ginger, round pepper, and burnt toast are to be infused in vinegar or verjuice and then boiled.[19]

Gratonea is the Latin name for a fried dish that appears in many medieval cookbooks, especially in British, French, and Italian ones, as *gratonata, gratunee, cretonee,* and the like.[20] Although the recipes at times vary widely, they all seem to have chicken or capon meat and egg yolks as common ingredients, as well as milk or verjuice, as in the following example from Italy:

Gratonata of chickens [Chicken with Verjuice]

Cut up your chickens, fry them with pork fat and with onions; and while they are frying add a little water so that they cook nicely in the pan; and stir them often with a large spoon; add spices, saffron, and sour grape juice [verjuice], and boil; and for each chicken take four egg yolks, mix them with verjuice and boil this separately; and beat everything together in the pan, and boil everything together with the pieces of chicken; and when it boils remove it from the fire and eat it.[21]

Even more diverse than *gratonea* are the countless European recipes for dough or batter fried in hot grease in a pan or pot, such as crêpes, fritters, or doughnuts. They could be simple pancakes with garnish, or elaborate fillings of meat, vegetables, nuts, or fruits surrounded with dough. These dishes were especially popular in Germany where they were known as *krapfen*. To prepare fritters for Lent, *The Book of Good Food* recommends mixing ground nuts and diced apples with spices, filling the fritters with this stuffing, and frying them in a pan.[22]

To conclude this brief survey of international dishes, two food preparations must be named that the rich and famous of medieval Europe loved to indulge in at the end of a meal: marzipan and *hippocras*. Presumably of Arabic origin, the sweetmeat marzipan was by 1340 known in Italy and southern France, where the word referred to both the almond paste and the box in which it was kept. Its principal ingredients sugar, almonds, and rose water, marzipan has in common with many other Arab-Persian desserts.[23] No medieval banquet was complete, however, without a round of *hippocras*, the famous spiced wine named after the Greek physician Hippocrates. The recipe for *Ypocras* from the *Menagier de Paris* (Householder of Paris) is one of the shorter ones. It asks for an ounce of long tube cinnamon, a knob of ginger, and an equal amount of galingale to be pounded together with a pound of sugar. The spice powder is then left to steep in a gallon of the best Beaune wine for an hour, and subsequently strained several times through a cloth bag to clarify the wine.[24] From these international favorites we shall now turn our attention to the cuisines of the various regions of western and central Europe and try to outline their culinary preferences.

BRITAIN

When it comes to medieval Britain and the rest of Europe, the research of food historians is hampered by the fact that the cookbooks that have come down to us are from the very end of the period. Most of them were written between 1300 and 1500. Since nearly all of them originated in the aristocracy, they tell us little about the dishes enjoyed by the lower classes. In the case of medieval Britain, scholars face an additional problem: after 1066 the ruling class was Norman, and so was their language and culture. Not surprisingly then, the earliest cookbooks we have from the British Isles are Anglo-Norman rather than Anglo-Saxon. To find out about Anglo-Saxon food, especially the food of the lower classes, one must turn to other sources, such as literary, historical, religious, or medical texts, art, and archeology.[25] Rarely in the sources, however, does one find anything resembling culinary recipes that describe in detail how the dishes were prepared.

Manorial records and account books tell us that the diet of the peasants in Britain was not dissimilar to that of the peasants in continental Europe. It consisted mainly of plant food, namely bread made from barley and oats, some fruits and vegetables, butter, and cheese, with meat and eggs in rather short supply.[26] Most wine consumed in Britain was imported from the Continent, which priced it out of reach of the ordinary peasants, who drank mainly ale. Cereals that were not consumed in the form of bread or ale were turned into porridge or broths. The fourteenth-century English poet Langland describes the food his protagonist Piers the Plowman has in his cottage as "two green cheeses, some curds and cream, an oat cake, and two loaves of bran and beans. He also has parsley, leeks and much cabbage, but no money with which to buy pullets, no eggs and no salt meat."[27] The poorest of the poor ate vegetables cooked without meat and drank water, or ate bacon rind and beans if they could afford it. In her youth Griselda, the heroine of the *Clerk's Tale* in Geoffrey Chaucer's collection of stories known as the *Canterbury Tales,* supposedly survived on potages made from the edible greens she gathered from the wayside. Milk, brown bread, bacon, and an occasional egg are the diet of the poor widow in the *Nun's Priest's Tale.*[28] Peasants who were able to keep a cow or some sheep had access to milk and dairy products.

When it comes to the types of dishes that were prepared from such a limited range of foodstuffs, soups, potages, broths, and *porreys,* that is stewed vegetables such as peas, onions, or leeks with seasonings, predominated.

The food of manorial servants was generally more varied, with beef, herring, or cod as additional sources of protein, and bread made from rye and wheat. The yeoman in Langland's *Piers Plowman* was doing better with his "bacon flitches, eggs, cheese, butter, milk, cream, onions, garlic, and malt to make ale."[29] Tenants who did boon work such as plowing or harvesting for the lord of the manor were often quite well fed, enjoying soup, wheat bread, beef, cheese, and an unlimited amount of ale. At Christmas the lord would receive a hen or grain for the brewing of ale from his tenants, and in return would give them a meal that included not just the staple foods bread, cheese, and potage, but also various meat dishes. Among the fruits and nuts peasants in medieval England often had access to were cherries, apples, pears, plums, filberts, walnuts, and sweet chestnuts. Parsley and other potherbs, small birds, rabbits, some freshwater and salt fish, and cockles also found their way into many a villager's stewpot. Poaching was a problem throughout the period and was usually severely punished by the authorities. With sugar having the status of a luxury food along with spices, the only sweetener for the lower classes, aside from fruit sugar, was honey.

The central role ale played in the life of the English peasants becomes especially evident in the festivities where the drink flowed freely. It was also frequently used as a way to raise money. "Bride ale," for instance, was an ale brewed for a wedding. The profits from its sale were given to the bride. "Help ales" were designed to give financial support to villagers in need, and "scot ales," special events held by the lord or on his behalf, required tenants to pay money for the privilege of drinking there. Exceptions were sometimes made for village bachelors, who on the last day of a "scot ale" were allowed to drink free of charge for as long as they could stand. The end of plowing was celebrated with seedcake, pasties (meat pies), and hulled wheat boiled in almond milk, known as "frumenty."

The food on offer in the towns of medieval Britain was generally more varied than that available to the villagers. In 1300 London had a population of close to one hundred thousand.[30] It was supplied with grain and livestock from the surrounding countryside. Wheat, barley, oats, and malt were often transported by water, while live cattle, poultry, and sheep were driven to town. Pigs, on the other hand, were commonly raised in towns and roamed the streets. Dairy products, primarily butter and cheese, were brought into the city, as were delicacies such as rabbits, swans, venison, and pike enjoyed by the wealthier city-dwellers. Cheese came in four basic varieties: hard, soft, and "green," which referred to a very new soft cheese, as well as a herb-flavored cream cheese known as *spermyse*. Fruits, nuts, and vegetables, too, were brought in from the countryside or were grown in the suburbs. In addition to apples, pears, cherries, and nuts, more upscale fruits such as quinces, peaches, mulberries, and medlars (acidic fruit of a small European tree belonging to the rose family) were also cultivated and sold to the discerning consumer. The vegetables on offer included onions, leeks, beans, cabbages, turnips, parsnips, spinach, carrots that came in purple, yellow, white, and orange, and beets, of which only the leaves were used for cooking then. Unripe grapes and crab apples were turned into verjuice and used for cooking and pickling.

A housewife in the city probably had a wider variety of herbs to choose from to put in her potage than her peasant counterpart. Among them were sage, mint, fennel, parsley, marjoram, orach, borage, sorrel, and basil. Pimpernel, primrose, and groundsel, which have since fallen off the list of edible herbs, were also popular ingredients then. Livestock was mainly sold at the stockyards, with other locations reserved exclusively for fish, for grain, and for general groceries. The fish offered for sale in medieval London included a wide range of sea fish such as cod, conger, dory, turbot, bass, mullet, and lamprey (toothed, parasitic, eellike fish that suck the blood of larger fish), and freshwater fish such as roach, barbel, and dace. Among the preserved fish that were consumed in large quantities by the population on the many fast days were dried cod known as "stockfish," and salted and pickled herrings. Sea fish and shellfish, notably oysters and mussels, were sold by fishmongers or itinerant street vendors called *birlesters*. Bread that was not sold by bakers in the market was usually peddled by hucksters who went from house to house. These mostly female street sellers received a 13th batch for every 12 they bought, which is how they made their profit—hence the expression "a baker's dozen." The various kinds of bread that were sold ranged from the finest and most expensive white bread known as *paindemaigne*, and later as *manchet*, and the somewhat lower-grade white breads *wastel, bis* (also known as *trete*), and *cocket*, to the brownest bread, called *tourte* or, in Latin, *panis integer.*

Housewives had the choice of buying their food in shops, in the market, or from hucksters. Much like today, many foods were sold ready prepared, by pie bakers and cookshops of various kinds that were at times also in the catering business. Aside from geese, hens, and capons baked in pastry or without, these cookshops sold many different roast meats, among them thrushes, finches, plover, woodstock, teal (short-necked river duck), pheasant, heron, and bittern (small, shorter-necked, speckled heron), rabbit, and lamb, as well as sauces and puddings. Prepared food could also be bought in the many taverns that sold wine and often offered lodging to travelers as well. Ale was frequently brewed by women known as "alewives" and sold by hucksters or in alehouses. An alestake (pole in front of an alehouse) was used as a sign to announce a new brew, which usually came in two qualities, "double" and "single," also known as "small ale."[31] Instead of an alestake, taverns had a pole with leaves, called a "bush," that projected from the building to attract customers.

Judging from the city ordinances, the sale of wine in London was closely regulated; these laws forbade wine sellers to sell both red and white wine, or sweet wine with any other kind. In medieval England, as in the rest of Europe, the wine was drunk relatively new, presumably because it deteriorated fast. Most wine consumed in the British Isles was a strong red wine from Gascony, but Alsatian, Rhenish, Moselle, and other German wines were also available, as were Italian, Sicilian, and Spanish wines. Some of the names under which these imported wines were known are *Riboldi* or *Rybole*, for wine from Rivoglio in Italy, *malvezyn, malvesie,* or *malvoisie* for a malmsey from Crete, *romeney* for an inferior malmsey, *de la Rivere* for a wine from Ribera in northern Spain, *bastard* for a sweet Spanish wine, *oseye* for a sweet French, Alsatian, or Spanish wine, and *vernage* or *vernaccia* for a sweet wine probably from Italy. Distilled alcohol was by the fourteenth century already added to spiced wines in England.

Even if the richer households made extensive use of high-end foodstuffs, such as dried fruits, spices, premium meats and fish, especially for their banquets, the meals of the average city dweller were still rather simple, as the "Act on the Diet and Apparel of Servants" of 1363 illustrates. In it the food for servants of the nobility, artisans, and tradesmen is described as "meat or fish once a day, the remains of other foods, milk, cheese, and 'other provisions' according to the employee's rank."[32] These provisions probably referred to bread, ale, and some sort of vegetable soup.

In the *Canterbury Tales* Chaucer not only hints at the food for the poor, he also provides the reader with a detailed picture of the cuisine that was representative of the gentry. The general prologue, written around 1387, contains the following description of the Franklin and his culinary delights.[33] As Epicure's son, the Franklin was both a good householder and a good host. In the morning he loved a piece of "sop," that is, bread dipped in wine. His bread and ale were always of the highest quality, and no other wine cellar was better stocked than his. Fish, meat, and baked food were plentiful: it literally "snowed" food and drink, and all the delicacies one could think of. He changed his diet according to the season, had many fat partridges in his coop, and a fishpond well stocked with bream and pike. Woe to the cook if his sauce was not piquant or his utensils were not ready. Instead of a temporary trestle table that was dismantled after the meal, as was customary, the Franklin had a dormant or permanent table in the hall that was set for a meal all day long. In the *Boke of Nurture* written in the fifteenth century, John Russell gives a model menu for a "Feast for a Franklin."

> Russell's first course consists of brawn (boar's flesh or pork) served with mustard, pea soup with bacon, a beef or mutton stew, boiled chicken or capon, roast goose or pork, and either a capon pasty (baked in a pastry crust) or an open tart with an egg-thickened filling: a total of six dishes, mostly simple ones. The second course was to start with either "mortrewes"—a bland, thick pudding of meat or fish—or "jussell," a pudding or dumpling made with bread crumbs and herbs; then came more roasts—veal or lamb, kid or rabbit, chicken or pigeon; and another tart or pastry.
>
> The final course included fritters and other dishes considered to be special treats, followed by apples and spiced (stewed) pears, served with cheese. The meal would have been accompanied by bread throughout and washed down mostly with ale, although some wine may have been available to higher-ranking diners. A drink of mead or sweet spiced wine came after the meal along with candied nuts and other "confits," and "wafers," which resembled small, thin waffles.[34]

This type of feast would have been typical of the lesser gentry, but certainly not of the nobility, whose dishes tended to be more intricate and in the form of *sotelties* often contained an element of surprise. The Franklin's standard of living would, however, have been comparable to that of two priests in fifteenth-century Dorset whose account books provide some interesting insights in their diet.[35] They ate a lot of bread and meat, beef, mutton, and pork mainly. Veal and lamb were reserved for special occasions. During Lent, and on Wednesdays, Fridays, and Saturdays, the three weekly fast days, they ate fish. Mackerel, haddock, herrings, and conger eel they bought fresh; ling, cod, and whiting as salt fish; and hake either fresh or salted. The two priests also ate a lot of shellfish, especially mussels, whelks, cockles, and oysters. Eggs, butter, cheese, and milk they bought; vines and fruit trees they cultivated in their own garden. Crab apples and other fresh fruits, peas, beans, and honey they bought; pigeons they kept; and some vegetables such as onions they grew themselves.

Their drink of choice was ale, of which they bought five or six gallons a week. When visitors came they drank wine. Perry, the juice of fermented pears, they made themselves, and perhaps cider as well. Suckling pigs and chickens they indulged in occasionally on meat days, and figs, raisins, dates, and almonds on fast days. Almond milk must have played a significant role in their diet judging from the quantities of almonds bought. The two priests also purchased a number of different spices, namely pepper, ginger, cloves, cinnamon, saffron, and mustard, and paid a baker for pies and flour. In wealthier households most of the foodstuffs were the same as those bought by the two priests, with the exception that on large estates ale and bread were produced on the premises. Additional luxuries mentioned in account books of the nobility and high clergy include capons, kids, calves, deer, often from the estate's deer park, porpoise, salmon, sturgeon, mace, as well as more and pricier wines, especially the sweet wines from the Mediterranean.

The sources—account books, manorial records, ordinances, literature, and the like—from which information on Anglo-Saxon food can be gleaned provide considerable detail but they are lacking in one important point: they do not contain any recipes. The only place where we can find collections of recipes from Anglo-Saxon England are the medical texts which, of course, were not aimed at the healthy diner but at a person with a specific ailment. The medical recipes do, however, yield some information on the processing of ingredients that would not have been too dissimilar to what went on in the kitchen, a case in point being the use of the mortar and pestle. They also tell us about a number of herbs and spices that were considered medicinal foods, and that found their way into drugs as well as regular dishes in the Middle Ages. (See Chapter 6.)

When it comes to actual cookbooks, the earliest collections from England date back to the end of the thirteenth century. They are hence among the oldest in Europe.[36] Since they are written in Anglo-Norman French, it has long been believed that they reveal more about French than English cuisine. And yet, a closer inspection of the recipes

Pie bakers with movable oven. From *Ulrich von Richental. Chronik des Konstanzer Konzils,* ca. 1470. Cod. Vind. 3044, fol. 48v. Courtesy of Österreichische Nationalbibliothek, Vienna (Photo: Bildarchiv, ÖNB Wien).

and their counterparts in France, the *Viandier* of Taillevent and the *Menagier de Paris,* for instance, has shown that rarely are they identical. To be sure, they are related to French cookery, but they also are evidence of the emergence of a new style of cookery that was distinctly English.[37] One example is the use of shellfish as an alternative to fish in English *blanc manger* recipes, something that would have been foreign to the French. A dish that is a close relative to *blanc manger* but is only found in England is called *Blandissorye.* Some of the different spellings of the name, such as the oldest Anglo-Norman *Blanc desirree,* suggest that it was believed to come from Syria.[38] In one of the two Anglo-Norman cookbooks it is followed by two other colored dishes "from Syria," *Vert desire,* that is "green food from Syria," and *Jaune desire,* or "yellow food from Syria."[39] Given the Arab influence on European cooking in general, that, as we shall see, was even stronger in Britain than in northern France, Middle Eastern provenance of these dishes is quite likely. The following is a fast-day version of the Syrian white dish:

Blank Desure [White Dish from Syria]

Take the yolks of boiled eggs and mix them with cow's milk, and add cumin, saffron, rice flour or crumbled white bread, and grind in a mortar and mix it with the milk; and make it boil and add to it egg white chopped up small, and take fat cheese and cut it in when the liquid is boiled and serve it.[40]

Although it would not have been suitable for Lent, this dish would have been acceptable on the weekly fast days, when eggs and dairy products were permitted. From England also comes a fast-day version of the international dish *mortrews,* which in France and elsewhere on the Continent was usually a meat dish.[41] Another typically English dish is a stew of oysters in ale that is thickened with bread crumbs. Given the importance of ale in the English diet, it should not be surprising that it was used by cooks as an alternative for wine. Where French and Anglo-Norman cookbooks differ greatly is in the use of sugar and sweet ingredients, such as fruits. The number of desserts that are neither confections nor medicinal recipes is much greater in England than in France. An English characteristic appears to be the presence of strawberries, cherries, apples, plums, and the like as ingredients in cooking. Such fruits were frequently turned into potages, sauces, and tarts. Flowers and flower petals, too, are included in some of these recipes, notably rose petals, hawthorn, and elderflowers; the latter two seem to be a particularly English trait. Often these fruit and flower dishes were garnished with the appropriate fruits or flower petals before they were served. The name of an elderflower dessert contained in the *Forme of Cury* is *Sambocade,* derived from *sambucus,* the Latin word for elderflowers. It consists of a piecrust filled with curds, sugar, egg whites, and elderflower blossoms. The pie is then baked, and rose water is added before it is served.[42] English cookery of the late Middle Ages would be unthinkable without the many sweet and savory custards and tarts. Some of them, such as the *Torte de Bry* that has a cheese and egg yolk filling, are the ancestors of our modern quiche, others had fruit fillings and were made into wonderful desserts.[43] Among the most famous is a custard purportedly from Lombardy. It was served at the feast of King Richard II and the duke of Lancaster on 23 September 1387:

Crustade Lombarde [Lombardy Custard]

Take good cream and leaves of parsley and eggs, the yolks and the whites, and break them into the cream. Beat the mixture until it is so stiff that it will stand by itself. Then take fresh marrow and dates cut into two or three, and prunes, and put the dates and the prunes and the marrow into a fair coffin (pastry crust for pies) made of fair paste, and put the coffin into the oven until it is a little hard. Then draw it out of the oven. Take the liquid and put it into the coffin and fill it up and cast enough sugar on. If it is Lent, leave the eggs and marrow out, and then serve it forth.[44]

Also characteristic of English cooking, it would appear, is the use of wheat starch, or *amidon*, which along with rice flour was a popular thickener in the cookbooks. *Amidon* was a feature of Roman, and later of Arab cooking, but is not mentioned in medieval French recipe collections. A sweet dish that contains fruit and rice flour, and that can easily be transformed from a dessert into a meat dish is the *Viaunde de Cypre* from the *Forme of Cury*. *Cypre* refers to Cyprus, the island in the Mediterranean which was a major sugar producer in the Middle Ages. According to the recipe, pitted dates are ground up small, put through a strainer, and mixed with mead or wine sweetened with sugar, and seasoned with spice powder and salt. The preparation is then thickened with rice flour. On meat days the dish can be made with boiled chicken and pork that is finely ground.[45]

Vegetable dishes are notoriously underrepresented in European cookbooks of the Middle Ages, especially French ones. And yet, in collections from England they are relatively abundant. What is more, they show a close affinity with Italian recipes. Fresh salad, practically unheard of in most of medieval Europe, with the exception of Italy, is already included in the fourteenth-century *Forme of Cury*. To prepare *Salat*, parsley, sage, garlic, chibol (a type of onion), onions, leek, borage, mint, porret (a young leek or onion), fennel, and watercress, rue, rosemary, purslane, and laver (edible purple seaweed) are washed, picked over, plucked into small pieces, and mixed well with raw oil. Vinegar and salt are then added, and the salad is ready to be served.[46] Also included in the *Forme of Cury* are recipes for ravioli and lasagna, two pasta dishes that today we still associate with Italian cooking. In fact, the oldest recorded recipe for ravioli anywhere is contained in one of the two Anglo-Norman cookbooks dating back to around 1300.

Ravieles [Ravioli]

Take fine flour and sugar and make pasta dough; take good cheese and butter and cream them together; then take parsley, sage, and shallots, chop them finely, and put them in the filling. Put the boiled ravieles on a bed of grated cheese and cover them with more grated cheese, and then reheat them.[47]

That Italian dishes would have found their way to the British Isles is not as unusual as it may seem if one considers that aside from conquering Britain, the Normans also occupied Sicily for over a century, from 1091 to 1194 A.D. In 1130 Roger II was crowned king of Sicily, and in 1140 he entered Naples, where he established a Norman court as part of his campaign to unite Sicily with the southern Italian mainland. It is believed that Italian cookbooks and recipes came to England via the court at Naples.[48] But the Norman rule of Sicily and southern Italy helps explain another peculiar feature of British cuisine in the Middle Ages, namely its strong affinity with Arab cookery. Prior to the arrival of the Normans, Sicily and southern Italy were ruled by the Arabs, whose sophisticated culture, far from being destroyed by the Norman invaders, was eagerly emulated by them. And so it happens that the recipe for fried spinach in the *Forme of Cury,* for instance, is in the end closer to a recipe in the *Baghdad Cookery Book* than to the *Menagier de Paris* from just across the English Channel. The ancestor of the English *Spynoches yfryed* ("fried spinach") is the Arab dish *Isfānākh mutajjan.* To prepare it, spinach is washed, boiled lightly in salt and water, and dried, then cooked with sesame oil and chopped garlic, and finally sprinkled with ground cumin, dry coriander, and cinnamon.[49] English cooks replaced the exotic sesame oil with olive oil, omitted garlic, and did not specify the spices to be used. In this example they gave the recipe an English name, but this was not always the case. One of the most common recipes in medieval English cookbooks is called *Maumenee.* Like the spinach dish, it can also be found in an Italian cookbook written in Latin, the *Liber de Coquina,* where it appears as *Mamonia.* The dish name goes back to Arabic *ma'mūnīya,* originally a sweet porridge that sometimes also contained yogurt.[50] The amazing transformations this recipe underwent in England over the centuries have been summarized by one scholar in this way:

> Dishes also changed in nature. In the case of "Mawmenny," for example, which dates from Anglo-Norman times, this was originally a dish containing ground beef, pork or mutton boiled in wine, served in a wine-based sauce which was thickened with capon meat and almonds. The sauce was seasoned with cloves and sugar, fried almonds were added and the dish colored with indigo or with a red dye. About sixty years later it had changed into a dish made from beef broth (no wine), capons cooked in milk of almonds and the whole thickened with rice flour or breadcrumbs. It was seasoned with somewhat stronger spices and coloured yellow with saffron. After another fifty years the wine had returned, together with a great deal more sugar, the beef had vanished but the capon remained. There were more spices, the almonds had been replaced by pine nuts and dates, and the colour was now a reddish orange. This was part of a process in which it appears that, as time went by, a dish tended to become

sweeter, spicier and more complicated. For example, more dried fruit was added by the fifteenth century.[51]

One thing these transformations of the dish make clear is the emphasis on color. And that, too, medieval Britain adopted from the Arabs. The *Baghdad Cookery Book,* like other Arabic texts on food, contains countless golden, saffron-tinted, red, white, scarlet, gold, silver, and vermilion-colored dishes.[52] Thanks to the crusaders who experienced Arab cuisine in Antioch and the crusader kingdoms in the eastern Mediterranean, the Normans in southern Italy and Sicily, and not to forget the Arab civilization in Spain, saffron became one of the most popular ingredients in England and on the Continent, and this primarily for the golden color it imparted on a dish. Another way of gilding food was by glazing it with egg yolk. This was the method used for *Pommes dorrées* ("gilded apples"), a standard dish in many late-medieval English cookbooks.[53] The older Anglo-Norman form *Poumes d'oranges* reveals the Arab origin of the dish even more clearly, which in the *Baghdad Cookery Book* appears as *naranjiya,* or "oranges." Ground mutton or chicken was formed into meatballs that were roasted on a spit and basted with egg yolk and saffron. Another original ingredient was the juice of bitter oranges, which in the late thirteenth century were still a rarity in northern Europe. In the fourteenth-century version from the *Forme of Cury* the dish has undergone some changes compared to its Arab ancestor, not the least of which being the option to use parsley to cover the meatballs. This would have turned them into green apples, rather than oranges, a fruit much more familiar to the northern Europeans:

For to Make Pomes Dorryle and Other Things [To Make Golden Apples and Other Things]

Take the flesh of raw pork and grind it small. Mix it up with strong powder, saffron, salt, and currants. Roll it into balls and wet it well in egg white and cook it in boiling water. Take them out and put them on a spit. Roast them well. Take ground parsley and press it together with eggs and plenty of flour and let the paste flow from above the spit. And if you wish, take saffron instead of parsley and serve it forth.[54]

These meatballs made to look like oranges or apples are just one example of the many *sotelties,* or foods meant to look like something else, that English cookery in the Middle Ages was famous for. Another, more elaborate dish designed to entertain, and in all likelihood also based on an Arab ancestor, is the multicolored "Turk's Head," an open tart with a filling and a top layer of nut paste in red, yellow, and green that showed a man's features, with the container in black representing his hair. One of the unusual ingredients in this Anglo-Norman recipe is pistachio nuts. They are common in Persian and Arab cookery, and figure prominently in a similar Arab dish called "Monkey's Head."[55]

To see how all these fancy dishes were combined in a meal, let us look at the menu of the feast of Richard II and the duke of Lancaster on 23 September 1387. The first course opened with venison and frumenty, followed by a meat potage called *Viaundbruse*. Then came boar's heads, roasted haunches of meat, and roasted swans and roasted pigs, presumably accompanied with the appropriate sauces. The first course concluded with the sweet Lombardy Custard, and a *sotelty*. For the second course a *Gele,* or jellied soup, and the White Dish from Syria were served as starters, to be followed by roasted pigs, cranes, pheasants, herons, chickens, bream, then tarts, carved meat, and roasted conies, that is, two-year-old rabbits. The second course, too, concluded with a *sotelty*. The third course opened with almond potage, and a stew in the style of Lombardy. It continued with roast venison, chickens, rabbits, partridge, quails, larks, a fritterlike dish called "Payne puff" (bread puff), a jelly dish, sweet curd, and egg fritters called *Longe Fritours,* and ended with the obligatory *sotelty*.[56]

Upper-class cuisine as it is reflected in the cookbooks from late-medieval England makes clear that it was highly cosmopolitan in nature. This may come as a surprise to some readers who still associate this period with the Dark Ages. Going way beyond the basic Anglo-Saxon diet of soups, potages, and stews accompanied with bread and washed down with ale, the cuisine of the aristocracy and the gentry was "fusion cuisine" of the best kind. As we have seen, it combined French, Italian, and Arab ingredients and modes of preparation with local preferences, and in doing so created many amazing dishes unique to Britain that were as much a feast for the eye as for the palate.

FRANCE

The diet of the lower classes in France was not dissimilar to that of their counterparts in Britain. The only major difference between them was in the type of drink they consumed. In Britain, as we have seen, ale was the drink of choice of the villagers, the urban middle class, and even the lower gentry. In France, where much of the wine was produced locally and was reasonably cheap, a greater proportion of the population could afford to drink it. For the poorest of the poor in both countries, however, water was the main beverage with which they quenched their thirst.

When it comes to the diet of the townspeople in France, many of the same types of sources as in Britain are available to researchers, with one important addition: a book on housekeeping from the late fourteenth century that a wealthy bourgeois from Paris wrote for his young wife. The work, commonly known as the *Menagier de Paris* (Householder of Paris), also contains an extensive cookbook section.[57] Paris in the fourteenth century was comparable in size to London, but it was not the only bustling city. France's central location on the crossroads between northern Europe and the Mediterranean, the Iberian Peninsula, and the Germanic world had made other cities, especially those in the county of Champagne, east of Paris, favorite destinations for merchants and moneymen from across the Continent. Most famous perhaps was the city of Troyes, which became the site of two of the annual Champagne Fairs, the "Hot Fair" in August, and the "Cold Fair" in December.[58] Troyes's permanent population was about 10,000, but when the fairs were on, the population soared to make it one of the biggest and wealthiest in Europe.[59] The connections between Champagne and England were not just commercial but also dynastic. Countess Marie de Champagne was the daughter of Eleanor of Aquitaine, who in her second marriage was wife to King Henry II of England. As an important patron of the arts, Marie supported a number of poets, among them Chrétien de Troyes, whose romances were masterpieces and made King Arthur and the Knights of the Round Table famous across Europe.

In Troyes as elsewhere, medieval housewives did their grocery shopping daily, and usually early in the morning.[60] Butchers sold the meat of large animals that were slaughtered on the spot, poulterers' shops sold geese, chickens, capons, and ducks, but also rabbits and hares. Wafers could be bought at the nearby pastry shop, and spices, vinegar, cooking oils, salt, sugar, and honey at the spice grocer's. The prices and weights of the different loaves of bread sold at the bakery were fixed, and the bread was marked with the seal of each baker. As in England, food shops were not the only places that sold foodstuffs. Peddlers in Troyes sold everything from "fish, chicken, fresh and salt meat, garlic, honey, onions, fruit, eggs, leeks, and pasties" to wine and milk.[61] French vintners used a "bush" (a pole with leaves) as a sign to attract customers as did the English taverns. In the wealthier households, live fish were kept in the kitchen in leather tanks, and the expensive spices, such as saffron, ginger, nutmeg, cinnamon, cloves, mace, cumin, and pepper in spice cupboards that were locked. Herbs grown by housewives in the city and in the country included basil, sage, savory, marjoram, rosemary, thyme, parsley, fennel, dittany (a plant of the mint family whose aromatic leaves were used in salads), hyssop, rue, coriander, mint, mallow, agrimony, nightshade, and borage. Flowers whose petals were used for cooking and as garnish were lilies, lavender, peonies, marigolds, violets, roses, and primroses. Also cultivated in French city gardens were currants, raspberries, pears, apples, medlars, and grapes.

The *Menagier de Paris* bears witness to the fact that extensive gardening was not just practiced in smaller towns but right in the middle of Paris. When around 1393 the author and compiler of the material, an elderly citizen of Paris, married his 15-year-old bride he was only too aware that one day she would be a widow.[62] The book of moral and domestic instruction he compiled was intended as a guide for his "dear sister," as he lovingly calls her, in a second marriage or to teach her daughters, friends, and others. Following a detailed discussion of matters concerning a woman's religious duties, her chastity, honor, love, and marriage, the book deals with more mundane subjects, such as a wife's care for her husband's bodily comforts, shopping, cooking, gardening, and other miscellaneous household matters. The reader learns, among many other things, when and what to plant in the kitchen garden. Broad beans and peas are mentioned, as are sweet marjoram, sage, lavender, costmary (a fragrant southern European herb, also used in salads), mint, clary (an aromatic Mediterranean herb of the mint family), sorrel, savory, parsley, fennel, basil, borage, orach, hyssop, house leeks, spinach, cabbages, cole (a plant of the same genus as cabbage), lettuce, gourds (a type of squash), beets, vines, raspberries, gooseberries, violets, gillyflowers, peonies, dragonwort, lilies, and roses.[63] The book advises to inspect and taste weekly the wines, vinegars, and verjuice kept in store, as well as the grains, oils, nuts, peas, beans, and other supplies. Judging from the various tips how to cure "sick" wine, spoilage must have been a major problem.[64] When it comes to the food of the servants, the elderly Parisian has the following advice for his bride:

> Nevertheless, dear sister, at appropriate times have them seated at table and have them eat amply of only one kind of meat, not several kinds that are fancy and dainty. Order them one nourishing beverage that is not intoxicating, either a wine that is not too strong, or something else. Bid them to eat heartily and drink well and sufficiently.[65]

How valuable spices were in the fourteenth century can be seen from the instruction to pound them in the mortar before pounding the bread that was used as a thickener for sauces and soups. That way not even the smallest amount of the powdered spices would be lost. Also of concern to the *Menagier* and cooks everywhere were the hazards of cooking on an open fire. Soups burned easily, and to remove the burned taste from them he suggests putting the soup in a new pot, and adding some leaven tied in a white cloth for a short period of time. His other culinary advice includes how to make soups less salty, take salt out of butter, and tips as to what makes the best broth.[66]

To ensure the foodstuffs that enter the kitchen are of the highest quality and are properly handled, the Parisian householder reveals how to choose the best eel, pike roe, shad, trout, carp, plaice, and dab. He explains how Parisian goose sellers fatten their geese, when capons and hens are to be killed, and when mallards, ringdoves, partridges, rabbits, hares, and pigs are the best.[67] Some of his culinary recipes address problems every housewife can relate to, for instance, what to prepare for supper when unexpected guests arrive, how to feed sick people, or how to make a preserve from nuts, fruits, and vegetables that are being added continuously as they come into season.[68] The instructions on how to turn a boar into a proper wild boar, contained in the section of miscellaneous recipes at the end of the book, are an indication that the *Menagier*'s household, especially on regular days, was a frugal one that lacked some of the trappings of the aristocratic lifestyle.[69] Content with his comfortable life and not one to aspire to a higher status, he admits that the dishes prepared by his cook are relatively simple, that a stuffed pig was something he had not seen before he started writing the book, and that some of the recipes he copied were too elaborate for the cook of a bourgeois to prepare.[70] And well they might have been, considering they came from the *Viandier* (The Provisioner) of Taillevent, whose credentials included chief cook of the king of France, no less. However, on special occasions even the *Menagier* and his friends splurged. In his book he gives the menus for the midday dinner and evening supper of a wedding feast for a certain Jean de Chesne, complete with shopping list for ingredients, their quantity and price, and the shops and markets to buy them from.[71] The feast was for 40 guests who ate in messes of 2. In its structure the wedding dinner tried to imitate the French aristocratic banquet, which in its basic form was made up of meat, potage, roasts, *entremets* (the French equivalent of the English *sotelties*), desserts, *hippocras,* wafers or fruit and cheese, and finally *boutehors* or "sally forth," that is, spiced wine and various spiced sweetmeats believed to aid digestion.

The soup was made from ground capon and almond milk, the roast was a combination platter of kid, duckling, and spring chickens, the *entremets* crayfish in jelly, loach fish (a small European freshwater fish, as a minnow), young rabbits, and pigs, and the dessert frumenty with venison. The supper was for half the number of diners and contained more luxurious dishes, among them *pasty* of two young hares, and two peacocks, and a dish of minced kid with halved and glazed kid heads. The items that were not prepared but bought ready-made were the cinnamon-based *sauce cameline*, candied orange peel, rose sugar, white *comfits*, that is sugar-coated aniseed and the like, *hippocras*, as well as 120 flat white loaves and 36 coarse, brown loaves for trenchers (slices of bread used as plates).

In the households of the French nobility, many of the same food-stuffs and dishes were eaten that were served at the bourgeois wedding feast. Some were probably eaten at regular meals, too, and not just on special occasions, or expensive spices like saffron were added to make the dishes more exclusive. Bread was a staple foodstuff for all classes, and was commonly used as a thickener in dishes.[72] The emphasis in the aristocratic kitchen was on local foodstuffs that often came from the estate itself, such as lamprey, carp, chicken, or rabbit. It is perhaps surprising to the modern reader that by the fourteenth century most of the meat eaten in European castles came from domesticated animals, and only a small percentage from wild animals. Among the French upper class, pork and poultry were especially popular. Cured pork in the form of bacon and ham was a staple, and lard was the preferred cooking fat. Beef was used little in kitchens of the wealthy, presumably because the medical community considered it too coarse a meat for the delicate stomachs of the nobility. It does, however, figure prominently in bourgeois cooking, as the frequent mention of beef in the *Menagier* illustrates. What did appear regularly on the dinner tables of the French upper class, however, was mutton, of which the shoulder and the leg were favorites, as was mutton bouillon. As the wedding dinner in the *Menagier* indicates, young animals in general were highly regarded foodstuffs. The aristocratic counterparts to the kid, ducklings, and spring chickens of the bourgeois feast were lamb, piglet, and kid. Fowl was enormously important in medieval French cooking, mostly the domestic fowl hens, chickens, capons, ducks, guinea fowl, and geese. Of the wildfowl, pheasants, partridges, and herons are frequently mentioned in the culinary records. As in England, the French aristocracy raised doves in dovecots and on occasion indulged in larks, quails, thrushes, and other small birds.

A wide variety of sea fish and freshwater fish was available to the affluent French consumer. Mackerel, cod, and salmon were usually preserved in salt and transported in casks. Other sea fish included gurnard, mullets, brill, bream, plaice, and sole. And judging from the recipes, lobster, crayfish, and mussels were also prepared in various ways. More costly, but not impossible to buy inland, were live sea fish delivered in vats of seawater. Live fish that were cheaper and much more readily available were the different kinds of freshwater fish caught in rivers, lakes, and ponds. Often the carp, tench, pike, lamprey, and eel prepared by the aristocratic cook came from his master's own fishpond.

Animal milk played a minor role in the aristocratic diet, but in the form of butter and cheese, made more durable through the addition of salt, it was a frequent ingredient in dishes. France was no different from the rest of late-medieval Europe with its love, not to say addiction, to almonds and almond milk. Eggs were used in great quantity by French cooks as secondary ingredients, but not as the main ingredient in a dish, as is so typical of Italian cookery. As in much of medieval Europe, vegetables do not figure prominently in the upper-class cookbooks of northern France. To the list of vegetables and legumes cultivated in the kitchen garden of the *Menagier*, we must add the brussels sprouts, watercress, garlic, scallions, and shallots that occasionally make an appearance in aristocratic recipe collections. Of the different fruits, grapes were by far the most versatile and the most widely used. They were dried and used as raisins, and unripe grapes were turned into verjuice, which along with wine, vinegar, must, and syrup were important ingredients in the kitchen. The fruits mentioned by the *Menagier* were representative of what was on offer during aristocratic meals as well. Most fruits were eaten raw or coated in sugar; apples were made into applesauce, and quinces into a paste known in France as *codignac*. Oranges, lemons, and pomegranate seeds are listed, but often just as garnishes. Dates, figs, and pine nuts were added to meat dishes. Sugar was used more and more in northern France as the Middle Ages drew to a close. The one area in which France, especially the north, differs significantly from the rest of Europe, is in the use of grain of paradise, which by the fourteenth century had largely replaced pepper. Mustard is another spice that the French aristocratic palate slowly lost interest in. Spice powders, a popular feature in recipes from Britain, also appear in French cookbooks, often in the form of strong spices, or *grosses espices,* that is, ginger, cinnamon, grains of paradise, and pepper, and lesser spices, *menues espices,* that is, cloves, galingale, nutmeg, and mace.

To find out how all these exquisite ingredients were turned into dishes fit for a king, let us take a closer look at the most famous French cookbook of the Middle Ages, the *Viandier,* usually ascribed to a certain Taillevent, or "slice-wind." His real name was Guillaume Tirel, and unlike the careers of most medieval cooks of which we know nothing, his is well documented:

> He first appeared on the culinary scene as a kitchen boy in a royal household in 1326; by midcentury he was in the service of Philip VI and a few years later of the dauphin whose father was John II. The dauphin ascended the throne as Charles V in 1364, and by 1373 Taillevent is described as chief cook (*premier queu du roi*). He is last mentioned in 1392, when the royal chefs were issued new pairs of knives. His documented career thus spanned some sixty-six years. When he died, around 1395, he was buried between his two (successive) wives, beneath a splendid tombstone, depicted wearing armor, as befitted a man who had received land and a title from his king, and holding a shield that bore three marmites [large, covered cooking pots].[73]

It is interesting to note that the oldest manuscript of the *Viandier* goes back to the thirteenth century; in other words, there was a "Taillevent before Taillevent."[74] What this tells us is that many of the recipes were already in existence decades earlier, and that Taillevent probably added his own recipes to an existing stock, and/or refined older ones. One reason why the cookbook was such a success for centuries to come was its organization. While many medieval recipe collections show no apparent order (at least to the modern reader), or at most differentiate between dishes for feast days and fast days, the *Viandier* uses the categories "Boiled Meats," "Thick Potages," "Roast Meats," "*Entremets,*" "Thick Meatless Potages," "Dishes for the Sick," "Freshwater Fish," "Round Sea-Fish," "Flat Sea-Fish," "Unboiled Sauces," and "Boiled Sauces" to arrange the material.[75] The influence of the *Viandier* is felt not just in the *Menagier,* which contains a substantial portion of the recipes, but also in the fifteenth-century French cookbooks, one entitled *Du fait de cuisine* (On Cookery), written by Maistre Chiquart, chief cook to Amadeus VIII, first duke of Savoy, later to become Pope Felix V, and a more modest mid-century cookbook from northeastern France called the *Vivendier.*[76]

If there is one type of dish that is characteristic of late-medieval French cuisine, it is the potage or broth. The *Viandier's* two extensive sections on "Thick Potages," and "Thick Meatless Potages" underline their importance and great variety. What is meant by "meatless" potages is not vegetable dishes, however, but potages made from fish, dishes that were suitable for fast days. Potages and *brouets,* or broths, were a favorite first course, judging from the French menus of the time. These dishes would have followed a starter, often in the form of seasonal fruit whose function it was to "open" the mouth of the stomach and prepare it for the main dishes that were thought to take longer to "cook," that is, to digest. The *Viandier's* white capon broth is a typical example of this genre of dish. To prepare this *Blanc brouet de chappons,* the capons are cooked in wine and water, broken into pieces, and fried in bacon grease. The dark capon meat, chicken livers, and almonds are ground up, steeped in the broth, and boiled with the other meat. Then a mixture of ground ginger, cinnamon, cloves, galingale, long pepper, and grains of paradise is added, followed by well-beaten and strained egg yolks.[77]

When these potages contained the spice cumin they were called *comminee.* For the fish *comminee* that opens the section "Thick Meatless Potages," the fish is cooked in water or fried in oil, and then boiled in almond milk to which ground ginger and cumin infused in wine and verjuice are added.[78] The recipe concludes with the remark that sugar is required if this *comminee* is served as a dish for the ailing. In a bourgeois household such as that of the *Menagier,* the broth might have been followed by a *porée,* a soup of leafy greens. *Porée blanche* was prepared from leeks and onions that were fried and cooked in cow's milk or almond milk, depending on whether it was a meat day or fast day.[79] The *Menagier* may have continued his meal with a civet of hare. To prepare it the hare was first roasted on a spit, then cut in pieces, fried in grease with chopped onions, and subsequently boiled in a dark broth made from toasted bread infused in wine and beef broth or pea puree. Ground ginger, cinnamon, cloves, grains of paradise, and saffron are the spices Taillevent lists in his civet recipes.[80]

At an aristocratic banquet the first course, *le premier mets,* containing the broths would have been followed by a variety of roasted meats accompanied with the appropriate sauces as the second course. In the *Viandier,* the sauce most often mentioned in the section on roasts is *sauce cameline.* Sometimes the meat is simply eaten with fine salt or verjuice. For his list of roast meats Taillevent starts with pork, veal, calf's tripe, mutton, kid, and lamb. He continues with the domestic fowl geese and goslings, pullets, chicks, capons, hens, and cockerels. From hare, rabbit, and wild boar he moves on to wildfowl, such as partridge, swan, pheasant, stork, heron, and many others. The section concludes with stuffed suckling pig.[81] With his next group of recipes Taillevent parallels the progression of an actual French feast, in which the roasts of the second course, *le second mets,* would have been followed by the *entremets,* dishes that could be sweet or savory and whose primary function was to entertain. Gilded foods, roasted birds returned to their plumage, boars' heads with flames shooting from their mouths, and pies filled with live birds are some of the more spectacular *entremets* in French cookbooks. An interesting showpiece combining two animals, a cock and a piglet, is called *Coqz heaumez,* or "Helmeted Cocks." To prepare them, piglets and poultry are roasted, the latter then stuffed, glazed with an egg batter, and seated on the piglets. As a finishing touch, the cocks or hens are equipped with paper helmets and lances.[82] While most of this preparation is still edible, the trend in the fifteenth century, as was shown earlier, was toward more and more complex constructions, often made of wood,

Boar's Head at Arthurian Feast, ca. 1340. From Cod. Vind. 2599, fol. 33r. Courtesy of Österreichische Nationalbibliothek, Vienna (Photo: Bildarchiv, ÖNB Wien).

with people enacting historical, or mythical scenes. *Entremets* were then purely a feast for the eye, and no longer for the stomach.

Following the *entremets*, a French banquet would continue with an assortment of dishes ranging from the prized venison to the lowly frumenty. Made from hulled wheat berries, milk, egg yolks, and ginger, frumenty was equally at home on the dining tables of the rich and the poor.[83] The *Viandier* does not have a separate section on sweet desserts in the modern sense of the word; Taillevent's focus is clearly on meat and fish dishes. The reason for this may be that some food-stuffs served did not need any special preparation, such as fruits and nuts, and that other individuals were specialized in the pastries and confections typically eaten at the end of a banquet. The *oubloyer* (maker of *oublies,* or wafers), for instance, provided the waffles and thin wafers which, along with cheese, candied fruits, *hippocras,* or sweet malmsey, formed a course the French called *issue de table,* or "departure from the table." The *épicier* delivered the *épices de chambre* or "parlor spices" eaten at the *boutehors* in a different room.[84] They included *dragées,* candied aniseed or coriander seed, and gingerroot.[85] Aside from aiding digestion they were intended to freshen the breath, much like the mints served at the end of a restaurant meal today.

In studying the handful of cookbooks from northern France that have come down to us, some features emerge that can be considered typical of the aristocratic cuisine in this region.[86] French cooks excelled in the preparation of meat and fish dishes, especially potages, broths, civets, roasts, and the sauces that went with them. The use of dough is relatively rare with the exception of some standard pies. Pasta dishes, so popular in Italy, and even found in England, are not part of French cookery. Equally lacking are the dumplings and stuffed fritters found in central European cookbooks. Omelets are not particularly common in the French sources, and the same is true for candied foods, compotes, and jams. What we do find in the French recipe collections, however, are a plethora of dishes named after specific places and peoples, some of them exotic. This may be a reflection of northern France's location on the crossroads of so many trade routes.

When it comes to the flavor of French cuisine, it was probably shaped more than anything by the addition of its characteristic spices and spice powders, and the liquid food additives almond milk, must, verjuice, wine, and vinegar. The taste of many dishes must have been sweet-sour with some being distinctly bitter, especially those that contained sorrel or the ubiquitous verjuice. Aside from their aroma, many of the herbs and spices used in the French aristocratic kitchen imparted to the dishes a wide array of colors, and it would appear that some of these ingredients were used more for their color than their culinary or medicinal properties. A gaudy green, known as *vert gai,* was achieved by mixing the green of parsley with the yellow of egg yolk or saffron, violet flowers were used to produce a violet coloring, ground sandalwood gave a dish a russet color, and red cedar colored it pink. Ground burned toast and roast liver were used to make black or dark brown dishes, or to tone down some of the brighter colors. For reds, cooks used lichen orchil (a crustlike fungus on rocks and tree trunks), alkanet (the root of a European perennial), or animal blood. Some of these colors were especially dazzling when used for transparent jellies. Much effort was spent on giving dishes a golden appearance. Saffron lent itself particularly well to this purpose, which may explain its popularity; glazing with egg yolks was another option. For an even grander effect, gold and silver leaf was sometimes applied to piecrusts, to the heads and feet of animals, or to whole animals that were used as showpieces. The late-medieval French fashion of wearing parti-colored outfits, a tradition that has lived on in the jester costume, also made itself felt in the aristocratic kitchen. The *Viandier* contains a *Blanc mengier party* which combines on a plate *blanc manger* dyed red on one-half, and dyed blue on the other, to which other colors can be added at will.[87] In Chiquart's cookbook *Du fait de cuisine* we even find an *entremets* recipe for boar's head with one-half colored green, and the other golden yellow.[88] It may have been the Arabs who turned medieval Europe on to coloring their food, but it was the French who embraced the idea with abandon. They perfected the technique and used it to create some of the grandest effects.

The French cuisine outlined is in essence that of the north. If we move south to the regions known as Languedoc and Provence the climate becomes Mediterranean, and so does the food. Southern French cuisine is in many respects more akin to Italian and Catalan than to northern French cooking. As far as medieval cookbooks are concerned, the source material for the south is sparse. Only one little collection of 51 recipes exists from the late fourteenth century; it is written in a mixture of Latin and Occitan, and is known as the *Modus viaticorum preparandarum et salsarum* (How to Prepare Food and Sauces), or *Modus* for short.[89] This may be surprising to some, considering that Languedoc was such a cultural center in the High Middle Ages; this region gave Europe the troubadours whose love poems were admired and imitated for centuries. But the area was also a Cathar stronghold. The Cathars, sometimes called Albigensians after the town of Albi in southern France, were considered heretics and ruthlessly persecuted by the Catholic Church. (See Chapter 5.) When the church mounted the Albigensian Crusade with the goal of stamping out the movement, much of its culture was destroyed in the process, and cookbook manuscripts may have been among the casualties.[90] Apart from the little recipe collection, various historical documents, and archeological records, there is one source that for a long time remained largely untapped: the records kept in the Vatican Archives in Rome that deal with the food supply of the papal court in Avignon, where between 1316 and 1378 six popes resided in succession.[91]

With regard to food preferences these records confirm much of what the cookbook suggests.[92] Foodstuffs not found in the northern French cookbooks but in the *Modus* from the south are chickpeas and lemons, both of which are typical of Arab, Catalan, and Italian cookery. Only the seeds of pomegranates are used, and mainly as garnish, in northern France and England, while in the south pomegranate juice is added to dishes. Introduced to Europe by the Arabs, pomegranate trees were actually cultivated in the south of France in the Middle Ages. Another ingredient in many Arab dishes is eggplant, but this does not appear in the cookbook from Languedoc. Also conspicuously absent are some basic ingredients in northern French collections, above all peas, butter, and pork fat. In Catalan cookbooks and in one of the southern French recipes salted meat is used as an animal fat.

Many of the above foodstuffs show the cooking style of southern France indebted to Mediterranean cuisines, and yet the situation is more complicated when it comes to spices and other seasonings. As in the north, ginger is the most frequently used spice in the *Modus*, but instead of grain of paradise, the more traditional pepper is used, and this in nearly half of the recipes. Pepper was also a favorite spice in Catalan and Hispano-Arabic cooking, as was saffron, which appears in close to 50 percent of the recipes from Languedoc. Mint rarely shows up in northern French recipes, but occurs repeatedly in the *Modus* and in Hispano-Arabic cuisine. With more than a third of the southern French recipes asking for sugar, the percentage of sweet dishes is quite high, especially if one considers that must and fruit, in particular figs and dates, had a sweetening effect, too.

When it comes to the preparation of dishes, the south also differed considerably from the north. Instead of frying in lard or stewing in a pot, people in Languedoc preferred roasting their meat in a dry medium, such as an oven or a frying pan without any liquid. Ovens were expensive and only found in upper-class kitchens. The middle and lower classes primarily used communal ovens or bought baked goods ready-made. In the south, however, portable ovens called *trapa* were used, in which pies and *tourtes* were cooked. Made of pottery or metal, these portable ovens were filled with the dish or dishes to be cooked, and then buried in coals. Interestingly, the records of the popes who resided in Avignon also list a *trapa* as part of the kitchen equipment.[93]

Among the recipes included in the little Occitan cookbook, the *Modus,* there are a handful that are even today still regarded as typical of the region and prepared in more or less the same way. One of them is *escabèche,* or *Scabeg* as the dish is called in the manuscript. The word is derived from Arabic-Persian *sikbag,* which in medieval Arabic described a dish made with vinegar. Similar to a *galantine,* or fish jelly, the *escabèche* is a sauce made from ginger, pepper, cloves, and cinnamon, ground and diluted in wine, to which boiled saffron is added, as well as ground bread diluted in vinegar, and fried onions, ground and diluted in wine. It is served together with fish fried in oil.[94] Another sauce typical of the south is the *aillade,* a garlic sauce made with walnuts. The white garlic sauce found in so many other European cookbooks of the time is normally made with almonds.

Other sauces in the *Modus* that are not generally found in northern French cookbooks are the *eruga,* or rocket sauce, which contains rocket (arugula) seeds ground and diluted in wine, and the *salsa de cerpol,* or serpolet sauce, which contains serpolet (wild thyme), mint, sorrel, costmary, sweet basil, and marjoram.[95] The Arab influence is especially strong in Mediterranean recipe collections when it comes to meat dishes. Two of them, *romania* and *limonia,* which can be found in several Catalan and Italian cookbooks, are also included in the *Modus.* The dish name *romania,* or *raymonia* as the Occitan scribe spelled it, is derived from the Arabic word for pomegranate, *rummān,* which in the form of pomegranate verjuice is one of the principal ingredients. As *Garnade,* the second part of the word "pomegranate," the dish even appears in England, in the aristocratic cookbook *The Forme of Cury.*[96] The Occitan version of the dish is as follows:

Raymonia [Pomegranate Dish]

If you want to make a *raymonia,* take hens and cook them with salted meat. And take unblanched almonds, and wash them in lukewarm water, and grind them very strongly, and dilute with hen's broth, and strain. Afterwards, take pomegranate verjuice or pomegranate wine and add it. Then boil it and add enough sugar.[97]

The white *limonia,* or *Limonieyra blanca* as it is entitled in the *Modus,* is another meat dish, but instead of pomegranate it uses lemon juice, almond milk, and rice, as additional ingredients.[98]

If there is one dish that epitomizes medieval Spanish cooking it is the *adafina,* and it would appear that the *matafeam* of the cookbook from Languedoc is a Christian version of this originally Hispano-Arabic-Jewish dish of chicken and meatballs.[99] In the *Modus,* pork is used for the meatballs, which would have made them unkosher. Jews traditionally prepared the dish on Friday and buried it in coals to keep it warm for the Sabbath when they were not allowed to cook. (See Chapter 5.) The name of the dish goes back to the Arabic verb for "to bury."

To get an idea what foodstuffs were highly prized and what was eaten at court in Languedoc, the account books of the popes in Avignon provide some interesting insights. Ironically, since the papal court also maintained an alms office that fed some 50 poor daily, we also get a glimpse at lower-class food in fourteenth-century Avignon. Consisting of bread, legumes, and a small amount of wine, the diet was occasionally enriched with (coarse) meat, fish, oil, and cheese. The sick among them were even given chicken and other poultry to eat.[100] The daily meals of the pope and the cardinals would have been comparable to the festive meals in the bourgeois *Menagier de Paris.*

In 1343 Pope Clement VI, a pope known for his lavish lifestyle, was given a festive meal by one of his cardinals that consisted of nine courses of three dishes each. The third course was one of the more elaborate *entremets:* a giant castle filled with venison, a wild boar, goats, hares, and rabbits, all of which had been skinned and cooked but made to look as if they were alive.[101] As for the other dishes, we can assume that the standard roasts, pies, jellies, aspics, *tortes,* wafers, waffles, and confections were among them. The wine, vermouth wine, must, *agresta* (Latin for verjuice), and sugar used in the kitchen must have given many dishes the characteristic sweet-sour taste encountered in the other French cookbooks. Spices were bought in great quantity by the papal kitchen and the apothecary, which was also in charge of preparing or buying confections. For one wedding alone, some 90 pounds of spices were acquired. Spices and animals were also given away as gifts by the pope, especially at Christmas and Easter. Judging from the account books in which the bulk purchases were listed, ginger, pepper, cinnamon, and cane sugar were the leaders among the spices and sweeteners.[102] The place to buy these luxury items was Montpellier, which in the fourteenth century was part of the Kingdom of Mallorca that acted as middleman in the spice trade between the Orient and Europe. Montpellier was especially famous for its *éspices de chambre,* or "parlor confections," that were eaten at the conclusion of a banquet. Candied aniseed from Montpellier was sought after, and so was the ginger confection known as *gingibrat.* The latter was more than twice as expensive when it came from Montpellier.[103] Other confections bought by the papal court were *dragées,* gilded lozenges, almond pastilles, and candied orange peel. They were bought in quantities ranging from one hundred to several thousand pounds a year.[104]

Montpellier was not just famous for its spices and confections, but also for a variety of flavored wines often consumed at the end of festive meals. They were known under such names as *girofle* (from the French word for cloves), or *garhiofilatum* in Latin, *claret,* or *claretum* in Latin, and *hippocras.* In the papal records another drink is mentioned that is called *nectar.* What exactly it was made from is not known.[105] Red *hippocras* drunk during the *yssue* course at a French banquet, was a specialty of Montpellier, and perhaps of the Languedoc region as a whole. Even as far away as Paris the author of the *Menagier* was familiar with it and included a recipe for *hippocras* in the style of "Besiers, Carcassonne or Montpellier" in his book.[106]

SPAIN

Many of the characteristics of southern French cuisine are also found in medieval Spanish food, but given Spain's geographic, ethnic, and religious diversity, it is impossible to speak of one Spanish cuisine in the Middle Ages.[107] Just as the plains, mountains, and coastlines had an influence on the food that was produced and eaten, so did the different peoples that invaded the peninsula over the centuries. The Romans established two provinces in Spain, and the food consumed by the Roman army consisted largely of bread, cheese, olives, olive oil, wine, and some roasted meat. Remarkably, these are still the staples of modern-day Spain. It was not the Romans, however, that introduced olives to Iberia, but the Phoenicians and the Greeks, who had already produced olive oil along Spain's southern coast long before the Romans arrived. Even older is the evidence of bread production on the peninsula, which was, however, substantially improved by the introduction of the Roman ovens. Not the Romans but the Greeks had brought the Malvasia grape to Spain, and in doing so had created the foundation for a wine industry that was to become famous in medieval times. Aside from wheat, olive oil, and wine, Roman Spain was an important producer of salt fish, and salt fish products such as the salty fish sauce known as *garum* that was the preferred seasoning in Roman cooking. By the early Middle Ages, however, *garum* had slowly fallen out of favor with European cooks.

Christianity came to Spain with a new group of invaders, the Germanic tribes known as the Vandals, Alans, Swabians, Goths, and Visigoths, who arrived in A.D. 409. Their impact on Spanish cookery was relatively minor compared with that of the Romans before them, and especially that of the Arabs from North Africa who conquered Visigothic Spain and established Muslim rule on the peninsula. It was to last for almost eight hundred years, from A.D. 711 to 1492. In the ninth century the Arabs extended their domain beyond Spain to southern Italy and Sicily. During the time of Arab expansion in the Mediterranean, Baghdad was the center of Arab culture, and when the Arabs settled in southern Spain, in the territory they called Al-Andalus, or Andalusia, it was the court culture of Baghdad they tried to emulate in their capital Cordoba. Andalusia quickly became the gateway through which Arab and the surviving Greek and Roman cultures reached medieval Europe.

The Baghdad court was known for its refinement. Its officials were highly educated, and sophisticated when it came to poetry, music, food and drink, clothes, scent, and other pleasures of the body.[108] In the ninth century a court modeled after the one in Baghdad was created in Cordoba. There Ziryāb, a famous Arab poet and musician, played an important role in introducing Arab haute cuisine, knowledge in perfumes and cosmetics, and the use of glass goblets at table to Spain and eventually to the rest of Europe. He is also said to have established a new order of the menu, according to which courses progressed from soup to meat dishes, and ended with sweets—the order we still use today.[109]

We have some idea of what the famous cuisine of medieval Baghdad was like, thanks to *The Baghdad Cookery Book* written by a certain Al-Baghdadi in the thirteenth century.[110] Among its characteristic dishes are meat dishes made from cubed meat, chicken, or meatballs combined with chickpeas or lentils, and spinach, turnips, leeks, eggplants, or other vegetables. Meat is also frequently cooked with fruits such as apricots, quinces, peaches, dates, apples, or pears. Garlic and onion play an important role, as do many herbs and spices. Favorites among them were cinnamon, cumin, ginger, turmeric, mastic (a small Mediterranean tree and its resin), saffron, sumac, caraway, sesame, mint, rocket, and rue. Ground almonds and ground rice were the preferred thickeners, and sour grape juice, tamarind, and pomegranate gave dishes their typical sweet-sour taste. Sweets were made with orange blossom water or rose water, and a variety of dishes were garnished with raisins, pine nuts, blanched almonds, and pistachios. The dishes featured in *The Baghdad Cookery Book* were meat dishes, fish dishes, rice dishes, stuffed vegetables, savory pastries, and sweets.[111] The Arabs not only influenced the way dishes were prepared in medieval Spain, but also the Spanish language. The list of Spanish culinary terms that have Arab roots is virtually endless. Among the best-known examples are *naranja* for orange, *limón* for lemon, *arroz* for rice, *espinaca* for spinach, and *azúcar* for sugar.[112]

Not many cookbooks or recipes have survived from Arab Spain. The ones that have indicate that the Spanish Muslims may have tried to imitate the cuisine of Baghdad, and yet their cuisine also shows signs of a fusion with the established Roman and Visigothic cooking styles of Spain. One of these Hispano-Arabic cookbooks, given the name *The Almohade Cookbook* by a modern scholar owing to the historic period it originated in, is a good example of this fusion, especially in upper-class cuisine.[113] The first two chapters of the cookbook deal with "simple" meat dishes, in particular stews, pounded meat preparations, and roasts. The next four chapters are on thickened dishes, vegetables, fish, and starchy dishes made from couscous, rice, pasta, and the like; the last chapter gives recipes for pastries and sweets. The cuisine is based on olive oil as a cooking fat and uses wheat and wheat flour for a variety of leavened and unleavened doughs that were often baked or deep fried. Lamb and mutton were the preferred types of meat; also mentioned are goat and rabbit. Chickens and partridges are frequently listed fowl, and eggplant, introduced to Europe by the Arabs, is the favorite vegetable.

The dishes were seasoned with a number of herbs and spices, in particular coriander seeds and leaves, mint, thyme, fennel, cumin, caraway, citron leaves, saffron, pepper, cinnamon, spikenard (an East Indian herb of the valarian family), ginger, clove, nutmeg, galingale; sugar was used as sweetener. Instead of *garum,* the salty fish-sauce the Romans loved so much, Hispano-Arabs used the sauce *murri,* a highly concentrated salt solution made from fermented bread that was similar to soy sauce. In order to thicken sauces, the Arabs in Spain developed their own techniques and a special terminology: either eggs or starch in the form of bread crumbs or pounded almonds were used. Many Hispano-Arab dishes were given an *au gratin* finish not found in other parts of the medieval Arab World. "Sealed" dishes, with the lid sealed to the pot and left to cook on the dying ashes for a long time, were popular. This technique was also applied by the Spanish Jews for preparing the *adafina* and other elaborate dishes for the Sabbath, as described below. Pounded meat turned into spicy little meatballs and deep-fried dough preparations were two more features of Hispano-Arab cuisine. Where the fusion between Baghdad and the old Hispanic and Roman traditions is most obvious is in the use of olive oil, rather than the tail-fat of sheep that was customary in the Middle East, and in the European way of making cheese. The fact that many dishes in *The Almohade Cookbook*'s 220 recipes have no counterpart in Middle Eastern cookery of the time speaks for the unique character of Muslim Spain's cuisine.

One technique the Arabs introduced to Europe that became extremely popular in Spain and in time was exported from there to the New World was the *escabèche* technique encountered in the cookbook from southern France. Presumably derived from the Persian word for vinegar or acid food, the name described a method of preparing meat that preserved the food at the same time. Typically, meat or fish were first boiled and then marinated in oil, vinegar, spices, and herbs. The following is a recipe for *escabèche* contained in the *Libre de Sent Soví* (Book of Saint Sofia), a Catalan cookbook from the early fourteenth century.

Pex Frit Ab Escabeyg [Fried Fish with Escabèche]

Take good fish and fry it. Then take finely chopped onion, and fry in oil. Then take roasted bread soaked in vinegar, and some of the flesh of the fish with spices, and grind all these with the fried onion. Then, when well ground, blend it with hot water, and turn it into the pan in which the onion cooked; and add a little vinegar for seasoning. And when it boils, pour it over the fish on a platter. And if you wish, add ground parboiled parsley; and hazelnuts as well.[114]

Another technique brought to Europe by the Arabs was distilling. Associated with the rise of alchemy, distilling was initially used to produce medicinal potions and perfumes. Distilled wine, called *vino ardiente,* or "burning wine," is called the "water of life" by the Catalan physician Arnald de Villanova, and "aqua vitae," the Latin term for "water of life," is used to this day for certain alcoholic spirits. Rose water, a staple in Arab and Hispano-Arab cuisine, is a well-known example of a nonalcoholic foodstuff produced by distillation.[115] It was used in confections together with sugar and almonds, such as in the famous almond paste known as "marzipan" that was usually served as a sweetmeat at the end of dinner, or in variations thereof containing honey and pistachios.[116]

In addition to the Arabs, the Sephardim, or Spanish Jews, also had an influence on the cookery of medieval Spain. When the Arabs invaded the peninsula in the eighth century, the local Jews sided with the Arabs against the Visigothic Christians, and Jewish communities soon flourished in the cultural centers of Muslim Spain, such as Toledo, Cordoba, Granada, and Seville. When the Christians reconquered southern Spain from the Arabs, the Sephardim were severely prosecuted or forced to convert to Christianity. Those who by 1492 had not converted were given no choice but to leave Spain. Ironically, the records of the Inquisition, established in 1480 with the goal of identifying and destroying the converted Jews, or *Conversos,* who were still secretly practicing Judaism, provide a glimpse of what Hispano-Jewish food in the Middle Ages was like. Aside from the general Jewish prohibitions against eating pork or seafood and against mixing meat and milk, two specific Sabbath dishes are mentioned in the sources whose preparation, when discovered by the authorities, would land *Conversos* in front of the Inquisition. One is the *adafina,* or buried dish, an elaborate stew usually containing lamb, onions, and chickpeas; the other a cold dish made with eggs, cheese, and eggplant.[117]

The Almohade Cookbook contains five dishes that are labeled "Jewish." They include a "Jewish Partridge" with almond, pine nut, coriander, and egg stuffing that is also inserted under the skin of the bird. The sauce in which it is stewed is made with cinnamon, mint and citron leaves, vinegar, sugar, and *murri.* Pistachios, almonds, pine nuts, and hard-boiled egg yolks are also used to garnish the dish. To prepare "A Jewish Dish of Chicken," the bird is roasted and then marinated in *murri,* vinegar, rose water, onion juice, and other aromatic ingredients. It is served in a sauce made from the giblets of the bird, onion juice, coriander, pine nuts, vinegar, oil, citron leaves, and fennel stalks, thickened with eggs, flour, bread crumbs, and crushed chicken liver. A simpler dish eaten on the Sabbath was the *harissa,* a type of porridge containing meat, that could be bought ready-made from street vendors. Not surprisingly, a recipe for *adafina* is also included in the cookbook:

Adafina [Stuffed Buried Jewish Dish]

Meatballs flavored with cumin and other spices, rose water, and onion juice are cooked in a pot between two layers of cinnamon-flavored omelette and covered by a third omelette of egg combined with pounded meat, salt, pepper, cinnamon, and rose water. The dish is served garnished with pistachios, pine nuts, mint leaves, and a sprinkling of spices.[118]

Adafina was the traditional meal-in-a-pot prepared on Friday and eaten on Saturday. It was complex, and time-consuming to prepare. Even more than the Arabs, the Sephardim were fond of meat and fruit combinations, and of sweet-and-sour dishes whose characteristic taste was achieved by mixing sour pomegranate juice, tamarind, sour grapes, lemon, or vinegar with sugar or honey. These were also the hallmarks of Persian cuisine with which it had historical ties. Overall, Sephardic cookery has been described as "sensual, aromatic, and colorful," and as making use of "anything that gives flavor—seeds, bits of bark, resins, pods, petals, pistils, and flower waters."[119]

With the forced conversion of Jews at the end of the Middle Ages came a fusion of culinary practices in Spain. Like the Spanish Christians, *Conversos* began to mix meat and milk, add pork and shellfish to their traditional dishes, and use pork fat instead of olive oil as a cooking fat. This is what happened to the *adafina*, which in time became just one of the many types of stew of the *cocido* and *olla* type eaten all across Spain. Best known today is perhaps the *olla podrida,* a stew made with meat, chicken, chickpeas, a large pork sausage, cabbage, garlic, saffron, and cumin. The traditional way of eating this *olla*, and incidentally the *adafina,* too, was by eating the stock as a soup first and the meat separately later.[120]

No medieval cookbook from the Central Meseta in Spain has come down to us, but from the early-seventeenth-century work *Don Quixote* by the famous Spanish author Miguel de Cervantes we know that mutton, beef, bread, and wine were the staples eaten by the peasants of the plains.[121] One such stew mentioned in the text is made with calves' feet, chickpeas, onions, and bacon. Other common foodstuffs in *Don Quixote* are veal, kid, eggs, garlic, and cheese. Compared to this scarcity of culinary information from central Spain, the cuisine from the region of Catalonia on the Mediterranean coast is richly documented in several surviving cookbooks. Catalonia had close political and culinary ties with southern France and Italy, and like the rest of medieval Spain, its cookery was also strongly influenced by Roman and Arab cooking styles. The earliest Catalan cookbook manuscript we have was written in 1324, and is known as the *Libre de Sent Soví*.[122] It is one of the oldest European recipe collections and has survived in two manuscripts from Valencia and Barcelona. It contains a wide range of soups, sauces, roasts, and desserts but comparatively few seafood dishes. Popular ingredients are chicken, game animals, almonds, onions, and bitter oranges.[123] The following is a recipe for *Mig-raust,* meaning "half- roasted," a dish that was a favorite of cooks and diners not just in Catalonia but also in Italy:

Mig-raust ab let de melles [Mig-raust with Almond Milk]

If you want to make mig-raust with almond milk, do it this way: First roast some hens. Then take stock made from other hens, and make stock with the insides of the roasting hens, plus salted pork; and then take blanched almonds, and make milk with the stock. And take the livers and pound them well, and mix them with the said milk. And set this to boil with good spices: pepper, ginger, cloves, cinnamon, and then add a sour ingredient and white sugar. And boil all this, until you know that it is cooked. Then serve it in bowls together with the hens; and if you wish, serve the hens on platters.... And if by chance you don't want to add sugar, use good honey.[124]

The fish recipes are for both saltwater and freshwater fish. In addition to fish that was used fresh, the cookbook mentions dried eel and dried salted tuna. The *escabèche* technique described above is an example of the strong Arab influence in Catalan cooking; another is the use of bitter oranges, rose water, almonds, and onions, as well as the overall sweet-sour and sweet-salty character of many dishes. Recipes for vegetables introduced to Europe by the Arabs include asparagus and eggplant dishes. The instructions for preparing asparagus can be quite simple. In one recipe the vegetable is cleaned, parboiled, and coated in wheat flour, and fried until done. It is served on a platter with vinegar as an optional seasoning.[125]

Pies, a standard feature of English and French banquets, are also found in the *Libre de Sent Soví,* as the following poultry pie illustrates:

Panades de pols...ab aldem [Poultry Pie with Egg and Verjuice Sauce]

Take parboiled hens, and put them in pastry with slices of salted pork; and make the sauce. Take eggs, beat them, and add as much verjuice as necessary. When the pie is cooked, pour the sauce in the pie, and return it to the oven briefly, so the sauce thickens. And if you don't have verjuice for the sauce, use vinegar.[126]

A dessert contained in this Catalan cookbook that has stood the test of time is called *bunyols,* a name it still bears today. Similar in style to medieval Arab fritters, *bunyols* are made from well-risen dough, eggs, and grated cheese formed into egg-sized balls. They are fried in pork fat and served on a bed of sugar with sugar on top as well.[127]

Another important Catalan cookbook that became much more influential than the *Libre de Sent Soví,* thanks to the invention of printing, is the *Libre del Coch.* It was put together in the fifteenth century by a certain Mestre Robert, or Rupert de Nola, who calls himself cook to "don Ferrando, rey de Napols [king of Naples]." The latter was probably Ferrante I, who ruled Naples from 1458 to 1494.[128] Through Mestre Robert, Catalan cooking became more widely known in Italy, but the influence went both ways, with the Catalan cook also incorporating Italian recipes and cooking styles in his repertoire. The cookbook was published in Catalan in 1520, and in Castilian translation in 1525. It quickly became a bestseller and by the late eighteenth century had gone through several editions in both languages.[129] As a truly Mediterranean cookbook, the *Libre del Coch* combines recipes of Catalan, Italian, French, and Arab origin. Written for an aristocratic audience and influenced by the Italian Renaissance, the text contains much more than just recipes. In the first part instructions are given for the proper way of carving meat, setting the table, and serving, plus information on the cooking and serving staff.[130] The second part deals with dishes for meat days, including sauces and fruits, and the third part with Lenten food. Of the sauces in the *Libre del Coch* two stand out, one a peacock sauce that is praised by Mestre Robert as being among the best dishes in the world, and the other, called *Alidem,* for its versatility. The former is made with almonds, the liver of peacock or other fowl, bread, orange juice or vinegar, egg yolks, sugar, and cinnamon.[131] *Alidem,* served with anything from roast pork, kid, chicken, or small birds to fried eggs and pies, appears to be of Arab origin. It combines pepper, ginger, saffron, and other spices, with meat stock, eggs, and verjuice or vinegar.[132]

Nearly a quarter of the approximately two hundred recipes in the book are for fish and seafood; many of them are adaptations of meat dishes suitable for consumption on fast days. Trout, barbel, conger eel, tuna, dentex (a European marine fish), hake, spiny lobster, squid, cuttlefish, octopus, and swordfish are made into *empanadas,* or fish pies. Alternatively, they are grilled, boiled, or cooked in stews and casseroles. For the fast-day version of *blanc manger* the cookbook recommends fish stock instead of beef stock. Some maintain that *blanc manger* was actually invented in Tarragona in the eighth or ninth century.[133] The recipe for baked dentex, entitled *De Déntol en Cassola,* is typical of the way Mestre Robert seasoned a variety of fish. The cleaned dentex is cut in hand-sized pieces that are sprinkled with finely ground saffron, pepper, nutmeg, and some salt, and put in a casserole. When the fish is half cooked, some orange juice and a mixture of herbs are added. Currants, and almonds with some oil are optional.[134] The herbs to be added to these fish dishes are usually parsley, mint, marjoram, and at times dried coriander. Clearly of Arab origin, or at least inspired by Arab cookery, are the different recipes for eggplant; one of them even announces in the title that it is "in the Moorish style." To prepare these *Albergínies a la Morisca,* eggplants are peeled, quartered, cooked well, then squeezed between two boards, chopped, fried with salted pork, and then cooked with fatty meat stock, grated cheese, and powdered coriander. Egg yolks beaten together with verjuice are added just before the eggplants are fully cooked.[135]

The frequent use of orange and other fruit juice, and of nuts, especially hazelnuts, pine nuts, almonds, and almond milk, also point to Catalonia's rich Arab culinary heritage. Mestre Robert's recipes for sweets are divided into four groups: fruit desserts, creams, cooked fruits, and cheeses.[136] They include such items as little marzipan pies, and *Los flaons,* pies made from flour, cheese, and eggs, and topped with honey, as well as *Manjar Imperial,* a dish prepared with milk, eggs, and sugar. Boiled quinces and quince paste, also encountered in French cuisine, are mentioned, as are figs with rose petals, and different cheeses ranging from "green" or unripened soft to roasted ones.

From Castile an important manual dating back to the early fifteenth century has come down to us that is not primarily a cookbook but nevertheless provides useful information on Castilian foodstuffs, dishes, and eating habits. The book was written by Enrique de Villena, and is entitled *Tractado del Arte de Cortar del Cuchillo* (Treatise on the Art of Cutting with a Knife), or *Arte Cisoria* (Art of Cookery) for short.[137] It is first and foremost a manual for professional food carvers, but it also describes table settings and dishes to be served at court to kings, queens, and the nobility at large. Like the *Libre del Coch,* it distinguishes between food for meat days and Lenten food. Poultry, meat, fish, and fruit and the proper way of carving them are discussed in detail. The culinary recipes that are contained in the manual range from meat pies or *empanadas,* sausages, meatballs, and blood pudding, to pastries and *cabeza de Turco,* or "Turk's Head," a dish with Arab ancestry that was also known to the Anglo-Normans. The discovery of the New World revolutionized Spanish cookery, just as the arrival of the Arabs on the peninsula some eight hundred years earlier had done. And yet, none of the new foodstuffs from the Americas gained instant popularity in Spain—or anywhere else in Europe, for that matter. Spanish cookbooks do not mention them until the end of the sixteenth century. What Spanish cookery adopted first were beans, maize, chocolate, and the tomato, while the potato had to wait until the late seventeenth century to be accepted by cooks and diners.[138]

ITALY

The staple foods of medieval Italy were much the same as those of medieval Spain: bread, olives, olive oil, and wine. They were complemented with cheese, some meat and fish, and a variety of fruits and vegetables. In both regions the cookery of ancient Rome formed the basis or substratum that was gradually transformed by the cooking styles of different invaders. In the early Middle Ages, the southern parts of both the Iberian and Italian Peninsulas were occupied by the Arab Muslims, who introduced new foodstuffs and new agricultural and cooking techniques. In Italy the Arab influence is especially strong in Sicily and on the southern mainland. Given the political connections between Catalonia and Naples in the late Middle Ages, some Spanish and Hispano-Arab dishes also found their way into Italian cooking.

The diet of the ordinary Italians was largely vegetarian, as it was for most other ordinary Europeans. Fruits were eaten as an appetizer at the beginning of a meal, and often also at the end. Instead of expensive spices, average Italians used herbs cultivated in the kitchen garden. Thanks to trade and the growth of towns, Italy had a rich middle class, and many patricians from the powerful city-states of Florence and Venice, for instance, had the means to keep up with or even surpass the nobility in conspicuous consumption. Given that the Italian nobility often lived in towns and took part in town affairs, and that social acceptance was determined more by wealth than by noble birth, the aristocracy and bourgeoisie in late-medieval Italy intermingled more, and as a result Italian society was less hierarchical than that in the rest of Europe.[139]

Nowhere on the Continent was there a richer and more diverse and sophisticated cuisine in the Middle Ages than in Italy. And it was there that the fork first became part of the table setting. By the late fourteenth century it seems to have been in general use already, and no longer restricted to the tables of the rich. People in taverns even ate pasta with it, and this has prompted some food historians to speculate that the quick acceptance of the fork may be connected with Italy's love for a plethora of pasta dishes.[140] From the informal meal in the countryside consisting of salad, lasagne, and an omelet, to the luxurious feast in the city that began with ravioli and lasagne in broth, continued with boiled meat, game stews, roast game birds, *torte*, and other savory meat pies, and ended with dried fruits and spices, pasta always made an appearance on the table.[141]

The sources that allow us to study Italy's culinary past are manifold. In addition to a number of cookbooks from different regions of the peninsula, most of them from the fourteenth and fifteenth centuries, there are also account books that tell us exactly what a certain group of people ate at a certain time of the week, on feast days and lean days, when they ate alone or entertained guests. One such source are the accounts of the Signoria, the government of the City of Florence.[142] The Signoria was created in 1282 and consisted of nine priors who were elected for two months at a time. During this period they were obliged to work, sleep, and eat in the town hall. The accounts from the years 1344 to 1428 name many standard dishes that bear such well-known names as *torta*, *erbolato* (herb omelet), *migliacci* (pancake), *savore* (sauce), ravioli, *tortelletti* (medium-sized pasta), *biancomangiare* (white dish), *gelatina*, and *salsiccetti* (type of sausage). For all of them recipes can be found in contemporary cookbooks, which is a good indication that the recipe-collections did, in fact, reflect the cooking practices of the time, rather than a cuisine people only read about or dreamed about, and that bore no resemblance to their day-to-day meals. Another source for Italian food customs are the illustrations in a medieval health book known as the *Tacuinum sanitatis* (Tables of Health), from which some of the illustrations for this book are taken.[143] The text is the Latin translation of an Arab dietetic manual whose illustrations were made in northern Italy sometime at the end of the fourteenth century.

When it comes to Italian cookbooks of the late Middle Ages, one stands out as the most comprehensive and the most detailed: the *Libro de Arte Coquinaria* (Book on the Art of Cookery) by Maestro Martino de Rossi from Como.[144] As cook to the Sforza family in Milan, and later to Cardinal Ludovico Trevisan, Martino gained enormous experience. It is assumed that he did not write down the recipes himself but dictated them to a scribe sometime in the mid-fifteenth century. The cookbook echos some earlier Italian recipe collections, but it also contains recipes and cooking techniques that were original to Martino. How this cookbook rose to international fame as Europe's first printed cookbook is one of the more unusual and intriguing stories in the history of food.[145] Martino's recipes were translated into Latin by Bartolomeo Sacchi who adopted the name of Platina, which is Latin for Piadena, Sacchi's hometown. Sacchi more than doubled the length of the cookbook by adding an introduction, extensive material on diet and health based in antiquity, allusions to Virgil, folkloric attributes of plants, and a handful of recipes adapted from a Roman cookbook more than a thousand years older than Martino's, namely Apicius's *De re coquinaria* (The Art of Cooking) of the third century. In the true spirit of the Renaissance, Platina used Apicius's cookbook structure to organize Martino's recipes rather than divide them into feast and fast-day dishes as was customary in many cookbooks from Christian Europe written at the time. Titled *De honesta voluptate et valetudine* (On Right Pleasure and Good Health), the Platina cookbook was not just the first printed cookbook, but one of the first printed books anywhere. It was first published in Rome around 1470, and reprinted in Venice in 1475.[146] The combination of Latin and the invention of printing led to the dissemination of the cookbook throughout Europe in the sixteenth century, and its translation into a number of vernacular languages, including French, Flemish, German, Spanish, English, and back to Italian, the language in which Martino's recipes had been written in the first place.[147] Aside from Platina, Martino's collection of recipes was also incorporated into another Italian cookbook manuscript, the *Cuoco Napoletano* (Neapolitan Cook) of the late fifteenth century.

In *De honesta voluptate,* Platina propagates moderate Epicureanism. If it is true that the types of dishes he lists are in the order in which they would have been eaten at a feast, then fruits, salad, frittata, risotto, a small pasta serving, soft-boiled eggs, and the like would have opened the meal. What follows in the cookbook are vegetable dishes, dishes featuring organ meats, sausages, roast or boiled meat, poultry dishes, game, and various prepared meats, soups, stews and sauces. The last section of the cookbook deals with such items as *torte,* fritters, egg dishes, truffles, snails, tortoise, frogs, and finally fish. Martino has been credited with two important cooking innovations, the use of egg white to clarify jelly, and the invention of an edible piecrust that led to the proliferation of a whole host of sweet and savory pies and tarts called *torte,* some of which were popular as snack foods.[148] Prior to Martino, only the filling of a pie was traditionally eaten. The crust merely functioned as a container for cooking and serving and was discarded afterward. Martino's cuisine is one that tries to bring out the natural flavor of foods and that uses short cooking times and light seasoning. Meat dishes are plentiful, and often they come in the form of whole birds in a sauce. Vegetables are usually cooked whole or fried as fritters. Color and texture are important aspects in dishes, as are the use of sugar, rice, rose water, and fruit such as pomegranates and oranges, all of which point to the influence of Arab cookery.[149]

Pasta is probably the specialty most commonly associated with Italy. This was the case in the late Middle Ages and it still is today. Pasta was prepared fresh in the home, or bought dried from merchants such as the *lasagnai,* or pasta makers, who in those days even had their own guild in Florence.[150] Semolina was used to make lasagne and macaroni, and wheat flour for most other cheaper kinds. *Vermicelli, fidelli,* and *tria* were other popular types of pasta that were sold commercially. The word *tria* goes back to Greek *itria,* the earliest known word for "noodle" in the Mediterranean. The Arabs introduced the term to Catalonia where it appears as *alatria.* Gnocchi, too, were a form of pasta that is found in Italian cookbooks as early as the fourteenth century:

I gnocchi [Cheese Gnocchi]

If you want some gnocchi, take some fresh cheese and mash it, then take some flour and mix with egg yolks as in making *migliacci.* Put a pot full of water on the fire and, when it begins to boil, put the mixture on a dish and drop it into the pot with a ladle. And when they are cooked, place them on dishes and sprinkle with plenty of grated cheese.[151]

In this case the pasta is cooked in boiling water, but more frequently it was cooked in stock, or in water to which salt, butter, and oil were added; sometimes it was cooked in almond milk or goat's milk with sugar. Many pasta dishes were served with spices or grated cheese, as they still are today. An Italian invention is pasta filled with a meat, vegetable, or cheese and egg purée, cooked in broth and served with grated cheese. These dishes were known under the names "ravioli," *tortelli,* or *torteleti.* But the terms *ravioli* and *tortelli* were also used for fritters that contained similar fillings, and were normally served with sugar.[152]

Rice was the basis for a variety of Italian dishes such as risotto which, like pasta, was frequently cooked in stock. Some inventive pasta makers came up with a creation that was both: pasta and rice. Shaped like grains of rice, this pasta was called *orzo,* meaning "rice."[153] With the development of a tender, edible shortcrust pastry the art of pie making reached new levels of sophistication in Italy.[154] Traditional pies, for which the Italians used the terms *pastero, pastello,* or *coppo,* consisted

Pasta making. From *Tacuinum sanitatis in medicina*, 14th century. Cod. Vind. Series Nova 2644, fol. 45v. Courtesy of Österreichische Nationalbibliothek, Vienna (Photo: Bildarchiv, ÖNB Wien).

of a filling that was usually encased in pastry made from flour and water. The big change came when Maestro Martino and other Italian cooks began to use flour in combination with eggs and oil or butter for the pastry. Known as *torte*, these pies with an edible crust quickly became the rage, especially among the newly rich. Like the old-fashioned pies, they had both a top and a bottom crust. They differed from the earlier pie versions not just in the type of crust, but also in the type of filling, which was generally more elaborate and included more expensive ingredients such as sugar and spices. The following *torte* recipe for eel would have been suitable for fast days:

Torta d'anguille fresche [Eel Torta (Pie)]

If you want to make a pie of fresh eels, take the eels, half-boil them, and cook with them parsley and mint and purslane [?], then cool and take them apart by hand. Discard the skin and the bones. Take good walnuts, skin them with boiling water, then crush them slightly. And take a *libra* [pound] of almonds, make them into milk, and cook it until it becomes very thick; and set it aside to cool; it will be a junket. Then put these things in a pan; make a crust; herbs should be chopped, and add strong spices, saffron, and twelve chopped dates. And when it is cooked, remove it; and if [the eels] were not fat, add good oil.[155]

In addition to these savory pies, there were also various kinds of sweet pies, such as the *torta bianca,* or white tart, which has been described by food historians as "one of Maestro Martino's greatest gastronomic achievements."[156] The filling of the tart is made from finely cut fresh cheese, egg whites, sugar, ginger, pork lard, butter, and some milk. The covered pie is cooked with fire from both below and above, and served with fine sugar and rose water on top.[157]

Italian cookbooks, more so than those from many other parts of Europe, offer a wide range of recipes for vegetables and legumes. Broad beans, generally looked down upon as Lenten food for the poor, are the main ingredient in not just one but several recipes by Maestro Martino.[158] His preferred way of preparing broad beans is with sage, onions, apples, and figs. A tasty little vegetable dish in Martino's collection is called *Finocchio,* meaning "fennel." The white part of fennel, and a little white leek are finely chopped, and fried with oil or salted pork. Then a little water, saffron, and salt are added and the dish is brought to a boil. Beaten eggs, presumably used as a thickener, are optional.[159]

Overall more pasta, fish, and vegetables were eaten in the south of Italy, and more meat was eaten in the north. Lamb, kid, suckling pig, and veal were especially prized, in addition to capon, chicken, pigeon, and peacock, which for dramatic effect was roasted and then served in its original plumage. The sausage maker produced a variety of different fresh and dried sausages, some of them not dissimilar to today's Italian salami. The inclusion of recipes for tripe, liver, and other inner organs in many upper-class Italian cookbooks points to a special taste, one that was not shared equally by diners across Europe. Tripe has remained a favorite dish of the Milanese since the fourteenth century.[160] Another regional delicacy that has survived to this day is *Fegatelli*, a dish of pork liver in sauce that is still prepared in Tuscany as it was more than five hundred years ago.[161]

In Italy as elsewhere in medieval Europe, eggs were used in great numbers in the kitchen, but no other cuisine seems to have come up with as many egg dishes as the Italian one did. This may in part be due to the fact that a dish with eggs as its main ingredient was regarded as an integral part of an Italian meal. Maestro Martino's list of egg dishes is truly impressive, consisting of an omelet (*frictata*), fried eggs (*ova frictellate*), poached eggs (*ova sperdute*), eggs poached in milk or wine (*ova sperdute in lacte o vino dolce*), stuffed eggs (*ova piene*), an omelet recooked on a grill with fresh eggs, sugar, and cinnamon (*ova sopra la graticula*), whole eggs on a spit (*ova nel speto*), today's *oeufs en cocotte,* or coddled eggs (*ova in patelleta*), whole eggs in the coals (*ova in cenere calda*), boiled eggs (*ova tuffate con la sua cortece*), eggs fried on both sides (*ova frictellate a la fiorentina*), eggs broken on the coals (*ova spedute in la brascia accesa*), Florentine eggs with a herb-and-spice mixture replacing the egg yolk (*ova frictellate piene*), and eggs deep fried in a thin dough (*ova in forma de raffioli*).[162]

The Arab influence on Italian cookery manifests itself not just in the use of some characteristic ingredients, but also in a number of standard Arab dishes that have been incorporated in Italian cookbooks. Two of them are *romania,* or chicken with pomegranate juice, encountered earlier in Spain and England, and *limonia,* or chicken with lemon, whose name is related to *laymūn,* the Arabic word for lemon. According to one recipe, chickens are first fried with grease and onions, then skinned almonds are crushed, soaked in meat broth, strained, and cooked with the chickens and seasoning. Instead of almonds, egg yolks can be used as a thickener. The juice of lemons, limes, or bitter oranges is added just before the dish is ready to be served.[163]

No medieval cookbook has survived from Sicily, where the influence of Arab civilization was felt more strongly than in the rest of Italy.[164] It was in the period between 878 and 1091 while under Arab occupation that the island of Sicily flourished, and its capital city, Palermo, reached a population of three hundred thousand. It was famous for its Arab architecture and its walled gardens, in which lemon and orange trees blossomed. The Arabs greatly improved the island's water supply through irrigation, reservoirs, and water towers, and they revolutionized agriculture and fishing. Vegetables and spices introduced by the Arabs were buckwheat, carob, cumin, pistachios, spinach, sugarcane, saffron, and tarragon, all of which still bear their Arab names in Italian. Dates, melons, rice, and sugar were grown on a large scale. Expert fishermen, the Sicilian Arabs caught tuna and swordfish, and preserved the fish and fish roe by means of pressing, salting, and drying.

Sicilian cookery was enriched by Arab methods of preserving food that also included drying fruits and vegetables, by distillation, and by the use of flower essences, as well as pistachios and carobs, as flavoring agents. Early in the ninth century an Arab army is said to have brought durum wheat to Sicily, and it was from there that durum wheat pasta spread throughout the Italian Peninsula. A separate tradition of pasta making was supposedly centered on Genoa, and it, too, seems to have been strongly indebted to the Arabs.[165] Modern Sicilian food is known for being hot, spicy, and sweet, qualities that are also characteristic of Arab cuisine. With the arrival of sugarcane on the island Sicily became internationally famous for its sweets. Like Montpellier, it produced a variety of nut and seed confections called *comfits* that were eaten by the nobility at the end of a banquet. Other Sicilian desserts included sherbets (*sorbetta*), ice cream (*gelato*), nougat candy (*torrone*), marzipan (*marzapane*), almond clusters (*confetti*), elaborate cakes such as the *Cassata alla Siciliana*, and last but not least the *cappelli di turchi* or "Turkish Hats" that appeared as "Turk's Heads" in the Castilian and Anglo-Norman sources, illustrating once again the international flair that surrounds medieval European upper-class cookery.

GERMANY

The food of German-speaking Europe was quite different from that of the Mediterranean world in the Middle Ages. This was in part due to the fact that the climate was harsher, which made it impossible to cultivate olives, almonds, and citrus fruits, for instance. And with most of central Europe being far removed from any ocean, the main fish to be had were freshwater fish. Ocean fish, if available at all, were usually the lower grade herring and cod that were salted or dried before being transported inland. Straddling the northeastern frontier of the Roman Empire, the Germanic tribes never really adopted Roman cuisine and gastronomy, and unlike Spain and Italy, which endured Arab occupation, Germany never came into direct contact with the sophisticated Arab civilization, either, except perhaps for the odd knight who went on a Crusade or on a pilgrimage to the Holy Land, or the German physician who attended medical school in southern Europe.

The little written evidence we have concerning the food of the early Germanic tribes comes from the Romans, who tended to be quite biased against the "barbarians" to the north.[166] According to Caesar and Tacitus, the Germanic diet consisted mainly of meat, dairy products, fish, eggs, bacon, lard, and beer, and was a far cry from the sophisticated cuisine of Rome. Another writer even claimed that the Teutonic tribes ate their meat fresh and raw, in essence putting them and their culinary habits on the level of wild animals. While the Germans were familiar with fire in Roman times and used it for cooking, archeology has shown that the Germanic diet in fact was strongly meat based. Not until the tenth and eleventh centuries did the shift to a grain-based diet occur, which was much later than in the Mediterranean. By the High Middle Ages, however, bread and gruel had become staples in Germany, especially for the poorer segments of the population. The meat that was eaten by that time was no longer the game meat of the early medieval period, but the meat of domesticated animals, primarily pork and beef. Other meat sources were sheep and goats, rabbits, hares, ducks, geese, chickens, and the hunted animals mallards, barnacle geese, stag, and wild boar. The latter, however, were only a small fraction of the overall meat consumption. The fish eaten in the northern German town of Lübeck included carp, bream, pike, sturgeon, cod, and plaice.

The types of grains cultivated in thirteenth-century Germany were barley, oats, rye, wheat, spelt, buckwheat, and millet. Barley and oats were the most popular, and millet was the grain eaten by the poor and in times of famine. Archeologists have found evidence of a wide variety of fruits, nuts, vegetables, and herbs that were grown in medieval Germany. They include cherries, plums, damsons, peaches, sloeberries (small, bitter, wild European plums, the fruits of the blackthorn), apples, walnuts, hazelnuts, grapes, elderberries, blackberries, beechnuts, chestnuts, medlars, pears, strawberries, roses, raspberries, bloodwort, amaranth, dill, celery, hemp, carrots, linseed, peas, lamb's lettuce, and rose hip.[167] This information points to a diet that was substantially more varied than what medieval German literature of the time would have the reader believe. Disregarding the upwardly mobile urban middle class that already existed around A.D. 1200, literary texts invariably list game, fish, white bread, and wine as aristocratic food, and dark bread, porridge, turnips, side meat (cheap cuts of pork), water, milk, cider, and beer as peasant food. At times also *blanc manger* is mentioned as upper-class food, and hemp, lentils, and beans as lower-class food.

Bread was by far the most cost-effective of the foodstuffs in terms of the calories it provided, and many people in late-medieval Germany as elsewhere in Europe depended on it for their survival. Bad harvests brought on by natural disasters or wars often led to a steep rise in grain prices that easily pushed the less well-off into starvation. But not only availability and affordability determined what Germans were eating in the Middle Ages. Norms were also imposed by different authorities, including town councils, the church, and the medical community. Sumptuary laws were intended to curb conspicuous consumption among the nouveau riche burghers who were trying to flaunt their wealth. In the area of food these laws prescribed, for instance, how many courses were allowed at a festive banquet, and how many platters of food in total. For wedding banquets in early-fourteenth-century Berlin the limit was five courses, and 40 platters for the bourgeoisie.[168] At that time only the aristocracy was allowed eight courses, but by 1500 this rule was no longer observed.

A banquet given by a town clerk in Frankfurt, for instance, consisted of eight courses whose sequence was modeled after the aristocratic banquets encountered earlier in England, France, and the Mediterranean regions. An appetizer of strawberries with sugar was followed by six meat courses: chicken, mutton stew, boiled mutton, roast chicken, roast mutton, and half a goose in sauce. Cheese and cherries concluded the feast. It is true that some of the ingredients, such as sugar, raisins, cubebs (dried unripe berries of an East Indian shrub of the pepper family), and nutmeg, were expensive imports, but real high-end foodstuffs such as game and saffron are not mentioned. In its selection of dishes and the expenses incurred, the banquet was probably comparable to the festive meals in the *Menagier de Paris.*

For Germans, observing the fasting laws of the Christian church was much more difficult than for people of the Mediterranean. Fish and olive oil were expensive luxuries north of the Alps that only the rich could afford, and even they were hit hard in their pocketbooks if they tried to replace all their normal meat dishes with fish dishes. It was not uncommon for their grocery bills to double or triple during Lent. For the lower classes there was not much alternative to the protein and fat they usually got from eggs, dairy products, pork fat, and side meat. Legumes, above all broad beans, were the classic Lenten food for the poor.

One way for Arab and southern European foodstuffs and dishes to become known in Germany was through the medical community. Many German physicians received their medical training at the famous medical schools of Salerno, Montpellier, or Bologna, where they experienced firsthand the Mediterranean cuisine influenced by the Arabs. Moreover, their medical textbooks were Latin translations of works written and compiled by such Arab authors as Avicenna, Rhazes, and Averroës, who not only included foodstuffs used in Arab cooking but also a variety of Arab dishes, especially those that were believed to be beneficial for the preservation of health. Two German physicians who in the fourteenth century compiled regimens of their own from the works of Avicenna, Rhazes, and Averroës were Konrad von Eichstätt and Arnold von Bamberg.[169] Konrad attributes the German love for—not to say addiction to—alcohol to the northern climate. The warming quality of the wine allows people to drink more, he argues, which is why one German consumes more than twice as much alcohol as people in southern Europe. Konrad's regimen contains a handful of simple culinary recipes; half of them he seems to have copied from his Arab health books, while the other ones he may have remembered from his student days in Montpellier. Most of the recipes are for sauces or preparing fish, and feature verjuice, almonds, and almond milk.

Arnold von Bamberg's regimen contains an impressive 40 recipes, and like the recipes provided by Konrad, they tell us little about German cuisine at the time, but a lot about the places Arnold visited and the textbooks he used for his studies.[170] What he propagates is primarily French and Italian cuisine. His preferred method of preparing meat is boiling it and combining it with verjuice, vinegar, or sauces. He also approves of turning it into aspics, pies, or *blanc manger*. For fish he recommends boiling it in water or wine, roasting it on a grill, frying it in a pan, covering it with dough and baking it in an oven, or preparing it in aspic. His sauces are the standard sauces found in French cookbooks, namely white, red, and green sauce. *Blanc manger* must have been a fairly common dish in Germany by the fourteenth century, because he claims every cook knows how to prepare it. In the chapter on cheese he lists three dishes that are contained in many Italian recipe collections: *lagana* (lasagne), *rafioli,* and *tarte* (pie). Arnold even approves of turtles and snails, which were certainly not common fare in Germany at the time but were eaten by Germany's southern neighbors. The few recipes he singles out as typically German are for apples, grapes, or figs boiled in water or almond milk, and cheese soup. Perch and ibex (wild goat with long, recurved horns) also may have been part of his German heritage, since he uses their German names in the otherwise Latin text of his regimen.

To find out what the Germans of all social classes ate, we must turn to the dietetic literature of the sixteenth century. It informs us that asparagus, venison, chickpeas, pigeons, saffron, cranes, hares, peacocks, and pheasants were regarded as food for the rich, and oats, cabbage, chestnuts, beans, millet, and turnips as food for the poor, who in places like Bavaria ate cabbage three to four times a day.[171] The diet of the average German must have been rather fatty, judging from the nickname "Fat Germans" that the French had supposedly given their eastern neighbors. Apples, eggs, chickens, pork, bacon, suckling pig, jelly made from pigs' feet, and butter were favorites, and figs, oranges, limes, rice, raisins, and carob beans were special treats. Items that were an integral part of Mediterranean cuisine, such as capers, lemons, olive oil, and pine nuts, were by the mid-sixteenth century still rare in Germany.

Compared to most other parts of medieval Europe, the number of cookbooks from Germany is staggering. Some 50 manuscripts ranging in size from a few miscellaneous recipes to several hundred have come down to us, most of them written in the fifteenth century.[172] Often they are included in books together with other dietetic and household treatises such as health regimens, books on grafting, or books of horse remedies. The oldest German cookbook was entered in a parchment codex in Würzburg around 1350.[173] Known as *Daz buoch von guoter spise* or *The Book of Good Food,* the recipe collection is just one small part in what was originally a big two-volume home companion owned by the patrician lawyer Michael de Leone, who was the highest notary to the Bishop of Würzburg. Compiled from two different sources, the cookbook brings together dishes made from favorite German ingredients, among them pork, beef, chicken, bacon, lard, butter, freshwater fish, eggs, bread, salt, sage, and parsley, and expensive foodstuffs imported from the Mediterranean, above all almonds, rice, sugar, and saffron.

Following the rhymed prologue are 55 prose recipes and two recipe parodies, one in prose, the other in rhyme. They probably concluded the original cookbook, to which 44 more recipes were appended that are not just different in content but also in style. The first part of the cookbook was clearly intended for a novice who had to be given detailed instructions regarding spices, quantities, and cooking times. The second part, by contrast, was written with an experienced cook in mind. Gone are any hints of measurements, or what type of spice(s), meat, or fish was required for a certain dish. To conjure up images of the East, some dishes have the adjectives "Greek" or "Heathen" in their titles. They are "Greek Chicken" containing roses, "Greek Rice" seasoned with sugar, "Heathen Peas," a sweet dish of ground almonds and honey, also called "Bohemian Peas" in the recipe, and "Heathen Heads," an elaborate savory *sotelty* that has, however, little in common with the "Turk's Head" in the other European collections. A casserole that bears the name "of Jerusalem" is made from perch and almond milk sprinkled with sugar.[174] How Greek or Arab those recipes really were, is far from clear. It would appear that the mention of roses, sugar, almonds, or almond milk was already enough to merit such a designation in fourteenth-century Germany. Aside from the eastern Mediterranean, dishes are named after three German locations: Friesental, Swallenberg, and Rheingau.[175]

One way to get a sense of a region's cuisine is to analyze the ingredients and the frequency with which they occur in its cookbooks. *The Book of Good Food* lists a variety of herbs and spices that are used as seasoning: pennyroyal (a hairy, strong-scented herb of the mint family), galingale, mint, parsley, tansy, rose, sage, mustard, anise, ginger, caraway, nutmeg, cloves, cinnamon, pepper, and saffron. Of these sage and parsley top the list of herbs, and pepper, saffron, and ginger the list of spices. Pepper, saffron, and ginger are also the most frequently mentioned spices in the cookbook from southern France, the *Modus,* and they are not dissimilar to the northern French preference in taste, except that in the north pepper was replaced by the more fashionable grain of paradise. Almost a third of the recipes in the German cookbook are sweetened, 16 of them with sugar and another 16 with honey. The most popular liquid food additives are wine, milk, and vinegar. Almonds are the leading nuts and are required for 23 of the recipes, 19 of which ask for almond milk.

If the use of almonds points to the possible influence of Mediterranean cooking, the use of fruit certainly does not. Only apples, pears, and cherries are mentioned, but no citrus fruits, pomegranates, figs, or dates. Rarely in the cookbook does one come across recipes for vegetables or legumes. In addition to beans, chard, and turnips, cabbage and peas appear in one or two recipes each. There is one pea recipe, however, that seems to have been a favorite across German-speaking Europe, judging from its inclusion in so many medieval cookbooks from all dialect areas. To make this *guot gerihtlin,* or "tasty little dish" as it is called, boiled peas are pressed through a sieve, mixed with an equal amount of eggs, and cooked in butter. Once cooled off, the mixture is cut into bite-sized pieces that are then roasted on a spit and basted with eggs and herbs.[176] Eggs are used in nearly half of the recipes in the oldest German cookbook, but primarily as a binding agent and not as the main ingredient, as was such a dominant feature of Italian cuisine. Other thickeners in *The Book of Good Food* were bread, flour, and rice flour. When it comes to fat, lard, butter, and bacon are the leaders. Oil, which probably referred to olive oil, is only mentioned in one recipe.

The types of meat specified in the cookbook are suckling pig, pork, pork belly, bacon, lamb, beef, veal, goose, chicken, pigeon, wild boar, deer, hazel hen (game bird of the grouse family), partridge, pheasant, and heron. Of these chicken is by far the most popular meat source and is included in almost a quarter of the recipes. By contrast, game plays a minor role. One recipe each mentions deer liver, wild boar liver, a heron on a platter, and a sauce for hazel hen, and two recipes suggest venison as an alternative to the meat of domestic animals. Besides the generic term "fish," several species are named in the recipes, most of them freshwater varieties. Pike is the clear favorite, followed by perch, eel, salmon, and stockfish. Bream, trout, and lamprey only occur one time each.

Most dishes in *The Book of Good Food* have a creamy consistency, usually achieved by parboiling the ingredients and subsequently pounding them in a mortar or forcing them through a sieve cloth. Alternatively, meat is roasted on a spit, which the cookbook assumes cooks know how to do and therefore does not elaborate on. However, the cookbook does discuss the sauces meant to accompany such roasts. They include a garlic, egg, and vinegar sauce that is said to go well with grilled chicken or mushrooms, and two sour sauces called *agraz,* from Provençal *agras.* The first, made from wine and the juice of grapes and sour apples, is especially recommended for lamb roast, chickens, and fish. Another sour sauce listed is made from shallots, salt, wine, and vinegar. It is followed by a sour grape, sage, garlic, and bacon sauce. Hazel hens are supposed to be accompanied by a cooked sauce made from tansy, parsley, sage, bread crumbs, seasonings, eggs, and wine.[177]

Multiple cooking of meat and fish is one of the characteristic features of medieval German cuisine as evidenced in the oldest recipe collection. In one extreme case, a suckling pig is prepared by first skinning it, then cooking its meat and returning it to the skin. Afterward the piglet is boiled, and finally grilled over a low heat.[178] There are several reasons why medieval cooks may have opted for multiple cooking. It was a way to make sure the meat was fully cooked, especially that of larger animals that were to be roasted. It also gave cooks the opportunity to debone the meat, season it, and turn it into a delectable stuffing. And it added an element of surprise to the dining experience: not knowing what the inside of an animal may actually contain. The motivation for the multiple cooking of fish surely had less to do with fully cooking it than with the cook's desire to display his skills and imagination, as in the following pike recipe:

Von gefuelten hechden [About Stuffed Pike]

Stuffed pike you prepare in the following way: you take suitable pike, scale them, and pull the intestines out through the gills. Take fish of any kind, boil them, and remove the bones. Grind them in a mortar, and add chopped sage, ground pepper, caraway, saffron, and salt to taste. With this you stuff the pike, and sprinkle them with salt on the outside. Roast it on a wooden grill and grill it nicely.[179]

Eel is prepared in a similar fashion in the cookbook.[180] The number of cooking processes is limited to only one or two in the second half of the collection. This is mainly due to the types of dishes that predominate there. Many of them are for purees, puddings, or casseroles, for which the cookbook uses the collective term *muos*, for dough preparations similar to pizza, called *fladen*, and for doughnuts and fritters, called *krapfen*. Fish, fruits, nuts, vegetables, or mushrooms are turned into creamy purees and puddings that are ideal for the many fast days of the year. For a sour cherry puree the cherries are boiled with a little wine, then pressed through a sieve cloth together with bread crumbs. Then lard and beaten egg yolks are added and seasoning is sprinkled on top.[181] Fritters stuffed with fish, fruits, or nuts were also popular Lenten food in Germany judging from this collection. *Fladen*, literally "flat cakes," consisted of rolled-out dough topped with a wide range of ingredients, from fish on fast days to meat, liver, cheese, eggs, and the like on meat days. A typical example of a *fladen* recipe is the following:

Einen fladen [A Flat Cake]

> If you want to make a flat cake of meat, take meat which comes from the loin or from the belly, and take marrow. See to it that it is boiled well, and chop it small. Grate half as much cheese, add it, mix it with eggs so that it thickens, season with pepper, and put it on a thin dough. Put it into an oven, and let it bake. Serve it hot.[182]

These flat cakes are also the basis for the most luxurious dishes in the collection, such as the heron on a platter.[183] To prepare the dish, a baked *fladen* similar to the one described in the recipe above serves as the base. It is put on a platter, decorated with four roasts that are topped with pies, and surrounded by a golden fence made from eggs and saffron, and a baked wreath with leaves. Finally, the roasted heron is placed in the middle of the platter.

In the oldest German cookbook as in all the other European ones examined in this chapter, color plays an important role. The main coloring agents are saffron, parsley, violets, and cherries. And yet, compared to the vast array of colors used, for instance, by Taillevent or Maestro Martino in their multicolored dishes, the German application of color is still fairly basic. One type of dish that produced dazzling colors is jellies, and they are conspicuously absent from *The Book of Good Food*. Also missing from the German recipe collection are soups, which may have been considered too low class to merit inclusion. Overall the cookbook sends a mixed message concerning the social milieu from which it originated. It is definitely not a royal cookbook in the league of Taillevent's *Viandier;* it may not even have been an aristocratic cookbook, given the scarcity of game and venison. What it seems to reflect is the cuisine of Michael de Leone's employer, the bishop of Würzburg, and perhaps the cuisine of Michael's own patrician household.

In the course of the fifteenth century, *The Book of Good Food* was incorporated in several bigger collections that contained more and more international dishes favored by the aristocracy, such as the boar's head with hellish flames shooting from its mouth, pies and *tortes,* jellies, and other often intricately colored dishes. Two fifteenth-century cooks even attached their names to their respective compilations of recipes: Meister Hannsen and Meister Eberhard.[184] The latter's keen interest in nutrition manifests itself in his inclusion of the dietetic list of foodstuffs by the physician Konrad von Eichstätt in his text. Eberhard's culinary recipes are also remarkable in that they combine dishes found in *The Book of Good Food* with recipes from another cookbook tradition that was centered on the Tyrolean Alps. One dish that is recurring in several of the recipe collections from the Alpine region is the head of a roe deer:

Der ain rech hawp machen will [If You Want to Prepare Roe's Head]

Singe it first and (boil it) until the meat comes off so that you can cut it and remove the bones. Chop the meat and the skin finely, and prepare it with eggs, herbs, and wine. Then take the four bones and fill the top two with the brain, and chop the brain with hard grains, grapes, and herbs to taste. And make four good egg-crêpes for the four bones, make a good stuffing of meat, and put it on the crêpes. Wrap the crêpes around the bones so that the bones are stuffed with the hash. Then it is ready.[185]

Another feature of this cuisine is the frequent use of dough, which may signal the influence of Italian cooking. Some of the multicolored dough-preparations are a far cry from the simple doughnuts and fritters of the Würzburg cookbook.

Compared to the wealth of medieval cookbooks from southern Germany written in High German, the information we have on the cookery of northern Germany is sparse. Only one recipe collection from Eastphalia has come down to us; it is written in Low German.[186] Its ingredients, like those of its counterparts from southern Germany, reflect a wealthy cuisine that was, however, not overly luxurious. The types of dishes in the Low German collection are by and large the same as in most High German ones from the south: purees, sauces, pies, jellies, aspics, flat cakes, and roasts. The number of fish, fish roe, and seafood dishes seems higher in the cookbook, while the number of dough-based dishes is much lower, especially when compared to the manuscripts from the Alpine region.

With Platina's *De honesta voluptate et valetudine,* Italy gained the distinction of being the country where the first European cookbook was printed, but Germany was not far behind. When in 1485 the German recipe collection entitled *Kuchenmeysterey* (Kitchen Mastery) was printed in Nuremberg, it became an instant bestseller. By 1500 an impressive 12 more editions of the book had appeared. Its some two hundred recipes are arranged in five chapters that deal with Lenten food, meat, eggs, sauces and electuaries (sweet-tasting pastes made by mixing drugs with honey or syrup), and finally vinegar, herbal wines, and remedies against stomach ailments.[187] Forty-three editions of the *Kuchenmeysterey* followed in the sixteenth century, and so did translations into Czech, Polish, and Low German. In the Renaissance, the rather modest *Kuchenmeysterey* that originally reflected the cuisine of the bourgeoisie was transformed into an aristocratic cookbook. It now included information on lavish banquets, started the recipe part with the meat chapter rather than Lenten food, and concluded with a new chapter on confections, preserves, and *hippocras*. Under the new name *Koch und Kellermeisterey* (Cook and Cellar Mastery) the book was designed to give upwardly mobile burghers in towns all over Germany a glimpse of the lifestyles of the rich and famous, which was, no doubt, part of its appeal.[188]

THE LOW COUNTRIES

Not much is known of the food eaten by the lower classes who lived in the territory comprising today's Belgium and the Netherlands during the Middle Ages. Even researching the cuisine of the upper classes is difficult, given that the cookbook tradition in this part of Europe did not set in until the end of the fifteenth century. Food historians have therefore been forced to turn to other sources for information, such as the fourteenth- and fifteenth-century account books of the counts of Holland, the dukes of Guelders, the dukes of Burgundy, the bishop of Utrecht, and a customs house on the Lower Rhine, for instance.[189] What they found in their studies was that in the medieval period meat, poultry, fish, eggs, wheat, and rye bread were eaten in great quantity, and that milk, butter, and cheese played a significant role, but were not yet as dominant a feature of the cuisine as they were to become in the second half of the sixteenth century. In one respect, however, Dutch cooking seems to have differed from cookery in the rest of Europe even then: the use of butter as cooking fat. In the Mediterranean olive oil was the preferred fat, and in northern France and Germany pork fat and bacon, with butter only being mentioned occasionally. The French, who supposedly coined the term "Fat Germans" for the German people on account of their love for fatty foods, also came up with a nickname for the Flemish people: they called them "butter balls."[190]

In the course of the fifteenth century cattle breeding intensified in the Low Countries and in northern Germany, and as a consequence butter consumption went up in the whole region, from the Dutch and Flemish coast to Westphalia, and even Sweden. The sixteenth-century Dutch cookbooks reflect this abundance of milk and dairy products. In one collection from Ghent, milk and butter are used for a wide range of recipes including fish dishes, flat cakes, pancakes, curd, egg cheese, and the like. The members of the religious order known as the Hospitallers of Saint John, too, ate a lot of butter on meat days, and a dish called *soete eijerde melc* or *eyerde soete melc* which means "sweet milk with eggs." In the Ghent cookbook a dish of this type is called *Duijtse pappe,* or "German pap." Consisting of a combination of sweet cream, wheat flour, and a lot of eggs, it made small lumps when it was heated. This "sweet milk with little lumps" even made it into a children's song still sung today by Dutch children.[191]

An increase in the availability of cattle not only led to an increase in the consumption of milk and dairy products but also of beef. However, beef was regarded by the medieval medical community as inferior to other kinds of meat, notably chicken and pork, and especially harmful to the members of the aristocracy and their dainty stomachs. Not surprisingly, then, given this difference in status, high quantities of beef were consumed in the household of a Dutch customs officer from Lobith, judging from surviving records, but very little, mostly the superior veal, at the court of Burgundy. There, poultry, pigs, especially suckling pigs, venison, and sheep, played a much more prominent role.

In the sixteenth-century sources which originated in the upper and middle classes, beef was the most popular meat, followed by lamb, pork, poultry, rabbit, and hare.[192] The Hospitallers of Saint John prepared dishes not just from the meat, but also from the feet and rumen of the cow.[193] During Lent the Dutch substituted the meat of terrestrial animals with fish, which they prepared with olive oil if they could afford it, or with some other less expensive vegetable oil. On the minor fast days they fried their fish in butter. Even for people living near the coast, or near rivers or ponds, fresh fish was expensive. Salt herring and dried cod, the ubiquitous stockfish, were the cheaper alternatives for the less well-off. Instead of chicken eggs, fish roe was used in the Low Countries during Lent, as it was in northern Germany, judging from the recipes for fish roe in the only Low German cookbook we have. Other Lenten foods popular with the Dutch were almonds and almond milk, figs, dates, raisins, and citrus fruits, all of which were luxury items that only started to come down in price in the sixteenth century. They were imported along with spices and sugar via the ports of Bruges and Antwerp. This meant that they were readily available to the aristocracy and increasingly to the upwardly mobile bourgeoisie.

In the Low Countries the third course of a festive dinner was called "banquet." It usually consisted of cold dishes that were eaten in a different room. Literally the word "banquet" means a little bench or table, and it was on a little table that the delicacies of this cold buffet were displayed. They consisted of such things as pastries, pies, wafers, *comfits*, dried fruits, nuts, rice porridge, cold meat, fish in aspic, baked apples and quinces, and raw salads. It would appear that in the late Middle Ages this cold third course developed into a separate meal eaten later in the evening, and that in time the term "banquet" came to describe an entire festive meal.[194] In the Low Countries as in Germany, raw salads were practically unknown through most of the Middle Ages, and even when this Italian custom of eating raw vegetables moved north of the Alps, the recommendation was to eat the salad first, and the hot dishes afterward to counteract the salad's cooling effect.

Beer and wine top the list of beverages drunk in the Low Countries. Despite the fact that cattle breeding made cow's milk readily available, it seems to have been consumed by children only, not by grown-ups. Beer, the national drink of the Dutch, was brewed locally or imported from such Hanseatic towns as Hamburg and Wismar. Wine was drunk in great quantity by the Hospitallers of Saint John in the sixteenth century. Among the imported wines sold in the Low Countries were red wine from Poitou in France, known as *Putou*, the sweet Mediterranean wines that were also imported to England called *bastaert* and *Romenye*, and some white wines from the Rhine and Moselle regions in Germany.[195]

A look at the contents of the first printed cookbook from the Netherlands, entitled *Een notabel boecxhen van cokeryen* (A Notable Book of Cookery), shows just how international Dutch cuisine was at the end of the medieval period.[196] The book was printed in Brussels in 1510 or shortly thereafter by Thomas Vander Noot, who was also the author and compiler of the recipes.[197] Giving a brief description of the contents, but sparing himself a lengthy introduction or a chapter on banquets or the like, which was customary in other printed European cookbooks, Vander Noot begins immediately with his first recipe for a white sauce to be served with meat, such as capon or veal. The subsequent 174 recipes are not arranged in any strict order, and cover such standard medieval dishes as sauces, jellies, pies, tarts, *blanc manger,* potages, broths, and spiced wines. The collection includes no fewer than 23 *pasteien,* or pasties, and surprisingly also 6 ravioli recipes. Looking through the cookbook one is immediately reminded of the French and Anglo-Norman cookbooks, and their selection of dishes. And, in fact, a comparison of *Een notabel boecxken van cokeryen* with the *Viandier* of Taillevent brings to light 61 common recipes.[198] The Dutch cookbook shares another 61 recipes with a cookbook manuscript from Ghent, and the wine recipes are contained in a manuscript now housed in Leiden. Several recipes, among them the ones for ravioli, seem to point to a possible Italian source. Some 50 years after Vander Noot's cookbook was printed, 113 of the recipes reappeared in *Eenen Nyeuwen Coock Boeck* (A New Cookbook) that was compiled by a certain Gheeraert Vorselman and printed in Antwerp in 1560.[199]

For 25 of the recipes in Vander Noot's recipe collection scholars have so far been unable to find any sources or parallel transmissions. There are indications that some of them may have been local dishes, such as the following simple egg dish called *Stuer van Uccle*. The word *Uccle* in the title refers to a suburb of Brussels by that name.[200]

Stuer van Uccle te maken [To Make Sturgeon from Uccle]

Take eggs and hard-boil them. Then peel them and cut them lengthwise into equal halves and put them in a bowl with the yolks pointing down. Then take butter and melt it in a pan. When the butter has melted, add mustard and mix it well together. When it is well-mixed, pour it on the eggs. And it is ready.[201]

The sturgeon in the title can be explained by the fact that during Lent the dish was made from fish roe. Vander Noot's *Een notabel boecxhen van cokeryen* concludes this brief survey of European cuisines in the Middle Ages. It was a culinary discovery tour that started in Anglo-Saxon and Norman England, continued on the Continent in northern France, then moved south to the Mediterranean regions of Languedoc, Spain, Italy, and Sicily, and northward across the Alps to Germany and the Low Countries. What became evident was an openness of medieval Europeans toward new foodstuffs and culinary techniques, many of them introduced by the Arabs, and a talent for adapting them to suit their individual tastes, their religious beliefs, and their pocketbooks.

NOTES

1. Terence Scully, *The Art of Cookery in the Middle Ages* (Woodbridge, U.K.: Boydell Press, 1995), 205.

2. Lorna J. Sass, *To the King's Taste: Richard II's Book of Feasts and Recipes Adapted for Modern Cooking* (New York: Metropolitan Museum of Art, 1975), 23; opinions vary widely as to what spices went into mild and strong powder, however.

3. See Scully, *The Art of Cookery,* 205f.

4. Ibid., 207–11.

5. The French food historian is Jean-Louis Flandrin; see Odile Redon, Françoise Sabban and Silvano Serventi, *The Medieval Kitchen: Recipes from France and Italy,* trans. Edward Schneider (Chicago: University of Chicago Press, 1998), 198.

6. Sass, *To the King's Taste,* 70.

7. Melitta Weiss Adamson, *Daz buoch von guoter spise (The Book of Good Food): A Study, Edition, and English Translation of the Oldest German Cookbook* (Sonderband 9) (Krems, Austria: *Medium Aevum Quotidianum,* 2000), 92 ("If you want to make *blanc manger*").

8. Redon et al., *The Medieval Kitchen,* 183f. ("Green omelette").

9. Scully, *The Art of Cookery,* 212f.

10. Terence Scully, ed., *The Viandier of Taillevent: An Edition of All Extant Manuscripts* (Ottawa: University of Ottawa Press, 1988), 289f. ("German egg brewet").

11. Redon et al., *The Medieval Kitchen,* 80–83 (*"Le Menagier's* civet of hare"; "Civet of hare or rabbit"; "Sweet-and-sour civet of venison").

12. Scully, *Viandier,* 300f. ("Parmesan pies").

13. See Scully, *The Art of Cookery,* 214.

14. Lois Jean Ayoub, "John Crophill's Books: An Edition of British Library MS Harley 1735 (Ph.D. diss., University of Toronto, 1994), 120.

15. On jellies and aspics see Johanna Maria van Winter, "Interregional Influences in Medieval Cooking," in *Food in the Middle Ages: A Book of Essays,* ed. Melitta Weiss Adamson (New York: Garland, 1995), 45–59.

16. Barbara Santich, "The Evolution of Culinary Techniques in the Medieval Era," in *Food in the Middle Ages: A Book of Essays,* ed. Melitta Weiss Adamson (New York: Garland, 1995), 66–68.

17. Redon et al., *The Medieval Kitchen,* 190 ("Trout in aspic").

18. Sass, *To the King's Taste,* 91.

19. Scully, *Viandier,* 296 ("Black pepper sauce").

20. Scully, *The Art of Cookery,* 216f.

21. Redon et al., *The Medieval Kitchen,* 86 ("Chicken with verjuice").

22. Adamson, *The Book of Good Food,* 105 ("A fritter").

23. Redon et al., *The Medieval Kitchen,* 203f. ("Marzipan tart").

24. Ibid., 220 ("Hypocras, Claré, and Hypocras powder").

25. Ann Hagen, *A Handbook of Anglo-Saxon Food: Processing and Consumption* (Pinner, Middlesex: Anglo-Saxon Books, 1992); and idem, *A Second Handbook of Anglo-Saxon Food and Drink: Production and Distribution* (Pinner, Middlesex: Anglo-Saxon Books, 1995).

26. For the following information on peasant food see P.W. Hammond, *Food and Feast in Medieval England* (Stroud, U.K.: Alan Sutton, 1993), 26–39.

27. Ibid., 29.

28. See Constance B. Hieatt, Brenda Hosington, and Sharon Butler, *Pleyn Delit: Medieval Cookery for Modern Cooks,* 2nd edition (Toronto: University of Toronto Press, 1996), xvii.

29. Hammond, *Food and Feast,* 32; for the following see ibid., 32–39.

30. What follows is based on ibid., 40–62.

31. The *Oxford English Dictionary* defines the "alestake" as a "stake or post set up before an alehouse, to bear a garland, bush, or other sign, or as a sign itself; an ale pole." See *The Oxford English Dictionary,* 2nd edition, prepared by J.A. Simpson and E.S.C. Weiner, 20 vols. (Oxford: Clarendon Press, 1989), "alestake."

32. Hammond, *Food and Feast,* 61.

33. Geoffrey Chaucer, *Canterbury Tales,* ed. A.C. Cawley (London: J.M. Dent & Sons; New York: E.P. Dutton, 1976), 11, verses 334–54; the commentary to verse 331 defines a "franklin" as "a substantial landowner of the gentry class."

34. Hieatt et al., *Pleyn Delit,* xiv.

35. For the following see Hammond, *Food and Feast,* 63–67.

36. For an edition see Constance B. Hieatt and Robin F. Jones, eds., "Two Anglo-Norman Culinary Collections Edited from British Library Manuscripts Additional 32085 and Royal 12. C. xvii," *Speculum* 61 (1986): 859–82.

37. Constance B. Hieatt, "Medieval Britain," in *Regional Cuisines of Medieval Europe: A Book of Essays,* ed. Melitta Weiss Adamson (New York: Routledge, 2002), 23.

38. Constance B. Hieatt and Sharon Butler, eds., *Curye on Inglysch: English Culinary Manuscripts of the Fourteenth Century (Including the Forme of Cury)* (Early English Text Society S.S.8) (London: Oxford University Press, 1985), 172.

39. C. Anne Wilson, "Ritual, Form and Colour in the Medieval Food Tradition," in *'The Appetite and the Eye': Visual Aspects of Food and Its Presentation within Their Historic Context* (Edinburgh: Edinburgh University Press, 1991), 22.

40. Hieatt et al., *Pleyn Delit, "Blank Desure";* the modern English translation is my own.

41. For this and the following see Hieatt, "Medieval Britain," 24f.

42. For a modern English translation of the dish see Scully, *The Art of Cookery,* 222; and Sass, *To the King's Taste,* 48.

43. See Sass, *To the King's Taste,* 48.

44. Ibid., 104.

45. For a modern English translation see Scully, *The Art of Cookery,* 221.

46. See Sass, *To the King's Taste,* 80.

47. Hieatt et al., *Pleyn Delit, "Ravieles* [Ravioli]."

48. Cf. Hieatt, "Medieval Britain," 25.

49. See Hieatt et al., *Pleyn Delit, "Isfānākh Mutajjan."*

50. For "*Maumenee*" and its history see, for instance, Hieatt, "Medieval Britain," 26; and Hieatt and Butler, *Curye on Inglysch*, 9f.

51. Hammond, *Food and Feast*, 128f.

52. Wilson, "Ritual, Form and Colour," 16–27.

53. On the history of the dish see ibid., 20f., and Hieatt, "Medieval Britain," 27.

54. Sass, *To the King's Taste*, 82.

55. Hieatt, "Medieval Britain," 28f.

56. Sass, *To the King's Taste*, 31f.

57. Georgine E. Brereton and Janet M. Ferrier, eds., *Le Menagier de Paris* (Oxford: Clarendon, 1981); for the abridged English translation of the *Menagier* used here see Tania Bayard, trans. and ed., *A Medieval Home Companion: Housekeeping in the Fourteenth Century* (New York: HarperCollins, 1991).

58. Troyes is the subject of the book by Joseph and Francis Gies, *Life in a Medieval City* (New York: Harper Perennial, 1981).

59. Ibid., 21.

60. For the following see ibid., 46–53.

61. Ibid., 49.

62. Bayard, *A Medieval Home Companion*, 21.

63. Ibid., 75–86.

64. Ibid., 101f.

65. Ibid., 104.

66. Ibid., 112f.

67. Ibid., 114–17.

68. Ibid., 119–25.

69. Ibid., 137.

70. Hammond, *Food and Feast*, 61.

71. For the details on the wedding feast see ibid., 131–33.

72. The following overview of French upper-class foodstuffs in the late Middle Ages is based on Terence Scully, "Medieval France A. The North," in *Regional Cuisines of Medieval Europe: A Book of Essays*, ed. Melitta Weiss Adamson (New York: Routledge, 2002), 47–66, esp. 53–61.

73. Barbara Ketcham Wheaton, *Savoring the Past: The French Kitchen and Table from 1300 to 1789* (Philadelphia: University of Pennsylvania Press, 1983), 20f.

74. Scully, *Viandier*, 4.

75. See ibid., 277–305, for the English translation of the *Viandier*-recipes.

76. Terence Scully, trans., *Chiquart's "On Cookery": A Fifteenth-Century Culinary Treatise* (New York: Peter Lang, 1986); and idem, ed. and trans., *The Vivendier: A Fifteenth-Century French Cookery Manuscript* (Totnes, U.K.: Prospect Books, 1997).

77. Scully, *Viandier*, 282 ("White brewet of capons").

78. Ibid., 288 ("Cuminade of fish").

79. For an English translation of the *Menagier*'s recipe see Redon et al., *The Medieval Kitchen*, 66 ("White Porée").

80. Scully, *Viandier*, 283 ("Veal stew"; "Hare stew"; "Rabbit stew").

81. Ibid., 283–86.

82. Ibid., 300 ("Helmeted cocks").

83. For an English translation of the *Menagier*'s recipe for frumenty see Redon et al., *The Medieval Kitchen*, 199f. ("Frumenty: wheat-berry porridge").

84. Ibid., 17.

85. Ibid., 11.

86. For the following summary of the characteristics of northern French cuisine see Scully, "Medieval France A. The North," 61–63.

87. Scully, *Viandier*, 301 ("A particoloured white dish").

88. For the French recipe and modern recreation of the dish see Jean-Louis Flandrin and Carole Lambert, *Fêtes Gourmandes au Moyen Âge* (Paris: Imprimerie nationale éditions, 1998), 121.

89. An edition and modern French translation of the cookbook is contained in Carole Lambert, ed. and trans., "Trois Réceptaires culinaires médiévaux: *Les Enseignemenz*, les *Doctrine* et le *Modus*. Édition critique et glossaire détaillé" (diss., Université de Montréal, 1989), 134–80.

90. Barbara Santich, *The Original Mediterranean Cuisine: Medieval Recipes for Today* (Kent Town, Australia: Wakefield Press, 1997), 41.

91. Stefan Weiss, *Die Versorgung des päpstlichen Hofes in Avignon mit Lebensmitteln (1316–1378): Studien zur Sozial- und Wirtschaftsgeschichte eines mittelalterlichen Hofes* (Berlin: Akademie-Verlag, 2002).

92. The following analysis of southern French cookery is based on Carole Lambert, "Medieval France B. The South," in *Regional Cuisines of the Middle Ages: A Book of Essays*, ed. Melitta Weiss Adamson (New York: Routledge, 2002), 67–84.

93. Weiss, *Die Versorgung des päpstlichen Hofes*, 207.

94. For the English translation of the recipe and the explanation of the dish name, see Lambert, "Medieval France B. The South," 68f.

95. For these sauces and their recipes in English see ibid., 69–71.

96. See Constance B. Hieatt, "Sorting through the Titles of Medieval Dishes: What Is, or Is Not, a 'Blanc manger,'" in *Food in the Middle Ages: A Book of Essays*, ed. Melitta Weiss Adamson (New York: Garland, 1995), 28.

97. The English translation of *Modus*, "*Raymonia* [Pomegranate dish]" is contained in Lambert, "Medieval France B. The South," 69.

98. For *Modus*, "White *limonieyra* [Lemon dish]" in English translation see ibid., 70.

99. For *Modus*, "*Ad faciendum matafeam* [To make *matafeam*]" and detailed commentary see ibid., 71f.

100. Weiss, *Die Versorgung des päpstlichen Hofes*, 221–24.

101. Ibid., 220f.

102. Ibid., 409–23.

103. Lambert, "Medieval France B. The South," 77.

104. Weiss, *Die Versorgung des päpstlichen Hofes,* 418.

105. Ibid., 417.

106. See Lambert, "Medieval France B. The South," 77.

107. The following is based on Rafael Chabrán, "Medieval Spain," in *Regional Cuisines of Medieval Europe: A Book of Essays,* ed. Melitta Weiss Adamson (New York: Routledge, 2002), 125–31.

108. Santich, *The Original Mediterranean Cuisine,* 11.

109. Chabrán, "Medieval Spain," 132.

110. A. J. Arberry, trans., "A Baghdad Cookery Book," *Islamic Culture* 13 (1939): 21–47, and 189–214.

111. Claudia Roden, *The Book of Jewish Food: An Odyssey from Samarkand to New York* (New York: Alfred A. Knopf, 1996), 216.

112. Chabrán, 132.

113. For an analysis of this cookbook see Rudolf Grewe, "Hispano-Arabic Cuisine in the Twelfth Century," in *Du manuscrit à la table: Essais sur la cuisine au Moyen Âge et répertoire des manuscrits médiévaux contenant des recettes culinaires,* ed. Carole Lambert (Montréal: Presses de l'Université de Montréal, 1992), 141–48.

114. Santich, *The Original Mediterranean Cuisine,* 102; for an edition of the Catalan cookbook see Rudolf Grewe, ed., *Libre de Sent Soví: Receptari de cuina* (Barcelona: Editorial Barcino, 1979).

115. See Santich, "The Evolution of Culinary Techniques," 76; and chapter 1, "rose water."

116. Santich, *The Original Mediterranean Cuisine,* 13f.

117. Roden, *The Book of Jewish Food,* 222.

118. Ibid., 219f.

119. Ibid., 212.

120. Ibid., 222f.

121. Chabrán, "Medieval Spain," 137.

122. Grewe, *Libre de Sent Soví.*

123. Scully, *The Art of Cookery,* 231.

124. Santich, *The Original Mediterranean Cuisine,* 75.

125. Ibid., 108.

126. Ibid., 138.

127. Ibid., 150.

128. Ibid., 42.

129. Chabrán, 139; the cookbook is edited by Veronika Leimgruber, ed., *Mestre Robert, Libre del Coch: Tractat de cuina medieval* (Barcelona: Curial Catalanes, 1977).

130. Chabrán, 140.

131. Santich, *The Original Mediterranean Cuisine,* 55.

132. Ibid., 63.

133. For the above see Chabrán, 140f.

134. Santich, *The Original Mediterranean Cuisine*, 97.

135. Ibid., 111.

136. For the following see Chabrán, 141.

137. For an edition see Russell V. Brown, ed., *Arte Cisoria* (*Biblioteca Humanitas de textas inéditos,* 3) (Barcelona: Editorial Humanitas, 1984).

138. See Chabrán, 143–46.

139. See esp. Santich, *The Original Mediterranean Cuisine*, 6–10.

140. Redon et al., *The Medieval Kitchen*, 13.

141. Ibid., 11.

142. Allen J. Grieco, "From the Cookbook to the Table: A Florentine Table and Italian Recipes of the Fourteenth and Fifteenth Centuries," in *Du manuscrit à la table: Essais sur la cuisine au Moyen Âge et répertoire des manuscrits médiévaux contenant des recettes culinaires,* ed. Carole Lambert (Montréal: Presses de l'Université de Montréal, 1992), 29–38.

143. Luisa Cogliati Arano, *The Medieval Health Handbook (Tacuinum Sanitatis),* translated and adapted by Oscar Ratti and Adele Westbrook (New York: George Braziller, 1976); and Franz Unterkircher, ed. and trans., *Das Hausbuch der Cerruti: Nach der Österreichischen Nationalbibliothek* (Dortmund: Harenberg Kommunikation, 1979); for a brief introduction to the *Tacuinum* see Melitta Weiss Adamson, *Medieval Dietetics: Food and Drink in Regimen Sanitatis Literature from 800 to 1400* (Frankfurt am Main: Peter Lang, 1995), 83–91.

144. Santich, *The Original Mediterranean Cuisine*, 42f.

145. For the following see Simon Varey, "Medieval and Renaissance Italy A. The Peninsula," in *Regional Cuisines of Medieval Europe: A Book of Essays,* ed. Melitta Weiss Adamson (New York: Routledge, 2002), 85–112.

146. See Mary Ella Milham, ed. and trans., *Platina: On Right Pleasure and Good Health: A Critical Edition and Translation of De honesta voluptate et valetudine* (Tempe, Ariz.: Medieval and Renaissance Texts and Studies, 1998).

147. Varey, "Medieval and Renaissance Italy A. The Peninsula," 88; Redon et al., *The Medieval Kitchen*, 33.

148. Santich, "The Evolution of Culinary Techniques," esp. 66–74.

149. Varey, "Medieval and Renaissance Italy A. The Peninsula," 92.

150. Santich, "The Evolution of Culinary Techniques," 75; and Santich, *The Original Mediterranean Cuisine*, 28f.

151. Redon et al., *The Medieval Kitchen*, 63 ("Cheese gnocchi").

152. Santich, "The Evolution of Culinary Techniques," 74f.

153. Varey, "Medieval and Renaissance Italy A. The Peninsula," 98.

154. For the following see Santich, "The Evolution of Culinary Techniques," 68–74.

155. Redon et al., *The Medieval Kitchen*, 152 ("Eel *Torta* [pie]").

156. Ibid., 158.

157. Ibid., 157f. ("*Torta bianca:* white tart").

158. Santich, *The Original Mediterranean Cuisine,* 112–15.

159. Ibid., 119.

160. Varey, "Medieval and Renaissance Italy A. The Peninsula," 93.

161. Redon et al., *The Medieval Kitchen,* 97 ("*Fegatelli:* pork-liver bundles").

162. For the list of egg dishes see Scully, *The Art of Cookery,* 212.

163. Redon et al., *The Medieval Kitchen,* 86 ("*Limonia,* or chicken with lemon").

164. For the following see Habeeb Salloum, "Medieval and Renaissance Italy B. Sicily," in *Regional Cuisines of Medieval Europe: A Book of Essays,* ed. Melitta Weiss Adamson (New York: Routledge, 2002), 113–23.

165. According to Salloum, see ibid., 118.

166. The following is based on the extensive study on German cuisine by Melitta Weiss Adamson, "Medieval Germany," in *Regional Cuisines of the Middle Ages: A Book of Essays,* ed. Melitta Weiss Adamson (New York: Routledge, 2002), 153–96.

167. For further archeological data see the study by Walter Janssen, "Essen und Trinken im frühen und hohen Mittelalter aus archäologischer Sicht,' in *Feestbundel voor prof. Dr. J. G. N. Renaud* (Zutphen: De Walburg Pers, 1981), 327–34.

168. For information on food and class see Harry Kühnel, ed., *Alltag im Spätmittelalter* (Graz, Austria: Styria [Edition Kaleidoskop], 1984), 214, 217.

169. Adamson, *Medieval Dietetics,* 142–9, and 150–60; see also chapter 6.

170. An edition of Ortolf's regimen is contained in Karin Figala, "Mainfränkische Zeitgenossen 'Ortolfs von Baierland': Ein Beitrag zum frühesten Gesundheitswesen in den Bistümern Würzburg und Bamberg" (Pharm. diss., University of Munich, 1969), 160–90.

171. See Adamson, "Medieval Germany," 163f.; the sixteenth-century German regimen is Guualterus H. Rivius [Walther Ryff], *Kurtze aber vast eigentliche nutzliche vnd in pflegung der gesundheyt notwendige beschreibung der natur/eigenschafft/Krafft/Tugent/Wirckung/rechten Bereyttung vnd gebrauch/inn speyß vnd drancks von noeten/vnd bey vns Teutschen inn teglichem Gebrauch sind/etc.* (Würzburg: Johan Myller, 1549).

172. See *Du manuscrit à la table,* 321–62.

173. For the following see esp. Adamson, *The Book of Good Food,* 12–19.

174. For an English translation of these recipes see ibid., 92 ("Greek chicken"; "This is called Greek rice"); 105 ("Heathen peas"); 111 ("If you want heathen heads"); and 105 ("A casserole").

175. For an English translation of these recipes see ibid., 93 ("These are hazel hens"); 102f. ("A good sauce"); and 103 ("About a roast").

176. Ibid., 102 ("A tasty little dish").

177. For English translations of these sauces see ibid., 99f. ("A dish"; "If you want to make *agraz*"; "An *agraz*"; "Another condiment"; "A sauce"); and 93 ("These are hazel hens").

178. For an English translation see ibid., 93 ("A stuffed roasted suckling pig").

179. Ibid., 95 ("About stuffed pike").

180. See ibid., 95f. ("About fresh eels").

181. See ibid., 108f. ("A pudding of sour cherries").

182. Ibid., 109 ("A flat cake").

183. Ibid., 111 ("A good stuffing").

184. For editions of the cookbooks see Trude Ehlert, ed. and trans., *Maister Hansen, des von wirtenberg koch: Transkription, Übersetzung, Glossar und kulturhistorischer Kommentar* (Donauwörth: Ludwig Auer, 1996); and Anita Feyl, "Das Kochbuch Meister Eberhards: Ein Beitrag zur altdeutschen Fachliteratur" (diss., University of Freiburg im Breisgau, 1963).

185. The recipe is included in Adamson, "Medieval Germany," 177.

186. For an edition see Hans Wiswe, ed., "Ein mittelniederdeutsches Kochbuch des 15. Jahrhunderts," *Braunschweigisches Jahrbuch* 37 (1956): 19–55.

187. For the reception of the *Kuchenmeysterey* see Adamson, "Medieval Germany," 183; for a facsimile of the edition of the cookbook see Rolf Ehnert, ed., *Kuchenmeysterey* (Passau: Johann Petri, ca. 1486; facsimile repr. Göppingen: Kümmerle, 1981).

188. See Julius Arndt, ed., *Meister Sebastian: Koch und Kellermeisterey* (Frankfurt am Main: Sigmund Feyrabend, 1581; facsimile repr., Stuttgart: Steingrüben, 1964).

189. The following is based on Johanna Maria van Winter, "The Low Countries in the Fifteenth and Sixteenth Centuries," in *Regional Cuisines of Medieval Europe: A Book of Essays*, ed. Melitta Weiss Adamson (New York: Routledge, 2002), 197–214.

190. Ibid., 198.

191. For the importance of milk and dairy products in the Dutch diet, see ibid., 200.

192. Ibid., 201.

193. This becomes evident in the meal plans of the Hospitallers of Saint John, an English translation of which is contained in Van Winter, "The Low Countries," 204–12.

194. On the history of the banquet see ibid., 203.

195. Ibid., 203f.

196. For an edition of the cookbook see Ria Jansen-Sieben and Marleen van der Molen-Willebrands, eds., *Een notabel boecxken van cokeryen. Het eerste gedrukte Nederlandstalige kookboek circa 1514 uitgegeven te Brussel door Thomas Vander Noot* (Amsterdam: De KAN, 1994).

197. Ibid., 8.

198. For the parallel transmission of the recipes see ibid., 9f.

199. Elly Cockx-Indestege, ed., *Eenen Nyeuwen Coock Boeck, Kookboek samengesteld door Gheeraert Vorselman en gedrukt te Antwerpen in 1560* (Wiesbaden: Guido Pressler, 1971).

200. See glossary in Jansen-Sieben and Van der Molen-Willebrands, *Een notabel boecxken,* 77, "stuer van Uccle."

201. Ibid., 61 ("*Stuer van Uccle te makeu* [To make Sturgeon from Uccle]"); the English translation is my own.

CHAPTER 4
EATING HABITS AND FOOD IDEAS

People in the Middle Ages usually ate two meals a day: a substantial dinner around noon, and a light supper in the evening. In monasteries of the Benedictine order both dinner and supper had to be eaten during daylight. Dinner for the monks was originally after devotions at *none,* which was the ninth hour after daybreak.[1] Since the *none* could be as late as 3:00 P.M. depending on the time of the year, the general population moved the time of dinner up to noon or 1:00 P.M., sometimes even to late morning. In bigger households it was frequently the case that at least some of the staff that waited on the lord and lady had dinner beforehand. Supper was normally a simple meal, often just soup or *sops,* that is, bread dipped in wine or some other liquid.

Although not officially recognized as a meal through most of the Middle Ages and frowned on by moralists, breaking the overnight fast too soon for an early-morning breakfast was common practice among peasants and craftsmen, who started work at daybreak and found it hard to hold out until dinner. By the fifteenth century, the nobility, too, began the day with bread, meat, and ale.[2] Also traditionally allowed a small morning meal were children, the elderly, and the sick. Grown men, not wanting to be associated with these groups, tended to feel apologetic or embarrassed to admit that they had breakfast. In addition to these meals, workmen also had little snacks in the course of the day, for which they received an allowance from their employer.

In the wage sheets these snacks were referred to as *nuncheons*.[3] An afternoon meal the nobility would indulge in was known as *drynkyngs*.[4] Judging from the name it must have included some form of liquid refreshments.

If breakfast and little in-between meals drew the ire of the moralists, how much more so the late meal after supper known as the *reresoper*. It was condemned unanimously by the church and heads of households as an unnecessary extravagance and an indulgence. Ranging from a full meal to just some snacks accompanied by lots of alcoholic drink, the *reresoper* was usually enjoyed by a few friends in a private room rather than the whole household in the hall, as was proper. Loud laughter, crude jokes, gambling, and flirting were some of the vices associated with this meal, which often dragged on until after midnight and resulted in many a hangover the following day.[5]

In households large and small, the morning was normally spent preparing the big midday meal, the dinner. Cook and kitchen staff of nobility, gentry, and rich bourgeoisie would get the various types of meat roasted, and the soups, stews, pies, pasties, fritters, sauces, and jellies ready that together made up the different courses of the meal.[6] In smaller households the housewife would do her early-morning shopping and then prepare the soup or stew she would serve her family for dinner. Even in castles and manor houses space was limited, and rooms including the great hall were used for other functions beyond dining.[7] It is for this reason that dining tables were rarely permanent in the Middle Ages. Usually they consisted of trestles and boards that were cleared out of the way once the meal was over. Permanent tables, such as our modern dining tables, were called "dormant tables" then. In the prologue to the *Franklin's Tale* Chaucer tells us of such a table, which its gourmet owner keeps set for a meal all day long (see Chapter 2). Diners usually sat on benches, with only the highest-ranking individual being given the privilege of his own chair in the middle of the high table. It would appear that more than the table itself, it was the tablecloth that was important for a great dining experience. Snow white and of the finest linen, it was supposed to cover the table generously. If one did not do the job because the table top was too wide, two or even three tablecloths would be used. Napkins and hand towels, too, were cut from the same linen that was bought in bulk. The illustrations found in medieval manuscripts at times show tablecloths with woven patterns or fringes. Even outdoor meals such as picnics of lovers or a hunting party were served on tablecloths. Paris, Avignon, Champagne, and Rennes, in France, and Aylsham in England were

A simple meal. From *Hugo von Trimberg*. Renner, 1426. Cod. Vind. 30896, fol. 73r. Courtesy of Österreichische Nationalbibliothek, Vienna (Photo: Bildarchiv, ÖNB Wien).

some of the places renowned for their fine linen. By providing napkins and hand towels it was hoped that diners would not wipe their hands on the tablecloth and soil it in the process. Given the hierarchical nature of a medieval meal, it should not surprise us to find that the best linen was used for the high table where the most important diners were seated. Well-worn linen, perhaps stained from previous meals, was given to the lowest-ranking diners.

Tables were usually arranged in an angular U shape and diners sat on the outer side only. This was done to facilitate serving which was done from the inside of the U. The lord and lady, together with their close family and important guest(s), occupied the dais, a raised platform at the end of the hall facing the room and the musicians' gallery. Beautiful tapestries framing the dais or the walls of the entire hall were a sign of distinction. Tables to accommodate all the other diners were placed lengthwise on both sides of the hall. The one right next to the dais on the right-hand side was known as the *rewarde* in England. Diners who had the privilege of being seated there received the premium dishes from the lord's own table. The first table to the left of the dais was called the *second messe*.[8] As with the napkins, the quantity and quality of the food and drink, too, diminished the farther away from the dais a dinner guest was seated. In the great hall differences in social status were measured, among other things, in the distance from the head table.

At the end of the hall, under the musicians' gallery and often hidden behind screens, were the doors used by the staff to serve the food. Aside from tables, benches, and the occasional chair, the hall usually had one other piece of furniture, the "cupboard." This buffet consisted of several shelves and a cupboard (in our sense of the word) under the top shelf.[9] Like the tables, this buffet would be covered with a cloth, and the pitchers used to replenish the drinks of the dinner guests were placed on top. If the host owned valuable gold or silver vessels, they would also frequently be displayed on the cupboard.

The table setting for each diner normally consisted of a napkin, a spoon, and a trencher. The latter was a thick slice of four-day-old bread that served as an edible or otherwise disposable plate. Soaked with gravy it could be eaten by a hungry diner, but more often it was given to the dog, or donated to the poor as alms. In the early modern period bread trenchers were gradually replaced by wooden or metal ones. According to the *Menagier de Paris* (Householder of Paris), the trencher, derived from the French verb for cutting, *trancher*, was to be "half a foot wide and four inches high."[10] Ordinary diners sometimes cut their own trenchers, but those of high station were always served their trenchers by the carver, who cut them in the desired square shape seen in many medieval illustrations. The function of the trencher was temporarily to hold the food taken from the shared bowl and to soak up the juices that would otherwise have soiled the tablecloth.

Another important item on the medieval dining table was the saltcellar. Salt was the main seasoning in the medieval kitchen, and to make sure diners would not have to endure bland food under any circumstances, salt was put on every dining table. The container in which it was served ranged in style from simplicity to grandiose luxury. In its basic form it was nothing more than a piece of old bread with a hollow for the salt. Small metal stemware used as a salt dispenser showed somewhat more class. Most memorable, however, were the elaborate saltcellars that adorned the high tables of nobility and royalty. Often in the shape of a boat, or *nef*, these vessels were designed by prominent silversmiths and were conversation pieces to be admired along with the precious dinnerware displayed on the cupboard. It has been suggested that a boat was the preferred design because it pointed to the sea as the place from which salt originated or across which it was transported.[11] In the status-conscious Middle Ages much importance was put on the distance one's seat at the dining table had from the lord's saltcellar. Placed either in front of the lord, or to the right, with the trencher to the left, the saltcellar contained salt that was produced mainly by evaporating brine or seawater.

The lord's knife was on the left of his place setting. Knives were not generally supplied for all diners, just for the lord and perhaps a distinguished guest. The others were expected to bring their own. Sometimes this was also the case with spoons. Italian hosts were the first in Europe to provide knives as part of the place setting. The wealth of many Italian towns and their proximity to Byzantium, which was renowned for its refined table culture, have been named as possible reasons for the change. It would appear that, at least some of the time, the knife was shared by two people.[12] But whether supplied by the host or brought along by the diner, the knife served several functions at table. It was used to cut meat into smaller pieces, or to cut meat off the bone, and to prong a piece of food from a serving dish. The tip of the knife, wiped clean, also served as a means to lift salt out of the saltcellar.

Different from the simple dining knife were the bigger and heavier carving knives. They were normally provided by the host and were used at table by the diners, who either carved meat for themselves or for the person next to them as a sign of courtesy. Official carvers attended to the most distinguished diners at the head table. Among their duties were the extraction of bones, the paring away of fat, and the shaping of food into perfectly sized morsels. Carving knives were often lavishly decorated with handles made of wood, horn, ivory, precious metals, and the like. In addition to the carving knives that were intended to cut the food, knives with a rounded blade, called *présentoir* in French, began to appear in the late Middle Ages. The name is a good indicator of their function: they were used to present the carved food to the noble diner.

The spoons found on medieval dining tables were for the most part simple spoons made of wood, or of the lighter horn, but more luxurious versions in silver are also mentioned in the sources. Shaped slightly differently from most modern spoons, they typically had a bowl resembling a fig, with the pointed part tapering into the shaft. The latter could be decorated at the end with coats of arms or other motifs, rather like the souvenir spoons that tourists nowadays bring back from their travels to Europe.

One piece of cutlery that today is part of every table setting and that people in the Western world cannot do without is the fork. This was not the case in the Middle Ages. For most of the period this utensil was conspicuously absent from dining tables all across Europe. This is not to say that forks were completely unknown. Since Roman times forks with a long reach had been used in the kitchen for various tasks. Medieval cooks, too, removed meat from the cauldron by means of a fork with clawlike prongs, and kitchen boys added wood to the fire with long-handled forks. As part of the cutlery, however, the fork seems to have traveled from the East to Byzantium, and from there made its way to Venice, where in the eleventh century it caused quite a stir. The incident has been described by one scholar in the following way:

> A Byzantine princess came to marry the future Doge, Domenico Selvo, and at one of the celebrations she scandalized society by refusing to eat with her hands like any ordinary mortal. Instead, after the food had been cut up into little pieces by her eunuchs, she fastidiously popped them one by one into her mouth with a golden fork. Total decadence.[13]

For the next few centuries the fork disappeared again, but reemerged in the late Middle Ages as a utensil with which to eat especially fruit and sweetmeats. Outside of Italy, however, forks remained a rarity even into the early modern period.

What made the dining habits of the Byzantine princess in the above quote so unusual was the fact that she did not use her fingers. Aside from spoon and knife, the fingers were the most widely used and most versatile dining utensil in the Middle Ages. For this reason, and because two or more diners would normally share their food, great emphasis was placed on clean hands. They were to be washed before and after the meal, and often also in-between courses, especially if they had become greasy from handling the food. Licking his fingers clean was not an option for the sophisticated diner. In noble households the *ewerer* was the person in charge of the towels, the *ewery*, which was a basin for the lord, and the cup to test the water for poison.[14] When money was no object, these items would be made of the finest materials and admired like the *nef*. Hands were either dipped in the water, or water from a jug was poured over them. This was more hazardous because the water could splash and stain the exquisite garment of the diner or one of his or her neighbors. These water jugs, too, could become art objects. Some versions were fitted with a lid, others covered with images of fantastic creatures, and in the case of the *aquamanile*, the jug itself was turned into an animal, such as a griffin or a lion.[15] The recipes for scented water that have come down to us suggest that in addition to hygiene, sensual pleasures were also derived from the ritual of hand washing in the Middle Ages.

Another important aspect of the medieval dining experience were the many different drinking vessels in use. They ranged from the traditional drinking horn rested on legs, and the *mazer*, a shallow wooden drinking vessel, often with a silver band around the rim, or a metal foot, to various types of cups and goblets. Glass was precious in the Middle Ages and rarely used at table. Pottery was much cheaper and more durable and therefore very popular, especially the rich and intricate designs from Malaga, in Andalusia, and Valencia, in Aragon, that were produced by skilled Arab craftsmen and combined Moslem and Christian motifs.[16] Pewter and silver cups are also frequently mentioned in the medieval sources. A few rich households boasted a wine fountain in silver or pewter. By means of a manual pump wine was channeled into spouts from which the precious liquid spewed into a basin that formed the fountain's base. Serving staff would replenish their empty pitchers at this fountain and continue serving the diners with wine.[17]

Since the more luxurious dinnerware was not just functional but also regarded as a status symbol, it was never left unattended in the great hall, but rather locked away only to be brought out on special occasions. Big medieval feasts were occasions when the great hall was transformed into a stage on which the diners were both spectators and actors. Along with the serving staff, musicians, singers, jugglers, jesters, actors, and dancers, the guests played their part in a spectacle that was minutely choreographed.

How important appearance was has been emphasized repeatedly in the description of the exquisite upper-class dishes in Chapter 3. In many cases, shape, color, and surprise effect played as big a role as flavor. But these dishes were not consumed in a vacuum, they needed the right setting to bring out their full splendor. This setting was provided by the great hall decorated with colorful tapestries, wall paintings, flower garlands, and representational objects, and populated by diners in luxurious outfits and servers in beautiful livery. The stage directions for these colorful pageants have come down to us in the form of ordinances for aristocratic families, and etiquette books for household staff and diners. For the host, a lavish feast was an opportunity to display his wealth and affirm his power, and for the guests the invitation to the feast attested to their importance, it established or cemented their place in the social hierarchy. It has been pointed out that medieval feasts were predominantly a male affair. Apart from the wives of the host and guest of honor, and their ladies-in-waiting, it was mainly men who attended.[18] Diners of lower rank, in particular, never brought their wives. And once the fireplace in the great hall moved from the center to the wall (between the twelfth and fifteenth centuries) and hence also heated the upstairs bedroom of the lord and lady, known as the "chamber," many a lord's wife and her entourage preferred to have their dinner in privacy, and only later appeared briefly at the high table in the hall. As the Middle Ages drew to a close, more and more lords followed suit, and the great hall became the place where only the lesser folk ate. The chamber was smaller and easier to heat, and since it was also the lord's bedchamber, it was an enormous privilege for guests to be invited to join the lord for a meal there. By physically separating themselves from the diners in the great hall, the select group that dined in the chamber could indulge in exquisite food and provide dishes of inferior quality to the masses in the hall below. Not being invited to the chamber and watching the best dishes being carried past the dais up the stairs to the chamber, however, had the potential of creating discontent in the household, which is why at really grand occasions the lord and lady did return to the hall to celebrate.[19]

Aside from the diners, the most important "actors" in the spectacle that was a medieval feast were the household staff.[20] From the top down they included the steward, who ran the entire household, the marshal, who was his chief official at dinner, the head waiter and taster, known as the *sewer*, the head of the pantry, known as the *pantler*, the person in charge of drinks, known as the "butler," the *ewerer* in charge of hand washing and linen, the carver, and the lord's cupbearer. Most of them had trained staff known as "grooms" under them. In the kitchen, the chief cook had assistant cooks, scullions, spit boys, pot boys, and bottle washers under his command, and the waiters and assistant waiters who transported the food from the kitchen to the hall. Normally it was the trained household staff that carried out all these tasks, but at royal feasts noblemen would be given some of the serving duties in the hall and be handsomely rewarded for their work.

After the *ewerer* had spread the tablecloths on all the tables, beginning with the high table, and prepared the *ewery cup* and towel, the *pantler* entered with bread rolls, trenchers, the ornate saltcellar, bread knives, and a spoon for the lord. He then proceeded to supply the other tables with trenchers, spoons, simple saltcellars, bread, and knives in cases when they were provided. Once this task was completed, and the dishes for the first course were ready to be sent to the hall, the lord sat down, grace was said, and the meal started with the staff charged with carrying out the first official duties: the *sewer*, the cupbearer, and the carver. With towels draped over one shoulder they subsequently approached the dais. Bowing three times in front of the lord, the carver then kneeled while uncovering the salt and the lord's bread. A small piece of both the white bread and the trencher bread that had been cut into neat squares was given to the *pantler* to assay, or test for poison. Simultaneously the cupbearer brought the lord's *ewery*, tasted the water, and kissed the towel. A cup made of agate or unicorn horn (in reality narwhale tooth), was believed to change color if it came into contact with poison.[21] Meanwhile, the dishes of the first course had reached the serving tables and the *sewer* cut off little pieces for the chief cook and the steward to assay. It was at this point that the other diners took their seats; the marshal, butler, and cupbearer tasted the ale and wine for poison, and the carver began to cut the various types of meat and fowl into appropriate portions.

A medieval menu normally consisted of two main courses, followed by a dessert course that was sometimes just for special guests at the dinner.[22] There was some variation in the number of courses, however, depending on the region, the occasion, and the social status of the host. A main course consisted not just of one dish, but of a variety of dishes such as several meat or fish dishes and two or more sweet ones. In the kitchen these dishes were arranged in compatible groups and put on platters or chargers which were then sent to the great hall. Two, four, or six diners shared such a serving or *messe*.[23] Here, too, one's place in the hierarchy determined how many people one shared the food with. Except for the high table, where the food was handed around by the serving staff, and where the carver cut the meat in appropriate portions, the rest of the diners had to help themselves to the food, either eating it directly from the shared platter or putting it on their trenchers first. For this reason, boiled or roasted meat on the platters came already cut in bite-sized pieces. Since meat was usually accompanied by a sauce, there were two ways of serving meat: with the sauce already poured over it, or served separately in a bowl for two or more diners to share. Beverages, too, were often shared by diners, who drank ale or wine from a common cup. Courtesy demanded that of those diners who shared a dish or drinking cup the one of lower rank would help the one above him, the younger the older, and the man the woman. Breaking the bread, passing the cup, and carving the meat were some of the activities to which these rules applied.[24]

In the event carving was required at the table, carving knives were provided and used by the diners to carve their own food or that of their fellow diners. The lord and distinguished diners at the high table were, of course, looked after by a professional carver. Of his various carving jobs, that of cutting the lord's trenchers into the desired shape and presenting them to him at the start of the meal and after each course, was probably among the easier tasks. Satisfying the whims of each diner was often next to impossible. Women in particular were known to constantly change their minds as to the type of food and size of portion they wanted.[25] Some animals, such as crabs, for instance, were a challenge for even the most seasoned carver, and were often cold by the time the carver had finished his job.[26] It was not uncommon to send a dish back to the kitchen for reheating after carving.[27] In courtesy books and special carver's manuals instructions were given for all aspects of carving, from the condition the hands of the carver and the carving knives had to be in, to the exact way of carving and presenting the various types of animals. Needless to say, the carver's hands and nails had to be impeccable, and his knives sharp. Protocol required that he hold the food which was to be carved in his left hand, and the carving knife in the right. Not only was the procedure for carving each animal spelled out in great detail, but a whole specialized vocabulary evolved around the carving of the various food items. English instruction books, for example, speak of "platting a pike," "undertranching a porpoise," "lifting a swan," "unlacing a cony," or "mincing a plover" when describing the appropriate carving method.[28] Besides carving, adding the right sauces was also one of the carver's tasks. Apparently carving knives were also used at the end of a course to remove crumbs from the table and into a container.[29]

Special treats, such as the *sotelties* mentioned in the previous two chapters, were served at the end of a course and before the beginning of the next one. The French name *entremets* points to their status as "between courses." In England they would normally be served to the distinguished diners seated on the dais, and mostly just admired by the dinner guests occupying the other tables. But food was not the only entertainment provided at a medieval dinner. The most basic form of dinner entertainment found in households of the rich and poor was, of course, conversation. One place where conversation was not allowed or at least discouraged, was the dining room or refectory of a medieval monastery, where monks were expected to eat in silence and if they had to, only communicate with one another by gestures. According to the Rule of Saint Benedict, supper in silence was to be followed by a reading from an edifying book, which was often the *Collationes* by Cassian. In fact, it is from the title of this work that the modern word "collations," meaning a light meal or repast, is derived.[30]

Outside monastery walls, however, dinner was one of the occasions for people to pass on the latest information and gossip, or simply to chat. That there were cultural differences in the amount of conversation at state banquets, for instance, can be seen from comments made by Venetian and Bohemian travelers to England who remarked on the unusual silence in which diners, who were probably overly concerned with etiquette, partook of their meal.[31] In the majority of cases, however, dinners were a noisy affair. Aside from conversation, there was the blow of the horn that announced the start of the meal, the music emanating from the musicians' gallery above the door opposite the dais, the singing of the latest love songs or political satires by minstrels, the performances of actors, jesters, tumblers or acrobats, jugglers, animal trainers, conjurors, comedians, and mummers or mimes.[32] Among the medieval musical instruments used were the harp, the lute, and the viele, a forerunner of the modern violin.

And then there were the oohs and aahs of diners expressing their amazement over the master cook's latest invention of a *sotelty*. That they could easily turn into shrieks of horror can be seen from the many practical jokes found among the medieval texts and household objects. The recipe in the *Menagier de Paris* for turning white wine into red wine at table, and Albertus Magnus's recipe for making a chicken leap in a dish may have been amusing, but the two recipes from an English cookbook describing the preparation of dishes made to look as if they were full of worms, or raw and bloody, more likely caused the squeamish female diner to turn away in disgust.[33] Similarly, guests in all probability marveled at a reusable puzzle jug that looked like a three-story building, with openings for the windows through which bishops and abbots could be seen on the first and third floors, a woman looking out of a window on the second floor, and musicians playing on the floor below her. The liquid that was poured into the jug flowed through the handle to the base and out the spout, bypassing completely the "open windows." Another such marvel was the "Tantalus cup" equipped with concealed hollows and tubes; when a person drank from it, the level of wine would sink, but the drinker would either be denied any wine or have it pour out from the cup's base all over his clothes.[34] Such medieval party games were not dissimilar in spirit to the whoopee cushions of today.

When it comes to *sotelties,* the trend in the later Middle Ages, as was shown in Chapter 2, was from an edible dish to a table ornament that over time became more decorative and less nourishing. When these surprises at a banquet moved from the table to the hall floor, and involved inedible props and people dressed up in costumes performing historical or mythical scenes, this was called a "pageant" in English. In French the word *entremets* was used for both types of dinner entertainment. One famous pageant, of which a beautiful illustration has survived, was performed on 6 January 1378 at a banquet hosted by Charles V of France in honor of his distinguished guests, Emperor Charles IV of Bohemia and his son, Wenceslas of Luxembourg. The pageant was nothing less than the recreation of the crusaders' conquest of Jerusalem, complete with a ship and European knights scaling the walls of the Holy City.[35]

Another memorable feast was that hosted by Philippe le Bon on 17 February 1454. Its theme was the loss of Constantinople, the capital of Christian Byzantium, to the Ottoman Turks in 1453. The description of the event is a vivid illustration of the way food, politics, and religion at times intermingled in the big spectacle of a medieval banquet:

> The feast was a lavish affair: guests entering the hall had to pass a chained lion before taking their seats at tables decorated with *automata,* described as *entremets,* including fountains, moving tableaux, and a pie crust containing twenty-eight musicians. During and after their meal, guests were entertained with similarly exotic scenes (also called *entremets*); a fire-breathing dragon flew over their heads, and a small boy mounted on a deer moved amongst them, singing a duet in which the deer took the melody line. Finally, the allegorical figure of *Sainte Eglise* [Holy Church] entered, mounted on the back of an elephant. She read a moving poem about her plight in the East following the Turkish capture of Constantinople during the previous year. Inspired by this spectacle, Philippe le Bon and his guests made vows to the Virgin and to a live pheasant, presented for this purpose, oaths intended to recapture Constantinople for the Christian faith.[36]

The quantities of food supposedly consumed at this feast were staggering, and included 9,000 loaves of white bread, 4,800 gourmet breads, 24 barrels of Beaune wine, 6 barrels of Germolian wine, 2 barrels of *hippocras* (spiced wine), 800 chicken pies, 1,600 roast pigs, 1,600 pieces of roast veal, 1,600 legs of mutton, 400 pieces of wildfowl, 600 partridges, 1,400 rabbits, 400 herons, 36 peacocks, and 6 horses carrying confectionaries.[37]

Giant pies often contained exotic animals, but jugglers, jesters, or musicians were also not uncommon at the time. The same was true of vows being taken before various kinds of birds. In the Burgundian example it was a live pheasant, while in similar accounts from England swans are frequently mentioned.[38] Some of the most lavish banquets were given on the occasion of marriages. Then even an English feast could contain as many as six courses of seven dishes each, followed by wafers and *hippocras,* by dancing, and pageantry of various kinds.[39]

During medieval meals tables were to be kept tidy and clean. For this purpose a vessel, called a *voyder* or "voider" in English, was always nearby where food fragments, such as the trencher crusts, could be dispensed of.[40] At the conclusion of the meal, tables were cleared by starting at the lower end and collecting the spoons, leftover broth and baked meat, and the voiders. Fruit and cheese, *hippocras,* wafers, and whole spices usually followed afterward. Once this dessert course had been consumed, the tables were cleared again, including the drinking cups, trenchers, napkins, and finally the saltcellar. Since every wealthy household in the Middle Ages had an almoner, a person in charge of the alms that were given to the poor, leftover food was collected in an alms dish and handed to the almoner. With all the food and dinnerware removed from the tables, the hand-washing ceremony that had marked the beginning of the meal was repeated, then grace was said, and the lord got to his feet as a sign that dinner had ended. The lord and distinguished guests would on occasion move to another room to enjoy more sugar-coated spices or *comfits* and other treats.

Whether big feasts marking special occasions or just the daily dinners eaten by the lord and his men in the manor house, most medieval meals were social affairs that required participants to behave in a "civilized" way. Courtesy, cleanliness, and moderation were the main virtues expounded in countless etiquette books, many of them addressed to children and adolescents, but also to household staff. Living in a world that was often violent, crude, and coarse, many Europeans in the Middle Ages believed that one's manners were the outer manifestation of one's inner worth.[41] Not wanting to appear as peasants who stuffed themselves when food was to be had and who belched contentedly when they were full, members of the upper class began to embark on a "civilizing process" at the end of which all bodily functions were closely controlled and subject to a myriad of rules and regulations. How people behaved in private largely eludes the eye of the historian, but in public, at least, the ideal was to appear elegant and refined at all times, especially when sharing a meal with one's peers.[42]

In the hierarchical society of the Middle Ages in which one's status and good manners determined one's place at the dinner table, being a glutton and looking after one's own belly without any consideration for one's fellow diners was unacceptable behavior. In fact, it was expected that the diner offer the best pieces to others, and that women should appear disinterested in food.[43] Given the lack of individual place settings and the arrangement of guests in messes of usually between two and six people, sharing was an important aspect of medieval dining. The very term "companion" originally meant the person one shared bread with.[44] Sharing with diners of lower rank was seen as gracious courtesy, but it did not mean sharing the actual dinner table with the really poor and destitute. In bigger households the almoner was the go-between who handed out the food donations to the less fortunate. There are indications in the sources, however, that people shared food with their pets at dinner, and judging from the famous illustration that shows the duke of Berry at a lavish banquet, little lap dogs could even be found running around on the high table in between the dishes of food.[45] Etiquette books, insofar as they address the issue of pets at all, discourage petting one's dog at dinner.

Cleanliness and hygiene were a concern for host and guests alike. In French courtesy books diners were advised to first look to see if their seat was clean before they sat down.[46] And of course, they were only allowed to sit down once the lord had taken his seat. Throughout the meal diners had to follow the cue of the lord at the high table. The hand-washing ceremony at the beginning of each dinner was a clear sign that utmost importance was placed on clean fingers and hands.[47] Hence spitting into the water basin, splashing water over one's neighbor, and making the common towel overly dirty were seen as improper behavior. Bread was to be cut or broken off a shared loaf, but never bitten off. Pieces of bread used to sop or soak up wine or other liquids were not to be dipped in a dish a second time, or more bread dipped in the liquid than one was prepared to eat. When bread was cut off a big round loaf, this was not to be done holding the loaf against one's chest. As is evident in the case of the trencher, bread was more than just a foodstuff at a medieval dinner. It could serve as a plate, a spoon, or a towel to wipe the actual spoon or knife clean. Using the tablecloth instead was not regarded as an acceptable alternative.

Strict rules governed the use of salt at the table. Ideally diners would lift salt out of the saltcellar with their clean knife and deposit it on their trencher for future use. Under no circumstances was meat or any other food to be dipped in the saltcellar. Once taken out of the common container salt was also not to be returned to it. When diners shared a cup, a number of rules applied, among them to wipe one's mouth before drinking and to drink quietly, and not to immerse one's beard in the cup or drink with one's mouth full. When passing a cup on to a fellow diner, one was to hold it from below, not to dip fingers in the wine, and to make sure the next person did not touch the cup with the lips in the same spot. Due to the absence of forks at the medieval dinner table, fingers, knives, and spoons were the primary means for handling food. All of them were expected to be clean at the start and to be kept reasonably clean throughout the meal. Licking them or a plate clean, however, was not acceptable behavior. Fingers easily became greasy when helpings of food were transferred from a shared platter to the trencher. For this reason women frequently ate in private first and only showed up at the high table toward the end of the meal, with spotless clothes and sparkling clean fingers. Courtesy demanded that the amount of food taken from a shared dish was not overly large, that diners did not fish around in the dish for a specific piece, take the best morsels for themselves, or return half-eaten food to the platter.

Since many medieval dishes were of liquid or semiliquid consistency, such as soups, broths, and gravies, they were either soaked up with bread, eaten with a spoon, or the bowl was tipped and the liquid drunk from it directly. Spoons were often provided by the host, and were not to be left in a common dish, but cleaned with bread and put next to the trencher. The high value of spoons can be seen from the fact that along with cups they were frequently stolen. To guard against theft, many households had them collected and counted by the steward after the main course. Even at the papal court in Avignon it was customary to keep the doors locked after a meal and not let anyone leave until all dinnerware was accounted for.[48] Many rules governed the use of knives at the table. Normally brought to the hall by the dinner guest, the knife was to be clean and sharp, and was to be used to cut, lift, and prong food. It was not to be used to pare nails, pick teeth, or push food into the mouth, or to carve at the table top. Meat, in particular, was to be cut into bite-sized pieces and not torn apart with one's fingers. Bones and food fragments were to be put in the voider and not discarded on the floor or table.

General rules of comportment at table included not to blow on food or drink for fear of bad breath, to consume the food quietly, not to offer or accept half-eaten food, not to blow crumbs of food from one's mouth or spit over the table, not to belch too close to the face of a fellow diner, and not to blow one's nose in the napkin. If fingers were used to clean one's nose, they were to be wiped on one's clothes afterward. Diners were to sit decorously at the table without stretching, leaning back, putting their elbows on the table, or their heads in their hands. That fleas and lice were a problem at the time can be seen from the rules not to scratch one's head or hunt for fleas under one's skirt. Overall, dinner guests were expected to be quiet and courteous at table, not to stare at their surroundings, not to engage in loud talk or laughter, which could be mistaken for drunkenness, or whisper, which could be mistaken for gossiping or for slandering somebody.

Since only the highest-ranking diners ate alone, many of the above rules were especially important for those farther away from the head table and lower down the social ladder who had to share their food with an ever-increasing number of people to a *messe*. Status also determined the quality and purity of the wine enjoyed at dinner. Apart from the fact that as a rule the best wine was always drunk first when all the participants were still sober, wine was mixed with more and more water the further down the pecking order a person found him- or herself. While those at the top had their wine and water at the table to combine at will, those of lower rank never had that choice, but were served the quantity and quality of diluted wine deemed appropriate for their position. Medieval cookbooks and etiquette books tell us a lot about the type of food and the way it was consumed by the wealthy in times of plenty, but they tell us next to nothing about the food eaten by the poor, or even by the general population in times of crisis. To find out what people ate in order to just stay alive, social historians must turn to other sources, among them medical texts, hospital records, and chronicles.

Before we look at the diet of the poor and indigent of medieval society, however, it is important to find out who belonged to this disadvantaged group of people. Throughout the period we find paupers hanging around the gates of cities, monasteries, and castles who were given alms by these institutions.[49] Often they were sick people such as lepers, cripples, the blind, or the mentally ill. While they were clearly on the fringe of society, they were nevertheless still part of it, unlike prostitutes, delinquents, vagabonds, and rebels roaming the forests, who were in most cases regarded as complete outcasts. To these two groups of involuntary paupers we must add the voluntary ones, such as hermits and mendicants. The latter, as well as peasants unable to make a living in the countryside, flocked to the booming towns of

Serving frumenty. From *Tacuinum sanitatis in medicina*, 14th century. Cod. Vind. Series Nova 2644, fol. 53r. Courtesy of Österreichische Nationalbibliothek, Vienna (Photo: Bildarchiv, ÖNB Wien).

late-medieval Europe in search of alms. But the towns were not always able to help, since many of their own inhabitants were constantly teetering on the brink of starvation. The working poor in medieval towns included many artisans, servants, textile workers, tanners, dyers, and craftsmen, but also intellectuals and civil servants, such as clerks, teachers, lecturers, poets, and artists of any kind. As we can see, the starving artist is by no means a modern concept.

In order to cope with the ever-increasing number of beggars in medieval towns, town councils tried to regulate the distribution of alms. Almoners and aldermen kept updated lists of paupers, who were given tokens that entitled them to receive social assistance in the form of money or supplies.[50] A typical annual stipend for such a pauper would include clothing, shoes, bread, meat, dried herring, peas, oil, wine or beer, and firewood.[51] Estimates of the number of poor and indigent in late-medieval towns range from 20 to 30 percent. In times of crises, often precipitated by wars or famines, the number could soar to 80 percent of a town's population.[52] In addition, studies of epidemics such as the plague have shown that it was the malnourished bodies of the poor that succumbed to diseases in much higher numbers than the bodies of the rich.[53]

For humans as for any other living creatures, food is the most basic need that must be met before any other needs can be addressed, and economists have known for a long time that the poorer a family is, the more of its overall income is spent on food.[54] For most of the Middle Ages a rise in wages went hand in hand with a rise in population. Only in the period immediately following the Black Death (1350–1450) was the opposite the case, with a third or more of the population dying of the disease, and labor becoming a hot commodity. For the working poor desperately trying to feed their families, or the town councils looking after the ever increasing number of beggars, bread was the most cost-effective foodstuff, rivaled only in modern times by the potato. A medieval mason's daily wage, for instance, would buy him three to four times as many calories if he spent it on bread than if he spent it on meat.[55] Furthermore, the body of a manual laborer burned far more calories than that of a member of the leisure class. It thus becomes clear that good or bad grain harvests had a much more dramatic effect on those at the bottom than those at the top of the social hierarchy. Grain prices in the Middle Ages fluctuated more widely than those of other foodstuffs, and peasants were thus usually caught between a rock and a hard place. In times of bad harvests when prices were high, they had little or no grain to sell, and when they had a bumper crop, they were forced to sell it at bargain prices. Townspeople, on the other hand, did at least benefit from low grain prices because they allowed them to supplement their caloric intake from bread with additional higher-priced foodstuffs such as meat or fish.

When grain was in short supply, however, it was not uncommon for conflicts to arise between townspeople, town councils, and the local millers and bakers. In Lübeck, for instance, bakers baked the bread too small, and in Constance they mixed bran and stones in with the flour. What usually followed were threats, punishments, and even strikes. In Basel in the spring of 1438, millers shut down all the mills, and were subsequently banned from the city for half a year. In Cologne bakers refused to sell bread at the old weight and price, but were forced by the town council to do so or risk losing their bread and the right to deal in grain in the city ever again. Cities like Frankfurt, Zurich, Nuremberg, and Erfurt hired bakers, sometimes from outside, to turn the grain stored by the city into bread and sell it to the indigent at a moderate price.[56] Despite these measures, people continued to suffer from periodic starvation well into the modern period.

To make the most of what little grain there was in times of crisis, people tried to extract more flour than usual from it and used the remaining bran for soups and gruel. Another way to stretch the supply was to add ground beans, lentils, green beans, and even sawdust to the flour for bread making.[57] According to a German proverb, salt and bread were the most basic foodstuffs in periods of need.[58] During extreme famines, however, people were at times reduced to eating grass, bread from weeds, dead animals, or filth, the medieval chronicles tell us.[59] One sixteenth-century German physician even hints at cannibalism as a consequence of severe starvation. Under "pork" he writes: "they say pork is similar to human flesh. This is why we read in chronicles and old stories that those suffering from unbearable hunger brought on by a rise in prices or a lack of supplies, when a town is under siege, for instance, had to eat human flesh."[60] But even when grain was available, wet summers could lead to a contamination of the crop with ergot (a fungus). If poor people weakened by malnutrition consumed these grains they would fall victim to a debilitating disease known as "ergotism" or "Saint Anthony's Fire."[61]

The doubling and tripling of grain prices when harvests were poor also posed a problem to the skilled workers and craftsmen of medieval towns, who on average spent more than half of their income on food. Baking bread from barley, oats, peas, and beans is what people in Cologne did during a famine.[62] But when even these ingredients were lacking, the population resorted to boiling cabbage and turnips, often without any meat or fat added. In the Middle Ages, meat was up to four times as expensive as bread, which usually put it out of reach of the poorer segments of society. Only after the Black Death, when up to 70 percent of the fields lay fallow and were eventually used as grazing land for animals, did more animal products, such as meat, milk, butter, and cheese become available, and in the following decades meat consumption rose to levels that exceeded even those of western Europe in the late twentieth century.[63] Apart from this anomaly, meat was relatively expensive and in short supply for most of the medieval period. Even more exclusive, however, was fish. For the average consumer trying to meet the daily intake of calories, fish was only approximately 1/32 as cost-effective as bread, since in addition to being roughly 16 times as expensive as bread, it had only less than half the calories of bread per 100 grams.[64] During Lent, fish was therefore not an option for most of the poor. Even for the better-off, Lent caused dietary hardship, given that hardly any green vegetables, root vegetables, or fruit were to be had in February and March as the winter supply ran out, and animal products such as eggs and cheese were banned from the menu by the church.[65]

Disruptions of the food supply as a result of natural disasters and diseases, but also manmade crises such as wars, were a constant in the Middle Ages. To these we must add the severe dietary restrictions imposed on the population by the Christian church for a large part of the year. It is therefore no wonder that fantasies of a paradise on earth with food aplenty were popular and widespread. Whether the threat of starvation was real or just imagined, a dreamland in which food was always available, easily accessible, and varied was in all likelihood part of the collective memory of Europeans for thousands of years. Passed on orally at first, descriptions of tasty drinks and roasted birds flying into one's mouth are already found in ancient Greece.[66] And the notion of the Golden Age invoked by various classical authors is not dissimilar to that of Paradise in the Bible before the fall of man. Feeding on both these traditions, the mythical *Land of Cockaigne* was thought to be found in the West rather than the East where the Bible located the Paradise of Adam and Eve. What both places have in common is food in abundance and animals serving man, with the only difference being that before the Fall, Adam and Eve were vegetarians, while for the inhabitants of *Cockaigne* animals are definitely on the menu, in fact, they willingly serve themselves up for consumption. One negative consequence of the expulsion from Paradise that is rectified in the *Land of*

Cockaigne is God's commandment that man henceforth had to work for a living. *Cockaigne* is always portrayed as a place where idleness reigns supreme and reaps handsome rewards. Not only does it allow its inhabitants to eat well, it also provides them with shelter—and edible shelter, at that. In the oral tradition of the *Land of Cockaigne,* eternal idleness, superabundant food, and edible architecture are the three most common features that are nearly always present. Others that were added in time include communally owned property, self-cooking animals, a delightful climate, an excessive number of holidays at the expense of fast days, and gratuitous sex.[67]

By the fourteenth century, rhymed poems describing the *Land of Cockaigne* began to appear in written form in various parts of Europe. There is a Middle English poem called the *Land of Cockaygne* from the fourteenth century that made ironic references to the fall of man, there were French versions that expanded greatly on the food aspects in the poem, and from the second half of the fifteenth century a Middle-Dutch version has come down to us whose contents, in brief, are as follows: In the *Land of Cockaigne* work is banned, women are beautiful, sleep is long, and despite the lack of work there are no shortages of any kind. Walls are made of sausages, windows and doors of salmon, sturgeon, and cod, tabletops of pancakes; jugs are made of beer, plates and platters of gold; there is bread, wine, and sunshine; the beams of houses are made of butter, distaffs and spools of the crispiest cracknel, benches and chairs of meat pies, attics of gingerbread, rafters of grilled eels, and roofs tiled with tarts. There are rabbits and hares, and wild boar and deer are available all year round. Clothes are lying in the streets or piled on tables free for the taking, and when it rains, precipitation takes the form of custards, pancakes, pies, and tarts. The rivers that flow through *Cockaigne* carry wine, beer, claret, muscatel, and sherry. Of ginger and nutmeg people can eat as much as they want. Hate and envy are unknown, and it is May all year long. But time is tampered with in more ways than one. There are four times as many church holidays than normal, fasting happens only once in a 100 years, and even then it only lasts half a day. And last but not least, the river Jordan runs through this land whose water makes people forever young. Together with music and dance, the conditions are ideal for eternal revelry.[68]

Such were medieval man's dreams of the good life. One element the author of this Middle-Dutch poem does not elaborate on that is, however, found in many other versions, is the "self-preparation" of food, and the "pushy way" roasted birds and pigs with knives sticking in their backs offer themselves up for dinner.[69] That of all the fantasies—from eternal idleness to eternal youth—found in the various descriptions of *Cockaigne*, food was by far the most prominent, an obsession almost, can be seen from the fact that on average 35 to 40 percent of a given text is dedicated to it.[70] In 1546 a Dutch prose version appeared which called the dreamland *Luilekkerland* or "lazy-luscious-land." This prose text is not, as one might expect, based on the earlier rhymed poem in Middle Dutch, but on the German prose text by Hans Sachs called *Schlaraffenland* that in turn goes back to two earlier German versions from around 1500.[71] Among the new elements in this group of texts are the mountain of buckwheat porridge three miles thick that one has to eat through to get to this land, the amazing capability of farm animals to produce excrement in the form of figs or pancakes, and the remarkable fact that farmers and money grow on trees.

Descriptions of the *Land of Cockaigne, Schlaraffenland,* or *Luilekkerland,* whatever its name may be, inspired various artists to try and depict this dreamland. Best known among them is perhaps Pieter Bruegel the Elder who in 1567 painted his vision of the *Land of Cockaigne.*[72] And yet, by the sixteenth century the character of *Cockaigne* began to change. Hans Sachs and those writing in his tradition no longer portrayed it as an idyllic place, as an escape for the average medieval worker from the daily grind, but as a paradoxical place that symbolized the vices gluttony and sloth, and which was used to teach the children of early modern Europe the value system of the middle class.

NOTES

1. See P.W. Hammond, *Food and Feast in Medieval England* (Stroud, U.K.: Alan Sutton, 1993), 105; Bridget-Ann Henisch, *Fast and Feast: Food in Medieval Society* (University Park: Pennsylvania State University Press, 1976), 20. The *none* lives on in the modern English word "noon"; see *The Oxford English Dictionary,* 2nd edition, prepared by J.A. Simpson and E.S.C. Weiner, 20 vols. (Oxford: Clarendon Press, 1989), "noon."

2. Henisch, *Fast and Feast,* 23.

3. Ibid., 24.

4. Hammond, *Food and Feast,* 105.

5. Henisch, *Fast and Feast,* 17f.

6. According to the *Oxford English Dictionary,* a "pasty" is "a pie, consisting usually of venison or other meat seasoned and enclosed in a crust of pastry, and baked without a dish; a meat-pie."

7. For the following on the dining hall see Henisch, *Fast and Feast,* 147–89; Terence Scully, *The Art of Cookery in the Middle Ages* (Woodbridge,

U.K.: Boydell Press, 1995), 166–79; Hammond, *Food and Feast,* 106–25; and Maggie Black, "Medieval Britain," in *A Taste of History: 10,000 Years of Food in Britain,* eds. Peter Brears, Maggie Black, Gill Corbishley, Jane Renfrew and Jennifer Stead (London: English Heritage in association with British Museum Press, 1993), 112–19.

   8. See Black, "Medieval Britain," 114.

   9. Hammond, *Food and Feast,* 106f.

  10. Quoted in Henisch, *Fast and Feast,* 161.

  11. Scully, *The Art of Cookery,* 171.

  12. For the following see esp. Henisch, *Fast and Feast,* 178–85.

  13. Ibid., 185.

  14. See Hammond, *Food and Feast,* 111; Black, "Medieval Britain," 116.

  15. Henisch, *Fast and Feast,* 168f.

  16. Ibid., 171.

  17. A detailed description of this wine fountain is contained in Scully, *The Art of Cookery,* 173.

  18. C. Anne Wilson, "From Medieval Great Hall to Country-house Dining-room: The Furniture and Setting of the Social Meal," in *'The Appetite and the Eye': Visual Aspects of Food and Its Presentation within Their Historic Context,* ed. C. Anne Wilson (Edinburgh: Edinburgh University Press, 1991), 33.

  19. See ibid., 34–36.

  20. For the dining ritual, see the excellent and concise description in Black, "Medieval Britain," 115–19; as well as Scully, *The Art of Cookery,* 170–74; and Hammond, *Food and Feast,* 111–16.

  21. See, for instance, Hammond, *Food and Feast,* 111.

  22. Black, "Medieval Britain," 115.

  23. Scully, *The Art of Cookery,* 172.

  24. See Joseph and Francis Gies, *Life in a Medieval Castle* (New York: Harper & Row, 1979), 116.

  25. Henisch, *Fast and Feast,* 179.

  26. Ibid., 200.

  27. For this and the following see Hammond, *Food and Feast,* 112; this work also provides references to medieval sources.

  28. Ibid., 112; and Henisch, *Fast and Feast,* 179.

  29. Henisch, *Fast and Feast,* 179.

  30. *Oxford English Dictionary,* "collation."

  31. Henisch, *Fast and Feast,* 199.

  32. See ibid., 208; and Gies, *Life in a Medieval Castle,* 118f.

  33. Henisch, *Fast and Feast,* 213; see also chapter 2; and Melitta Weiss Adamson, "The Games Cooks Play: Nonsense Recipes and Practical Jokes in Medieval Literature," in *Food in the Middle Ages: A Book of Essays,* ed. Melitta Weiss Adamson (New York: Garland, 1995), 183f.

  34. For the puzzle jug and "Tantalus cup" see Henisch, *Fast and Feast,* 213–15.

35. See Henisch, *Fast and Feast,* 234.

36. Catherine Emerson, "Who Witnessed and Narrated the Banquet of the Pheasant (1454)? A Codicological Examination of the Account's Five Versions," *Fifteenth-Century Studies* 28 (2003): 124.

37. Herman Pleij, *Dreaming of Cockaigne: Medieval Fantasies of the Perfect Life,* trans. Diane Webb (New York: Columbia University Press, 2001), 136.

38. Hammond, *Food and Feast,* 148.

39. Ibid., 150.

40. For this and the following see ibid., 112–16.

41. Henisch, *Fast and Feast,* 190.

42. For an edition of a number of English books on table manners, many addressed to children, see Frederick James Furnivall, ed., *Early English meals and manners: John Russell's Boke of nurture, Wynkyn de Worde's Boke of keruynge, The boke of curtasye, R. Weste's Booke of demeanor, Seager's Schoole of vertue, The babees book, Aristotle's A B C, Urbanitatis, Stans puer ad mensam, The lytille childrenes lytil boke, for to serve a lord, Old Symon, The birched schoolboy, &c. &c.: with some forewords on education in early England* (London: N. Trübner, 1868; repr. Detroit: Singing Tree Press, 1969).

43. Henisch, *Fast and Feast,* 196.

44. *Oxford English Dictionary,* "companion."

45. Henisch, *Fast and Feast,* 192.

46. Ibid., 198.

47. For the overview of medieval table manners see Hammond, *Food and Feast,* 116–19; Henisch, *Fast and Feast,* 159–203; Gies, *Life in a Medieval Castle,* 116; and Hans Sachs, "Ein Tischzucht," in Astrid Stedje, *Deutsch gestern und heute: Einführung in Sprachgeschichte und Sprachkunde* (Lund: Liber Läromedel, 1979), 130.

48. Stefan Weiss, *Die Versorgung des päpstlichen Hofes in Avignon mit Lebensmitteln (1316–1378): Studien zur Sozial- und Wirtschaftsgeschichte eines mittelalterlichen Hofes* (Berlin: Akademie-Verlag, 2002), 164.

49. Michel Mollat, *The Poor in the Middle Ages: An Essay in Social History,* trans. Arthur Goldhammer (New Haven, Conn.: Yale University Press, 1986), 64f.

50. Ibid., 140.

51. Ibid., 276.

52. Ibid., 175–77; 296 et passim.

53. Ibid., 193.

54. Wilhelm Abel, *Massenarmut und Hungerkrisen im vorindustriellen Deutschland* (Göttingen: Vandenhoeck and Ruprecht, 1972), 14.

55. Ibid., 23.

56. For the above see Wilhelm Abel, *Strukturen und Krisen der spätmittelalterlichen Wirtschaft* (Stuttgart: Gustav Fischer, 1980), 93.

57. Hieronymus Bock, *Teutsche Speißkammer: Inn welcher du findest/was gesunden vnnd kranncken menschen zur Leibsnarung von desselben gepresten von noeten/Auch wie alle speis vnd dranck Gesunden vnd Krancken jeder zeit zur Kost vnd artznei gereichet werden sollen* (Strasbourg: Wendel Rihel, 1550), fol. 44r.

58. Ibid., fol. 47r.

59. Mollat, *The Poor in the Middle Ages,* 61f., 159–61.

60. Guualterus H. Rivius [Walther Ryff], *Kurtze aber vast eigentliche nutzliche vnd in pflegung der gesundheyt notwendige beschreibung der natur/ eigenschafft/Krafft/Tugent/Wirckung/rechten Bereyttung vnd gebrauch/inn speyß vnd drancks von noeten/vnd bey vns Teutschen inn teglichem Gebrauch sind/etc.* (Würzburg: Johan Myller, 1549), *pvrcus;* the translation is my own.

61. Mollat, *The Poor in the Middle Ages,* 63.

62. Abel, *Strukturen und Krisen,* 89.

63. Ibid., 41–45.

64. Ibid., 52.

65. Barbara Ketcham Wheaton, *Savoring the Past: The French Kitchen and Table from 1300 to 1789* (Philadelphia: University of Pennsylvania Press, 1983), 13.

66. Pleij, *Dreaming of Cockaigne,* 27.

67. Ibid., 67.

68. For the above see ibid., 33–35.

69. Ibid., 90.

70. Ibid., 89.

71. Ibid., 59 et passim.

72. Ibid., 66.

CHAPTER 5
FOOD AND RELIGION

In order to survive, human beings must eat, and fortunately the world is full of edible plants and animals. Yet, since time immemorial, humans have made certain selections from the many foodstuffs available. Diets differ from one culture to another, even if they are in the same climate zone where the same plants and animals flourish. In fact, diets differ even within a culture, with individuals showing preferences for particular foodstuffs from the accepted and acceptable list of options. Food therefore is elementary in the formation of a person's identity within a group, and it defines a group vis-à-vis other groups and their dietary habits. The verdict is still not in as to whether the first humans were herbivores or carnivores or the omnivores we are today, but thanks to its fundamental importance, food took on symbolic meaning very early on in human history. The type of food eaten and the way it was eaten made individuals either members of a group or outcasts, gave them power and status within the group, and as a form of sacrifice food defined the group's relation to the universe, its religion.

With certain foodstuffs being more highly prized than others, many cultures soon developed food hierarchies. In the majority of cases meat was ranked at the top and plant food at the bottom of these hierarchies.[1] That medieval Europe subscribed to this value system becomes clear from looking at the cookbooks of the time, which feature an endless stream of meat dishes but hardly any recipes for vegetable dishes. And yet, not all meat that was edible was actually used for food. Then as now eating fellow humans was taboo. The term "cannibalism" did not yet exist in the Middle Ages, but reports of people eating human flesh can sometimes be found in accounts that tell of extreme famines and starvation.[2] Survival cannibalism of this kind, though still eliciting a certain emotional response, has always been socially more acceptable in the West than the ritual cannibalism of an obscure tribe in a faraway land, for instance, or the criminal cannibalism committed by Westerners in their own society.[3] But the meat of fellow humans was not the only food that was taboo in the Middle Ages. The consumption of carnivorous animals and of uncastrated animals was also generally frowned upon in Europe. The taboo was not as strict as it is today, as is evident from the consumption of rodents, for instance, among the lower classes, especially in times of need.[4]

The idea that what we eat has an effect on our behavior, our character, goes back to the beginnings of human history, and can be explained by the fact that what we eat literally becomes part of our body, transformed into muscle, fat, nerves. Meat has traditionally been associated with virility, strength, aggression—those qualities hunters needed to kill animals and establish dominance over nature. Men were not just the main providers of meat but also the main consumers. And yet, medieval hunters did not eat raw meat or drink blood. Through cooking, a practice that is peculiar to humans, raw meat was turned into a product of culture. When one anthropologist developed his theory of the raw and the cooked, he was primarily thinking of meat, because plant food has always been eaten raw as well as cooked in cultures where cooking is practiced.[5]

Throughout history a diet based primarily on plant food has been the norm in world cultures. This has been largely a question of wealth, as becomes evident from the fact that once a society's wealth increases, an increase in meat consumption follows.[6] With meat being a relatively rare and high-prized commodity in ancient and medieval Europe, those who had access to it, be it through hunting or animal husbandry, were powerful individuals, most famous among them, perhaps, Odysseus, whom Homer describes as the owner of an impressive herd of 30,000 animals.[7] Not surprisingly, it was also animals that the Greeks sacrificed to their gods, and the consumption of specific types of meat is one important element that separates Christianity from Judaism and Islam.[8] The first five books of the Bible lay out the dietary laws of the Hebrews. The Paradise from which Adam and Eve were expelled was a vegetarian one, whose living creatures in the form of sacrifice were God's prerogative. Not until after the Flood are Noah and those that came after him allowed to eat meat. Blood alone is henceforth the new signifier of the vital principle that is now reserved for God. The dietary laws are modified again under Moses, when in addition to the blood taboo certain animals are declared unclean. It has been observed by scholars that these animals that were not fit for the altar and for human consumption were carnivores and omnivores, and any other animals that showed anomalies within their own classes, such as fish with no scales, terrestrial animals that wriggle, airborne ones with four feet, and cloven-hoofed ones that did not chew the cud.[9]

If it is true that any form of disorder, such as hybridization, was against Mosaic law, then Jesus, the Son of God who became man, must have been an offensive concept to the Hebrews.[10] But Christianity did more than introduce a God-man; it abolished the Hebrew distinction between clean and unclean food by declaring all food clean, it reaffirmed the dominance of man over nature, and it allowed gentiles to convert to the new religion. This repositioning vis-à-vis Judaism contributed significantly to Christianity's rise in popularity in the early Middle Ages. And with fasting and the Eucharist, the former in memory of Jesus's 40 days in the desert, the latter in memory of the Last Supper, Christians made food practices the focal point of their new faith.

Banquets and other festive meals were used in archaic cultures to define a community and give it stability, and in a certain way this was also the case in civilized societies such as classical antiquity. It should therefore not be surprising that it was a communal meal, the Pessach-meal shared by Jesus and his disciples, that formed the basis for the Eucharist, reiterated time and again in the Holy Mass when believers recall or repeat the words Jesus spoke at the Last Supper:

> And as they were eating, Jesus took bread, and blessed it, and brake it, and gave it to the disciples, and said, Take, eat; this is my body. And he took the cup, and gave thanks, and gave it to them, saying, Drink ye all of it; For this is my blood of the new testament, which is shed for many for the remission of sins. (Mt 26: 26–28)[11]

In the first and second century A.D. this holy meal of bread and wine that represented Christ's body and blood became the central act of the liturgy.[12] It was by no means a feast, but a rather frugal repast based on two main elements of the Mediterranean diet. Eating Christ's body and blood in the form of bread and wine, the products of culture rather than grain and grape, the products of nature, was designed to create community among the faithful. Christ, the sacrificial Lamb, was, in other words, consumed by his followers not as flesh, but as vegetarian foodstuffs that, unlike the manna sent from heaven, were processed by man, and therein lay the root for a centuries-long debate: If Christ was present in substance in the bread and wine, when exactly did this act happen?

In 1215, at the Fourth Lateran Council, the doctrine of transubstantiation was announced, which was followed in 1264 by the feast of Corpus Christi. What the doctrine confirmed was that at the consecration Christ's "body and blood are really contained in the sacrament of the altar under the species of bread and wine, the bread being transubstantiated into the body and the wine into the blood by the power of God, so that to carry out the mystery of unity we ourselves receive from him the body he himself receives from us."[13] This council also established yearly confession and Communion as the minimum observance for the faithful. While the doctrine of transubstantiation brought some clarification, it did not fully respond to an issue raised by Peter the Chanter in Paris in the twelfth century, who concluded that since a body cannot exist without blood, it required both bread and wine to be consecrated for Christ to be present. Consequently, if the wine had not been consecrated yet, but the bread had, the faithful were worshiping flour.[14] Determining the exact moment of Christ's appearance was therefore of enormous importance to Peter the Chanter and many of his contemporaries. In maintaining that the body and the blood of Christ were present in each element, Thomas Aquinas and other theologians responded to this type of criticism, and at the same time they placated the concerns of those believers who worried that chewing the host could hurt God, or that spilling crumbs of the host was tantamount to bits of Jesus falling off. In 1562 at the Council of Trent, the doctrine of concomitance was announced, which confirmed the presence of Christ's body and blood in both species, bread and wine.

With the cup of wine being withheld more and more from the faithful over the centuries, and only the priest receiving both, the host became the focal point for the laity, an object of adoration, a way of actually seeing Christ.[15] The practice of stamping pictures of Christ on the wafer which began in the twelfth century also contributed to making Christ visible. And so did the introduction in the fourteenth century of the monstrance, a vessel in which the consecrated wafer was displayed. It allowed believers to adore the host outside of the Mass as well.[16] The pious reacted to a Christ who was both edible and visible in the host with feelings ranging from "frenzied hunger for the host" to "intense fear of receiving it."[17] The God they were eating, according to the theology of the high Middle Ages, was the God who had become man, the bleeding and broken flesh of the crucified Jesus. Eating God was therefore for many faithful an imitation of the cross.[18]

One scholar has recently made the interesting observation that with the feast, the characteristic medieval meal whose aesthetic and social components overshadowed the gastronomic one, "Visual effects were more important to a medieval diner than taste and that vivid colors... were often applied at the expense of flavor."[19] The existence of food entertainment between meals, known as *sotelties* in English, and other illusion food such as imitation meat during Lent, made people used to the idea that what they ate was not what it seemed.[20] In other words, food that involved more than just the taste buds was a common experience not dissimilar to eating Christ in the form of the host. This raises the question, however, of whether Communion was not one of the reasons for the proliferation of illusion food.

But being a Christian in the Middle Ages implied more than going to confession and receiving the host at least once a year, it also meant observing regular fasts. The concept of voluntary fasting is an old one and is present in many of the world's religions. Since people in preindustrial societies regularly experienced hunger and famine, and were subjected much more than we are today to the rhythm of plenty and scarcity, they often believed that by intentionally controlling their hunger they could coerce the gods in some way to fulfill their hopes and dreams. With food being the most basic of needs, and hunger making itself felt only hours after the last meal, a wish by humans to defy the needs of the body and thereby defy corporeal limits also plays a role in ascetic behavior.[21] In addition, communal fasting, as the flip side of communal eating, had a similar effect of binding people to one another in a group.

As has been noted earlier, compared to the strict dietary laws of the Hebrews laid out in the first five books of the Bible, early Christianity offered a remarkable degree of dietary freedom. And yet, by the fifth century A.D. more and more rules for fasting and abstinence were being instituted. Why? Around A.D. 200 Tertullian was one of the first to link flesh with lust and carnal desire.[22] In the fourth century Saint Jerome maintained that a stomach filled with too much food and wine leads to lechery, and in the sixth century Isidore of Seville explained the connection between gluttony and lechery as a consequence of the close proximity of the stomach and the sexual organs in the body. Indulging in food, therefore, also incites lust.[23] For this reason fasting was seen as a way of both cleansing the body and controlling sexuality.

Rooted in the ancient Pythagorean and Neoplatonic belief that the spirit is dragged down by the body, Christian writers early on began to praise fasting as food for the soul, as a way to make the soul "clear and light for the reception of divine truth."[24] Classical medicine, too, held that food and sex should be consumed in moderation, as the writings on dietetics and personal hygiene of Hippocrates and Galen illustrate (see Chapter 6). By circa A.D. 400 the idea had taken hold among Christians that gluttony was the sin committed by Adam and Eve that caused the fall.[25] Fasting coupled with charity was regarded as a way to recover what had been lost.

It is in this context that the asceticism practiced by monks of the early church has to be seen. To be precise, abstinence from food was a concept that meant "dry-eating," that is, living on bread, salt, and water alone, a diet occasionally supplemented with fruits and vegetables. Hermits, on the other hand, often subscribed to "raw eating," which has recently become fashionable again under the name "macrobiotic diet," meaning that no cooked food is consumed.[26] The dietary restrictions were generally more austere in the monasteries of the East than in western Europe. There the most famous monastic rule, the Benedictine Rule instituted by Saint Benedict around A.D. 530, regulates in chapters 39 and 40 the quantity and quality of the food to be consumed. Benedictine monks are allowed two meals a day and two dishes of cooked food each. The food includes one pound of bread and approximately half a pint of wine per monk. Animal flesh is prohibited except for the sick and the weak. The daily allowance of the monks can be increased at the discretion of the abbot. The sick, the old, and the young could get certain dispensations from these dietary rules.[27]

What these general guidelines make clear is that Benedict's aim was not to starve the monks to death, but to provide them with enough nutrition so they could go about their daily tasks, first and foremost among them prayer and study. What was eliminated from the menu almost completely was the consumption of meat, a measure designed to suppress feelings of lust in the monks and to purify their bodies. The rather moderate fasting proposed by Benedict as a group practice for his monks is in stark contrast to the reports of extreme asceticism that monks and hermits practiced in Egypt and Syria in the third and fourth centuries, and later also in Ireland.[28] Spurred on by the idea of the added-on fast, called *superpositio* in Latin, as a way to multiply merit, ascetics at times embarked on competitive fasting and in doing so tried to surpass the feats of other ascetics.

So what exactly did these famous ascetics of the Middle East, known as the Desert Fathers, live on? In 375 or 376 Jerome reports that Paul the Hermit lived for 113 years in the desert on dates from a date palm and water from a spring; during the last 60 years he supposedly also received half a loaf of bread a day, supplied to him by a crow.[29] To make this account more credible, Jerome backs it up with information on a recluse who had lived for 30 years on barley bread and muddy water, and another who survived in a well on five dry figs a day. While these acts of food deprivation may seem extraordinary to us, dates as a means of survival in the desert had been used by Bedouins, for instance, for a long time. In fact, a sufficient quantity of dates supplemented with a little camel milk has "traditionally supplied the basic nutritional needs of the rural and desert peoples of the region."[30] Nevertheless, Jerome's claim that a diet of dates, water, and some bread sustained Paul the Hermit for 113 years seems dubious, or miraculous, as the case may be. It also raises the question of how representative it was of desert ermeticism in general.

A medievalist who has studied the sources that describe the life of hermits in the desert points out that these individuals were frequently said to have small gardens in which lentils, chickpeas, peas, and broad beans grew, legumes that added protein to their diet of bread. He also found mention of "dried, salted, and fresh fish, cabbages, vetch (climbing vines of the bean family), cheese, olive oil, wheat and barley grain, and wine."[31] This suggests a much more varied diet as a norm than that of Paul the Hermit, in fact, a diet that is not too dissimilar to modern vegetarian or semivegetarian diets.

The early church did not particularly encourage extreme fasting of the kind Paul the Hermit, Anthony, or Jerome himself were famous for, but rather a more balanced diet that was less harmful to the body, as can be seen from the examples of the sin of vainglory found in the wisdom literature of the time. In the majority of cases, it is ascetics engaged in prolonged, ostentatious fasts and restricted diets that become guilty of this sin.[32] And for Christianity to grow as a religion, the asceticism of the early centuries was certainly too destructive a model for believers to emulate on a mass scale. Monastic orders and individual ascetics aside, a diet that included meat was still central to the Christian faith, and so was procreation. However, in order to bridle people's lust, make them atone for Adam's sin, and help them direct their spirits toward heaven, Christians were told by popes and bishops as early as the third century to renounce food temporarily.[33]

Fasting among the laity was a group practice, engaged in by all at certain times of the year, and like Communion, corporate fasting gave the individual a sense of belonging and a way of identifying with fellow Christians. Monday and Thursday had traditionally been the fast days of the Jews, and presumably using them as a model, Christians early on chose Wednesday and Friday as fast days. A later development was the choice of Saturday as an add-on fast day (*superpositio*). In the West this happened at the expense of Wednesday as a fast day. Lent as a 40-day fasting period evolved in the fourth century, and so did the Lent of Pentecost, albeit only in the East. As penitence at the end of the year, a third fast emerged that was to start on November 14. Fasting to prepare for baptism and Holy Communion was also established practice by the fourth century. The Ember Days were part of the Western church by the seventh century, and finally the feast days of the church came to be preceded by fast days.[34] Ember Days, from Latin *Quattuor Tempora,* meaning "four times," are fast days at the beginning of the seasons, specifically Wednesday, Friday, and Saturday after December 13 (Saint Lucia), after Ash Wednesday, after Whitsuntide, and after September 14 (Exaltation of the Cross). They were presumably introduced by the church to replace the pagan harvest festivals the Romans celebrated in June, September, and December.[35] All in all, fast days amounted to more than a third of the year for most Christians. Exempt from the fasting laws were children, the old, pilgrims, workers, and beggars. Not exempt, however, were the poor when they had a roof over their heads.[36]

But what exactly was meant by fasting in the early church? Fasting strictly speaking is refraining from eating, something even the most extreme ascetics would be hard pressed to keep up for the 40 days of Lent.[37] In Christianity, fasting took on the meaning of abstaining from certain foods, and eating one meal only after vespers.[38] This practice is still adhered to today by Muslims during Ramadan. Christians, however, from the early medieval period on moved the time for the daily meal up, initially to the ninth hour, known as *none*. The *none* was at 3:00 P.M. and had the added significance that it was the time when Christ had died on the cross.[39] By the fourteenth century the Lenten fast ended at midday, and people were also allowed a small meal in the evening.[40] The dry fasts of some early Christian sects, which excluded meat, fish, eggs, milk and dairy products, wine, and oil, soon proved too rigorous for the majority of Christians, and so from the beginning of the Middle Ages on fish was already permitted.[41] Over time the list of forbidden foodstuffs was trimmed down further and in medieval times essentially included the meat of warm-blooded animals, milk, dairy products, and eggs. In 1491 the curia in Rome relaxed these dietary strictures even more and allowed eggs, milk, and dairy products on certain fast days.[42] That this had already become common practice long before can be seen from the fact that the oldest German cookbook, written around 1350, recommends the use of butter on fast days and lard on meat days. In these recipes we also find mention of milk, eggs, and cheese, and in one instance even bacon.[43] The Benedictine monastery of Tegernsee in Germany, too, lists on its meal plans as fast dishes cheese soup and milk soup. At Easter, however, the emphasis in Tegernsee was on eggs: eggs in their shell, egg soup, and Easter cake, known as *fladen praepositoris*.

It is interesting to note that for Christians throughout the Middle Ages the issue was not so much the quantity of food eaten on fast days, but rather the type of food. How to suffer the least dietary deprivation while adhering to the fasting laws of the Catholic Church became a preoccupation for cooks and diners alike. Cookbooks often give fast-day variants of dishes, such as the famous *blanc manger* prepared with pike instead of chicken meat, or they group dishes for fast days and feast days together.[44] For the lower classes these periods usually meant an endless stream of cheap fish, herring or dried cod, if they were lucky enough to live in a region that was relatively close to the ocean. Further inland they had to make do with various types of plant food, bread, vegetables, legumes, and oil pressed from nuts and seeds, since olive oil was not an affordable alternative. The meal plan of the leprosarium Grand-Beaulieu in Chartres, France, in the thirteenth century lists as food during Advent herring; during Lent on Mondays, Wednesdays, Fridays, and Saturdays herring; and on Sundays, Tuesdays, and Thursdays herring and dried fish. On the fast days before the big feast days the diet was more varied, with cheese and eggs served on Mondays, Wednesdays, Fridays, and Saturdays, and fish and legumes on Tuesdays and Thursdays. In a normal week, the leprosarium prepared meat on Sundays, Tuesdays, and Thursdays, and potage on the remaining days.[45]

In upper-class households the expenses for food during periods of fasting could easily double, in large part because cooks would turn to higher-priced fish such as trout and pike than the lowly herring. The courses of a meal on lean days would often imitate those on meat days. The following is an example of a meal for an Austrian bishop from 1486:

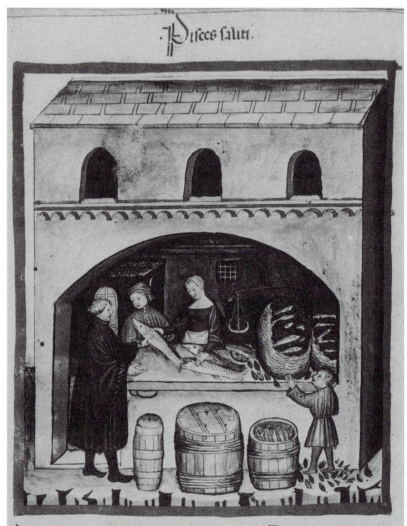

Buying fish. From *Tacuinum sanitatis in medicina*, 14th century. Cod. Vind. Series Nova 2644, fol. 82v. Courtesy of Österreichische Nationalbibliothek, Vienna (Photo: Bildarchiv, ÖNB Wien).

1. Almond puree with little balls of white bread
2. Fresh fish, boiled
3. Cabbage with fried trout
4. Crayfish cooked in wine, then pureed and sprinkled with cloves
5. Figs cooked in wine with whole almonds
6. Rice cooked with almond milk and decorated with whole almonds
7. Trout boiled in wine
8. Crayfish cooked in wine
9. Shortbread with grapes covered with dough, and sprinkled with icing sugar
10. Different kinds of pears, apples, and nuts[46]

To increase the variety of meat sources during Lent, medieval minds came up with some rather unusual classifications of animals. Not only were the warm-blooded porpoise, whale, and dolphin counted as fish, but so, more interestingly, was the tail of the beaver, on account of the fact that it spent a large part of the time in water. According to the thirteenth-century encyclopedist Thomas of Cantimpré, the beaver cannot survive for long without holding its tail in water. He argued that the tail resembles a fish, which is why Christians eat it during Lent but consider the rest of the body meat.[47] Also eaten on fast days was the barnacle goose. It was believed that rather than laying eggs, the bird procreated by spontaneous reproduction.[48]

Such ingenious reclassifications aside, most warm-blooded animals were still banned from the medieval dinner table on fast days. To satisfy their masters' cravings for meat, cooks came up with the idea of imitation meat dishes. Even if these creations did not always fool the palate, they nevertheless often did fool the eye of the diner. Found in medieval cookbooks from across Europe, such dishes frequently used ground seeds and nuts, especially almonds, as well as fish meat and fish roe, peas, bread, and various fruits to simulate the shape, color, and consistency of cooked meat. Of all the ingredients that lent themselves well to the preparation of imitation meat dishes, ground almonds were by far the most versatile. They were the basis for "almond milk, a substitute for cow's milk, almond butter, curds, cheese, cottage cheese, white, black, and red hedgehogs (colored almond paste in the shape of hedgehogs with almond slivers as quills), eggs, and egg dishes such as *verlorene eier.*"[49] Pike was used for the fast-day version of *blanc manger,* but also for imitation meat pies and roasts, often made to resemble game meat and game birds like partridges. Pike roe, too, was transformed into a host of imitation meat dishes. Mashed peas were a popular ingredient in simulated roasts, as were chopped grapes and figs.

If we ask for the reasons why imitation meat dishes for Lent were so popular in the Middle Ages, several come to mind: especially in the upper classes from which most of the medieval cookbooks originated, the concepts of food and entertainment went together. This is exemplified in the medieval banquet, which was as much an aesthetic and social event involving all the senses as it was a gastronomic one.[50] The idea of making dishes look like something else found its most vivid expression in the fantastic creations called *sotelties* that were an integral part of great feasts. Furthermore, by telling the faithful that the host is the body of Christ and stamping his picture on it, the Christian church, too, made use of the idea of imitation food. By indulging in imitation meat on fast days medieval diners may well have felt some titillation. After all, they were, on the surface at least, breaking the fast without the consequence of committing a sin. Another reason for the proliferation of imitation meat may have been the belief that by eating something that looked like the forbidden foodstuff, one could partake of some of the powers that were thought to be inherent in the actual meat dish.[51]

The internal struggle over fasting that Christians in the Middle Ages were engaged in, and that led to such phenomena as imitation meat, also found its expression in art and literature, where it is often portrayed as a literal battle. Long before Pieter Bruegel the Elder's famous 1559 painting of the *Battle between Carnival and Lent,* in which corpulent Carnival and gaunt Lent are involved in a joust, the Spanish writer Juan Ruiz, the archpriest of Hita who died in 1350, describes in an elaborate allegory the battle between Sir Flesh (Don Carnal) and Lady Lent (Doña Cuaresma), and their respective armies. In the Spanish narrative poem, Lent's armor consists of roach, salmon, pike, plaice, and lamprey. With fish bones as her spurs and a thin sole as her sword, she rides humbly on a mule. Carnival, by contrast, wears pork, mutton, partridge, quail, and a boar's head as a helmet, and rides on a proud stag in the poem. Attacks by roast capons, beef, eggs, lard, and animal milk which form Don Carnal's army, are countered by Doña Cuaresma's troupes of whiting, halibut, mackerel, herring, olive oil, and almond milk.[52] Lent's victory on Ash Wednesday is only temporary, because after 40 days the battle escalates again and this time the army of meat gains the upper hand and celebrates its victory in a sumptuous feast on Easter Sunday.

As this poem makes abundantly clear, food was on the minds of medieval Christians practically all the time, and the deprivations endured on fast days could easily lead to excesses on feast days. To counteract

the temptations of the flesh, and to make moderation a guiding principle on lean and meat days alike, the church declared gluttony and
the other vice it was thought to beget, namely lechery, cardinal sins.
The fact that Evagrius in the fourth century and Cassian in the fifth
listed these two carnal sins before all others underlines their enormous
importance in early Christianity. Not until Gregory the Great in the
seventh century was there a shift in emphasis when the sins of the flesh
gluttony and lechery took a back seat to the spiritual sins pride, envy,
anger, sloth, and avarice.[53] For Cassian gluttony was the "primal sin . . .
which led to the fall of humankind and which the devil first tempted
Jesus to commit in the desert."[54] In his *Confessiones,* Saint Augustine
gives us a vivid description of his struggle to resist the temptation of
food, a temptation he considers much stronger than sexual temptation
because man must eat to stay alive.[55]

Eating without falling prey to gluttony was a delicate balance for
Christians to achieve, and it raises the question what exactly the
church meant by the term "gluttony." The *Catholic Encyclopedia* describes it as eating "too soon, too expensively, too much, too eagerly,
and too daintily."[56] In an Old English poem, *The Seasons of Fasting,*
gluttony is defined as "eating and drinking too soon, or consuming
more than necessary, or preferring more exquisite food and drink."[57]
This put especially the upper classes, among whom conspicuous consumption was king, at the risk of committing a deadly sin every time
they sat down for a meal. And taking part in a banquet or feast could
be construed as tantamount to committing gluttony.

In the homiletic or sermon literature of the Middle Ages much
room is given to one aspect of gluttony, namely the sin of drunkenness. According to Saint Jerome, drunkenness takes a central position
among man's vices and can be seen as representative of all vices because "inasmuch as all the vices turn the mind from God they are all
ebrietas, overthrowing reason in the mind."[58] Paulinus of Nola,
Isidore of Seville, Ælfric, and Alcuin take an equally strong stance
against drunkenness, and yet none of them condemns outright the
consumption of any alcohol. Not only was wine in moderation regarded as medicine by the medical community, wine as a symbol of
Christ's blood was also an important part of the Eucharist. Even the
Rule of Saint Benedict in chapter 40 allows for a *hemina,* or approximately half a pint, per monk per day.[59]

In addition, there is the issue of water-to-wine miracles performed
first by Jesus at the Marriage of Cana, and then by various saints after
him. In an interesting twist to this type of miracle, Saint Cuthbert,

who himself abstained from drinking any alcohol, is reported by Bede to have caused water to merely taste like wine. Those who drank it apparently thought it was the best wine they ever had. This "imitation wine," reminiscent of the imitation meat dishes medieval cooks conjured up, appears to have provided the pleasures of wine without the negative physical and spiritual side effects.[60] Some medieval writers went to extraordinary lengths to illustrate to their audience what disastrous consequences a life of gluttony can have for the soul. The Old English text *Soul and Body* describes in graphic detail how after death the tables are turned and the body becomes itself a banquet for worms.[61]

In order to keep the seven cardinal sins in check, medieval theology came up with the concept of the seven cardinal virtues. They had their roots in the four cardinal virtues, fortitude, prudence, temperance, and justice, which are already mentioned in classical antiquity by Plato and Cicero, and the three Christian virtues, faith, hope, and charity.[62] Among the moral virtues temperance stands out as the one that is characteristic of all of them, a fact that was recognized by Thomas Aquinas, who called it a "special" virtue.[63] Virtues subordinate to temperance are abstinence, chastity, and modesty. Abstinence is in direct opposition to gluttony and drunkenness, and chastity to lechery. Recognizing that self-restraint with regard to food and drink and sexual pleasures is harder to achieve than modesty in dress, speech, and general lifestyle, the Catholic Church calls abstinence and chastity the "chief and ordinary phases" of the virtue of temperance.[64]

We can assume that most lay people in the Middle Ages tried to follow as best they could the admonitions of the church to purify their bodies at regular intervals through fasting and sexual abstinence. Now and again, however, individuals or groups would carry these concepts to the extreme. This had the potential of costing them their lives, either because they were branded as heretics or because they were starving themselves to death, as especially young women were in danger of doing. Vegetarianism is not a modern idea; in fact, it already existed in the ancient world. Pythagoras and his followers refrained from eating meat, for instance. They were presumably under the influence of Indian philosophy and the belief of the transmigration of souls that reached Greece via Persia.[65] Going back as far as 800 B.C., abstinence from meat eventually became an integral part of some of India's major religions, Hinduism, Buddhism, and Jainism.[66] There is, however, a fundamental difference in what motivated Pythagoras to refrain from eating meat and the ascetics of the early Christian church whose meager rations were also essentially vegetarian. The driving force for Paul the Hermit, Anthony, or Jerome appears to have been not compassion for other creatures, but rather a burning desire to conquer the temptations of the flesh. Nevertheless, for the majority of Christians, especially for the laity, meat eating remained the norm throughout the Middle Ages, and the fasting laws of the church, rather than turn the faithful into vegetarians, served to confirm meat's central role. Those groups that embraced vegetarianism were more often than not branded heretics and persecuted by medieval church authorities.

Three of the most famous heretical movements that subscribed to vegetarian ideals were the Massalians, the Bogomils, and the Cathars. All of them had in common that they originated in the East and spread to western Europe. The Massalians, whose ideas were rooted in Manicheanism and Paulicianism, swore off meat, wine, and sexual intercourse.[67] The same is true of the Bogomils, who emerged in Bulgaria five hundred years later. Some of their ideas, such as the rejection of violence against animals and humans, and their belief in the equality of men and women, make them sound rather modern.[68] Since the consumption of meat was in the Middle Ages often associated with the ruling class, that is the aristocracy, Bogomil philosophy was attractive to the peasants, who only rarely could indulge in meat. The Cathars, whose name was derived from the Greek word *katharos,* meaning "pure," were the most famous and the most persecuted of these heretical groups. Their movement was especially popular in northern Italy and France from the eleventh to the thirteenth centuries. In Cathar doctrine the connection between meat and sexual intercourse is clearly stated: flesh, since it is the result of intercourse, must be avoided, and intercourse must be avoided because it begets flesh. The Cathars shared the Pythagoreans' belief in the rebirth of the soul in animals and humans.[69]

A desire for purity and the transcendence of their earthly existence were among the motivations that drove a number of young girls and women in the Middle Ages to starve themselves and inflict unspeakable pain and hardship on their bodies, often resulting in their premature deaths. Because of the similarities between this type of eating disorder and modern anorexia nervosa, one scholar has recently coined the term "holy anorexia" for the medieval phenomenon.[70] It must be pointed out, however, that in medieval society thinness was not the beauty ideal it is today. What did contribute to the decision of girls, often from urban centers and well-to-do families, to renounce food was the male-dominated society they lived in that left them with few other life choices beyond marriage or the convent. By the time they entered puberty and reached marriageable age, many girls felt trapped. In order to gain control over their lives, some began to deny themselves food. Why they chose food as a form of protest is easy to explain. Since time immemorial women have been associated with food. In the form of breast milk women *are* food, the food that feeds the next generation. In most medieval families women were also the ones preparing the food that men ate. In other words, food was the area over which women had control in their daily lives, and renouncing it gave them a sense of power. In addition, the church, as was shown earlier, portrayed fasting as a way to purify one's body, and women were by their very nature regarded as severely lacking in purity. In the literature of the time, women are frequently equated with physicality, lustfulness, materiality, and appetite, and men with spirituality, rationality, the soul, and the intellect.[71] To transcend the impurities of their physical existence, the Desert Fathers had chosen asceticism, and many medieval women followed the same path. The numbers are certainly impressive: of the 261 holy women from 1200 to the end of the twentieth century recognized by the Catholic Church as either saints, blesseds, venerables, or servants of God, there are 170 of whom we have detailed records. And of these more than half showed signs of anorexia.[72] To wage war against their flesh they would sometimes go to extraordinary lengths. Holy anorexics typically began their lives as happy and obedient children who were special in some way, sometimes by being the youngest, or by being the only surviving child. Initially their parents would support them in their spiritual quest, but would eventually turn against their daughters if they rejected the idea of getting married or taking religious vows. To become more beautiful in the eyes of God, these girls would do things to their bodies that had the opposite effect, namely to make them ugly and undesirable in the eyes of society. As one scholar put it: "Reading the lives of fourteenth- and fifteenth-century women saints greatly expands one's knowledge of Latin synonyms for whip, thong, flail, chain, etc."[73] Practices of self-imposed hardships included cutting their hair, scourging their faces, wearing coarse rags or hair shirts, binding the flesh tightly with ropes or chains, rubbing lice into self-inflicted wounds, walking around with sharp stones in their shoes, thrusting nettles or driving silver nails into their breasts, denying themselves sleep, flagellating themselves with chains, adulterating food and water with ashes or salt, drinking the pus of the sick, eating spiders, rejecting regular food, and taking nourishment only from the host. Some turned to even more extreme forms of torture, such as rolling in broken glass, jumping in ovens, hanging from a gibbet, or praying upside down.[74] Mastery of the body was achieved by obliterating all feelings of physical pain, fatigue, hunger, and sexual desire.[75]

Catherine of Siena, a saint who lived in the fourteenth century, is one of the most famous holy women who practiced extreme fasting. At the age of 16 she restricted her diet to bread, raw vegetables, and water, at 21 she stopped eating bread, and from 25 on she ate nothing, according to her biographer Raymond.[76] Even a mouthful of food in her stomach supposedly made her vomit. At the end of her life, she drank no water for a month, and subsequently lay on her deathbed for another three months before she died at the age of 33. Not all of those holy women starved themselves to death, some were cured. This was the case with Clare of Assisi, companion to Saint Francis and founder of the Order of the Poor Clares, and with Benvenuta Bojani. After Saint Dominic appeared to the gravely ill Benvenuta, she recovered from her eating disorder and happily indulged in a big bowl of rice cooked in almond milk that her relatives prepared for her.[77] Rice and almond milk were not only expensive foodstuffs for the upper classes, but also standard ingredients in dishes for the sick. Virgins were not the only ones to engage in extreme fasting. Married women and mothers are also known to have practiced it. How closely linked the carnal desires food and sex were in the medieval mind can be seen from the fact that one anorexic, Francesca, poured hot wax or pork fat on her vulva, which caused her excruciating pain during intercourse, and afterward she would vomit and cough blood in her room. Eventually her husband gave up any claims to her body.[78] The negative effects of sexual intercourse supposedly even manifested themselves in lactating women, as the story of Catherine of Sweden illustrates. As a baby she refused the breast of her sinful wet nurse, and even that of her saintly mother, Bridget, if her mother had had conjugal relations the night before.[79] Among the physical symptoms of anorexia are fatigue, anemia, and amenorrhea. When carried to the extreme, fasting can lead to a closing-down of a woman's normal bodily functions, and medieval accounts of holy anorexics are full of stories of women no longer menstruating, or excreting feces, urine, sweat, spittle, or tears, or shedding dandruff. Fasting was, no doubt, used by some of these women as a way to escape the medieval marriage market, since it not only made them physically unattractive, but also unfit for procreation. By taking only the host as nourishment, many hoped to achieve a much grander goal, the complete union with Christ, their heavenly bridegroom.

In addition to the Christian majority medieval Europe was also home to a sizeable Jewish minority, whose food restrictions were generally more severe than those of the Christians. In the Old Testament, specifically in Leviticus and Deuteronomy, a distinction is made between clean and unclean foods. To eat kosher or pure food extends beyond the mere choice of a certain foodstuff to its production and preparation. The correct handling of food is especially important in the case of animals, since it was animals that were ritually sacrificed in the temple of Jerusalem prior to its destruction in the first century A.D., the event that led to the Diaspora of the Jewish people throughout the Roman Empire. Animals considered clean according to the Jews are those that chew the cud and have cloven hooves, in other words, herbivores. This excludes the pig, the horse, the camel, and the rabbit. Carnivorous animals are forbidden because the Garden of Eden was a vegetarian one in which no killing was allowed. The list of unclean foods also includes all birds of prey and other birds such as owls and storks; it further excludes carrion and animals that have died of natural causes or disease, or have been hunted and killed by gunshot.[80] To be considered kosher, fish must have fins and scales, which excludes sturgeon, swordfish, shark, eel, lamprey, all shellfish and crustaceans, sea urchins, octopus, and squid. Reptiles, snails, and frogs are also forbidden.

Unlike Christians, Jews are strictly prohibited from consuming blood, which is regarded as the signifier of life and seat of the soul. This means that animals must be slaughtered in a ritual manner by cutting their throats and allowing as much blood as possible to drain. Large animals are killed by professional slaughterers who are not only good butchers but also familiar with rabbinical law. The slaughter is supposed to be painless, carried out in one slash that severs the trachea and the jugular. An inspector then determines whether the meat is kosher or whether the animal shows signs of disease. Fat from below the abdomen of the animal is not to be eaten, as well as the sciatic nerve or at times the entire hindquarter to which it is attached. To remove any remaining blood, the meat is soaked in water, then covered in coarse salt and rinsed again in water. But not only animals have traditionally been subject to strict laws. Fruits, for instance, were supposed to come from a tree that was more than three years old.[81] With regard to bread and wine, the restrictions for Jews were generally not as strict as for meat in the Middle Ages, with the exception of the unleavened bread eaten at Passover, of course.

When it comes to the preparation of kosher food, the most important law is that of the separation of meat and milk. The command in the Bible not to "seethe the kid in the mother's milk" has been interpreted to mean that meat and milk cannot be part of the same meal. Even utensils for meat and milk are supposed to be strictly separated, and meals of meat and milk must be eaten a certain time period apart: six hours for Eastern Europeans, three for Germans, and one for Dutch Jews. Despite the fact that the strict dietary laws of the Jews gave them a sense of identity and acted as a barrier between Jews and non-Jews, Jewish food throughout history has always reflected the culture(s) of the surrounding region as well. In the Middle Ages, two distinct Jewish food cultures evolved in Europe, one strongly indebted to the Mediterranean world, the other to central and northern Europe. Those belonging to the former have come to be known as Sephardim, and those belonging to the latter as Ashkenazim. The Sephardic or Spanish Jews are steeped in the rich cultural mosaic of medieval and early modern Spain, and their language, *Ladino,* is a Spanish dialect. The Ashkenazim, by contrast, speak Yiddish, a late-medieval German dialect with Hebrew words mixed in. While Sephardic cuisine is full of foodstuffs the Arabs had introduced to Europe, eggplant, artichoke, and chickpea among them, Ashkenazi cuisine shows a preference for bagels, gefilte fish, matzoh ball soup, and the like. It is these foodstuffs and dishes, exported to the New World by Jewish immigrants from central and eastern Europe, that today have become synonymous with Jewish food.

Both groups, however, observe the same Jewish festivals, in which food has an important ritual function. The Sabbath is the Jewish counterpart to the Christian Sunday. It begins on Friday at sundown and ends on Saturday at sundown. During this time work is prohibited, and this includes kitchen work such as lighting fires, cooking, curing, grinding flour, or baking.[82] This means that the festive meals for Friday evening and Saturday lunch, and the more modest meal on Saturday evening, have to be prepared beforehand, with most dishes normally eaten cold. Sephardic cuisine did develop a way for stews, known as *adafina,* to cook overnight from Friday to Saturday in communal ovens or buried in the ground. On Rosh Hashanah, the Jewish New Year, dates, figs, and pomegranates are traditionally eaten, as are pastries with sesame. To achieve purity, white foods are eaten, and golden ones, especially those colored with saffron, are supposed to ensure happiness. Sharp, bitter, and black foodstuffs are avoided. Ten days after Rosh Hashanah is Yom Kippur, the Day of Atonement, on which Jews fast.

Sukkot is also known as the Feast of Tabernacles or booths. Jews celebrate this harvest festival in huts made from plants and branches. The four symbolic plants that are part of Sukkot are the citron, the young shoot of the palm tree, the myrtle bush, and the branch of a willow. To celebrate Purim, the feast commemorating their deliverance from extermination in ancient Persia, the Jews exchange edible gifts, eat pastries, drink alcohol, and enjoy a main meal that is vegetarian and dairy in memory of Queen Esther's diet. Passover, which lasts a week and commemorates the Exodus of the Jews from Egypt, is celebrated with unleavened bread called "matzoh." The Ashkenazi also forbid rice and legumes because of their capacity to rise or ferment. Of central importance to Passover is the Seder meal. Set out on a decorative Seder plate are green vegetables representing new growth, which are dipped in salt water, bitter herbs in memory of the bitter days of slavery, a roasted egg and a lamb-shank bone, which both represent sacrificial offerings in the temple, and a fruit-and-nut paste to remember the building of the pyramids for the pharaohs.

Throughout the Middle Ages, the difference in food customs between Christians and Jews was the source of endless conflicts. Since Christians were the overwhelming majority, their use of food to exclude, stigmatize, and demonize Jews often resulted in persecution, forced conversion, or expulsion, most notorious perhaps the decree signed by Ferdinand and Isabella in 1492.[83] It expelled all Jews from Spain that had not converted to Christianity. In an effort to marginalize the Jewish minority, Christian Europe did everything in its might to portray Jews as hostile to the Christian faith, and often it was food that became the focal point.[84] If a Christian cleric ate with a Jew, for instance, he faced excommunication. But the laws of exclusion started much earlier, namely at the very beginning of life, with breast feeding. It was Gregory the Great who forbade Christians to employ Jewish wet nurses, and at the Third Lateran Council in 1179 Jews were no longer allowed to employ Christian wet nurses. As part of the Christian propaganda, Jews were accused of making Christian wet nurses drain their breast milk in the latrine for three days after they had taken Communion. The Synod of Avignon in 1209 went even a step further, barring Jews from eating meat on Christian fast days.

One way of discrediting Jews was to identify them with their taboo foods, first and foremost the pig. Sculptures depicting the *Judensau* (Jewish pig) were found in churches of various German towns, including Nuremberg and Wittenberg. In Spain the term for the descendents of converted Jews was *Marranos,* meaning "swine." For hundreds of years they were subject to intense scrutiny, and often torture, by the Inquisition which suspected them of secretly holding on to their Jewish food rituals.[85] Perhaps most extreme of all the accusations made by Christians against the Jewish minority was that of blood libel. Targeting both the Jewish blood taboo and the Jewish and Christian taboo against eating fellow humans, it was alleged that Jews practiced a ritualistic form of cannibalism by stealing, torturing, and slowly killing Christian children for their blood, which they supposedly consumed with their friends. In a similar vein, Jews were at times also accused of desecrating the body of Christ in the form of the host by torturing it until it began to bleed or caused miracles to happen.[86]

NOTES

1. See Alan Beardsworth and Teresa Keil, *Sociology on the Menu: An Invitation to the Study of Food and Society* (London: Routledge, 1997), 200; and esp. Nick Fiddes, *Meat: A Natural Symbol* (London: Routledge, 1991).

2. See, for instance, Guualterus H. Rivius [Walther Ryff], *Kurtze aber vast eigentliche nutzliche vnd in pflegung der gesundheyt notwendige beschreibung der nutur/eigenschafft/Krafft/Tugent/Wirckung/rechten Bereyttung vnd gebrauch/inn speyß vnd drancks von noeten/vnd bey vns Teutschen inn teglichem Gebrauch sind/etc.* (Würzburg: Johan Myller, 1549), *pvrcus.*

3. On the different forms of cannibalism see Felipe Fernández-Armesto, *Food: A History* (London: Macmillan, 2001), 25–34. In his opinion most cannibals engage in the practice for reasons other than survival, seeking instead "self-transformation, the appropriation of power, the ritualization of the eater's relationship with the eaten." In targeting food for transcendent effects, the author compares cannibals with those following dietary regimes for the purpose of "self-improvement or worldly success or moral superiority or enhanced beauty or personal purity" (32).

4. Harry Kühnel, ed., *Alltag im Spätmittelalter* (Graz, Austria: Styria [Edition Kaleidoskop], 1984), 204.

5. Claude Lévi-Strauss, *The Raw and the Cooked,* trans. John and Doreen Weightman (London: Cape, 1970).

6. Beardsworth and Keil, *Sociology on the Menu,* 200.

7. Colin Spencer, *The Heretic's Feast: A History of Vegetarianism* (London: Fourth Estate, 1993), 34f.; and Melitta Weiss Adamson, "Imitation Food Then and Now," *Petits Propos Culinaires* 72 (2003), esp. 86–88.

8. For the following see Jean Soler, "The Semiotics of Food in the Bible," in Robert Forster and Orest Ranum, *Food and Drink in History: Se-*

lections from the Annales–Economies, Sociétés, Civilisations, vol. 5, trans. El-borg Forster and Patricia M. Ranum (Baltimore: Johns Hopkins University Press; 1979), 126–38.

9. Mary Douglas, *Purity and Danger: An Analysis of Concepts of Pollution and Danger* (New York: Praeger Publishers, 1966); and idem, "Deciphering a Meal," in Mary Douglas, *Implicit Meanings: Essays in Anthropology* (Boston: Routledge and Kegan Paul, 1975), 249–75; see also Fernández-Armesto, *Food,* 36f.

10. Soler, "The Semiotics of Food," 136.

11. The Holy Bible, King James Version.

12. Caroline Walker Bynum, *Holy Feast and Holy Fast: The Religious Significance of Food to Medieval Women* (Los Angeles and Berkeley: University of California Press, 1987), 48.

13. Quoted in Bynum, *Holy Feast and Holy Fast,* 50.

14. Ibid., 53.

15. Ibid., 56.

16. Ibid., 54f.

17. Ibid., 58.

18. Ibid., 54.

19. Ibid., 60.

20. Ibid., 61.

21. Ibid., 34.

22. Spencer, *The Heretic's Feast,* 119.

23. Hugh Magennis, *Anglo-Saxon Appetites: Food and Drink and Their Consumption in Old English and Related Literature* (Dublin: Four Courts Press, 1999), 95.

24. Bynum, *Holy Feast and Holy Fast,* 36.

25. Magennis, *Anglo-Saxon Appetites,* 94; Bynum, *Holy Feast and Holy Fast,* 36.

26. Bynum, *Holy Feast and Holy Fast,* 38.

27. See the *Catholic Encyclopedia,* "Rule of St. Benedict," http://www.newadvent.org.

28. Bynum, *Holy Feast and Holy Fast,* 38.

29. Kevin P. Roddy, "Nutrition in the Desert: The Exemplary Case of Desert Ermeticism," in *Food in the Middle Ages; A Book of Essays,* ed. Melitta Weiss Adamson (New York: Garland, 1995), 99.

30. Ibid., 104.

31. Ibid., 101.

32. Ibid.

33. Bynum, *Holy Feast and Holy Fast,* 38.

34. Ibid., 37.

35. See the *Catholic Encyclopedia,* "Ember Days."

36. Bynum, *Holy Feast and Holy Fast,* 41.

37. Simeon Stylites is one monk who supposedly accomplished this feat.

38. Bynum, *Holy Feast and Holy Fast*, 37.

39. See Bruno Laurioux, *Manger au Moyen Âge: Pratiques et discours alimentaires en Europe aux XIVe et XVe siècles* (Paris: Hachette Littératures, 2002), 105; and *The Oxford English Dictionary*, 2nd edition, prepared by J. A. Simpson and E.S.C. Weiner, 20 vols. (Oxford: Clarendon Press, 1989), "noon."

40. Bynum, *Holy Feast and Holy Fast*, 41.

41. Laurioux, *Manger au Moyen Âge*, 105.

42. Kühnel, *Alltag im Spätmittelalter*, 229.

43. For this and the following on the Tegernsee diet see Melitta Weiss Adamson, "Medieval Germany," in *Regional Cuisines of Medieval Europe: A Book of Essays*, ed. Mellita Weiss Adamson (New York: Routledge, 2002), 161.

44. Melitta Weiss Adamson, *Daz buoch von guoter spise (The Book of Good Food): A Study, Edition, and English Translation of the Oldest German Cookbook* (Sonderband 9) (Krems, Austria: *Medium Aevum Quotidianum*, 2000), 92 ("If you want to make *blanc manger*").

45. Laurioux, *Manger au Moyen Âge*, 110.

46. Kühnel, *Alltag im Spätmittelalter*, 229; the translation is my own.

47. For the exact quote of the passage in French see Laurioux, *Manger au Moyen Âge*, 115.

48. See ibid., 116; and Barbara Ketcham Wheaton, *Savoring the Past: The French Kitchen and Table from 1300 to 1789* (Philadelphia: University of Pennsylvania Press, 1983), 12.

49. Adamson, "Imitation Food," 91; Hans Wiswe, *Kulturgeschichte der Kochkunst: Kochbücher und Rezepte aus zwei Jahrtausenden mit einem lexikalischen Anhang zur Fachsprache von Eva Hepp* (Munich: Moos. 1970) 87–92; and chapter 2.

50. Bynum, *Holy Feast and Holy Fast*, 60f.; see also chapter 4.

51. Wiswe, *Kulturgeschichte der Kochkunst*, 92.

52. On the *Libro de buen amor* by Juan Ruiz, see Terence Scully, *The Art of Cookery in the Middle Ages* (Woodbridge, U.K.: Boydell Press, 1995), 62–64; and Rafael Chabrán, "Medieval Spain," in *Regional Cuisines of Medieval Europe: A Book of Essays*, ed. Melitta Weiss Adamson (New York: Routledge, 2002), 125f.

53. Morton W. Bloomfield, *The Seven Deadly Sins: An Introduction to the History of a Religious Concept, with Special Reference to Medieval English Literature* (East Lansing: Michigan State College Press, 1952), esp. 59–76.

54. Quoted in Magennis, *Anglo-Saxon Appetites*, 97.

55. See ibid.

56. See the *Catholic Encyclopedia*, "gluttony."

57. Magennis, *Anglo-Saxon Appetites*, 121.

58. Ibid., 103.

59. See the *Catholic Encyclopedia*, "Rule of St. Benedict"; and Magennis, *Anglo-Saxon Appetites*, 106.

60. Magennis, *Anglo-Saxon Appetites*, 111.

61. Ibid., 120–28.

62. Bloomfield, *The Seven Deadly Sins*, 66f.; and Melitta Weiss Adamson, "*Gula, Temperantia*, and the *Ars Culinaria* in Medieval Germany," in *Nu lôn ich iu der gâbe: Festschrift for Francis G. Gentry*, ed. Ernst Ralf Hintz (Göppingen: Kümmerle, 2003), 110.

63. See the *Catholic Encyclopedia*, "temperance."

64. Ibid.

65. Spencer, *The Heretic's Feast*, 43.

66. Ibid., 77.

67. Ibid., 153.

68. Ibid., 154, 157.

69. Ibid., 171.

70. Rudolph M. Bell, *Holy Anorexia* (Chicago: University of Chicago Press, 1985).

71. Bynum, *Holy Feast and Holy Fast*, 262.

72. Bell, *Holy Anorexia*, x.

73. Bynum, *Holy Feast and Holy Fast*, 210.

74. See ibid., 209f.

75. Bell, *Holy Anorexia*, 19f.

76. Ibid., 25.

77. Ibid., 129.

78. Ibid., 137.

79. Bynum, *Holy Feast and Holy Fast*, 214f.

80. Regarding Jewish dietary laws see Claudia Roden, *The Book of Jewish Food: An Odyssey from Samarkand to New York* (New York: Alfred A. Knopf, 1998), esp. 18–20; and Laurioux, *Manger au Moyen Âge*, 117–22.

81. Laurioux, *Manger au Moyen Âge*, 119.

82. For food on the Sabbath and other Jewish festivals see Roden, *The Book of Jewish Food*, 25–37; and Laurioux, *Manger au Moyen Âge*, 117f.

83. Roden, *The Book of Jewish Food*, 220–25; esp. 222.

84. For the following see Winfried Frey, "Jews and Christians at the Lord's Table?" in *Food in the Middle Ages: A Book of Essays*, ed. Melitta Weiss Adamson (New York: Garland, 1995), 113–44.

85. Roden, *The Book of Jewish Food*, 222.

86. Frey, "Jews and Christians," 135.

CHAPTER 6

CONCEPTS OF DIET AND NUTRITION

Medieval ideas regarding nutrition were firmly rooted in the medical theories of antiquity, which saw a close connection between food and medicine. Along with breathing, exercise, sleep, digestion, sweat, sex, hygiene, and emotional health, diet was considered an integral part of a person's overall well-being. The theory of maintaining or regaining one's health through a lifestyle of moderation and balance was called "dietetics." More than in our days, diet played a role in preventing and curing diseases, and in fact it was one of the main areas of study at medieval medical schools.[1] Not surprisingly, foodstuffs and dishes were seen in much the same way as simple and compound drugs, and like them were classified in accordance with the theory of the four humors, by which was meant a theory of the four bodily fluids. To find out the history of this early scientific theory we must go back to the sixth century B.C., to such Greek philosophers as Anaximenes, Heraclitus, and Thales.[2] In their attempts to find answers to the question of what the basis was for all life, they came up with various elements, including air, fire, and water. By the fifth century B.C. Empedocles postulated that there were four basic elements, fire, water, air, and earth, and four basic colors; and his contemporary Zeno spoke of four basic qualities, hot, cold, wet, and dry.

It was Hippocrates, the famous Greek physician, and his followers who around 400 B.C. added to the four qualities of Zeno the four bodily fluids blood, phlegm, black bile, and yellow bile, and formulated a prototype of what came to be known as "humoral theory." Blood was aligned with the basic qualities hot and wet, and the season spring; yellow bile with hot and dry, and summer; black bile with cold and dry, and fall; and phlegm with cold and wet, and winter. In time the four organs, heart, liver, spleen, and brain, and the four stages of life, childhood, adolescence, adulthood, and old age, were added to the system, and fire came to be associated with the quality hot, water with wet, air with cold, and earth with dry. Aristotle, who claimed that of the basic qualities only the four combinations hot and dry, hot and wet, cold and dry, and cold and wet were possible, was the first to speak of the four temperaments, one of the few remnants of humoral theory that has survived into the twenty-first century. When we describe a person's temperament today as sanguine, choleric, melancholic, or phlegmatic, we are, in effect, referring to their dominant bodily fluid or humor: blood (*sanguis*), yellow bile (*cholé*), black bile (*melaina cholé*), and phlegm.

The Greek physician who was the most prolific medical writer and who influenced medieval medicine more than any other was Galen of Pergamon of the second century A.D. In selecting and harmonizing elements of the humoral theory he found in Plato, Aristotle, Hippocrates, and others, he created a system that was capable of describing the world as a whole, and all inanimate and animate objects in it. Galen added to the system the four qualities of taste (sweet, bitter, sour/spicy, and salty) that he aligned with the fluids blood, yellow bile, black bile, and phlegm, respectively. When it comes to temperaments, Galen lists a total of nine, four with one prevailing quality, four in which two qualities are balanced, and the perfect state in which all qualities are balanced. Imbalance in the form of too much heat and dryness, for instance, was thought of as burning an organism to death, too much cold was thought of as freezing it to death. Other aspects found in Galen's system are different types of fevers assigned to the humors, as well as the male principle attached to yellow bile, and the female principle attached to phlegm. In the Christian Middle Ages the four temperaments were firmly linked with the humoral system, as were the four cardinal points, the four evangelists, and the Dorian, Phrygian, Lydian, and Mixo-Lydian modes of ancient music. As early as the second century A.D., the planets and signs of the zodiac had also become integrated in the system. In its most elaborate form, humoral theory would assign to blood, for instance, the prime qualities hot and wet, and in addition spring, childhood, red and sweet air, continuous fever, morning, a serene or unruffled disposition, the sanguine temperament, the apostle Mark, the planet Jupiter, the Lydian mode, and the signs of the zodiac Gemini, Taurus, and Aries.

Important for the description of foodstuffs and drugs was a refinement of the humoral system first documented in Galen, who further divided the basic qualities hot, cold, wet, and dry into four levels of intensity known in medieval Europe under the Latin term *gradus,* meaning "degree."[3] Galen applied this fine-tuning in his books on simple and compound drugs, but not in his description of the nutritional qualities of foodstuffs.[4] This was to come later when Arab physicians began using the Galenic system. For Galen, as for Hippocrates before him, drugs differed from foodstuffs in the effects they were thought to have on the body. Drugs supposedly altered the body, while foodstuffs merely increased its substance. "Weak" is the adjective used by Galen to describe the lowest level of intensity, or first degree (*gradus*), followed by "noticeable" for the second, "strong" or "violent" for the third, and "extreme" for the fourth. A further subdivision of degrees into beginning, middle, and end, suggested by Galen in his medical writings, would have led to a total of 12 levels of intensity, but this never caught on in late-classical and medieval Arab or Western medical literature.

What the Arabs did, however, was to extend the use of *gradus* to the description of foodstuffs, and the reason for this is that there existed a "gray" area between food and drugs where the two categories overlapped. Galen, for instance, listed a variety of herbs, spices, fruits, and vegetables, such as marjoram, dill, mint, caraway, cinnamon, saffron, fennel, poppy seed, mustard, squash, cucumber, wheat, barley, lentils, apricots, citrons, onions, and garlic in both his book on simple drugs and his book on foodstuffs. The majority of these items were herbs and spices. When the tenth-century Arab physician known in the West as Haly Abbas summarized and systematized Galenic medicine, he distinguished between the four different categories, remedies (*medicina*), poisons (*mortifera potio*), remedial foods (*medicinales cibi*), and pure foods (*solum cibus*), which he defined in the following way:

> 1) remedies in the absolute sense are the materials which the body at first changes but which then change the body and transform it into their temperament; 2) deadly poisons are those materials which change the body and gain power over it without the body being able to resist them; 3) remedial food materials are those which at first change the body until the body gains power over them and transforms them into its own nature. . . . 4) finally, the (pure) foods are those which the body changes and transforms into itself.[5]

Lettuce, garlic, and onions are examples of remedial foods in Haly Abbas. In his specific list of foodstuffs, the Arab writer follows Galen's book on foods but adds levels of intensity (*gradus*) to 30 items, 28 of them plants, plus honey and wine. Incidentally all of these 30 foodstuffs are also discussed in Galen's book on simple drugs. Historically, this is not unusual because many foodstuffs, especially exotic ones such as spices, were first used to make perfumes, perfumed oils, medicines or aromatic wines in ancient Greece, before they were incorporated in cooking.[6] The medical work that contains Haly Abbas's list of pure and remedial foodstuffs was translated from Arabic into Latin in Monte Cassino, Italy, by the monk Constantine the African, and given the Latin title *Liber pantegni* or *Liber regius* (Royal Book).[7] It became the textbook at the nearby medical school of Salerno, south of Naples, the first and for a long time the most famous medical school of medieval Europe. Haly Abbas's special blend of Greek and Arab medicine was thus disseminated throughout the Continent. Aside from Galen's lists of foodstuffs and simple and compound drugs, the herbal of the Greek writer Dioscorides from the first century A.D. was also mined for information on the properties of various plants, and "modernized" to include information on degrees of intensity (*gradus*).[8] The Arabic writer from Baghdad who made the most extensive use of the *gradus* system and who leaned heavily on Galen and the herbal of Dioscorides was known in the West as Ibn Butlan. In the eleventh century he put together a practical handbook for physicians in chart form called *Tacuinum sanitatis* (Tables of Health); it quickly gained popularity in Europe and in some versions was embellished with more than two hundred illustrations or miniatures depicting a wide range of foodstuffs used in the medieval kitchen whose humoral properties and effects on the human body the text describes.[9] In the *Tacuinum* Ibn Butlan extends the use of the *gradus* system beyond plants to meat and animal products, as well as the four seasons, clothes, scents, and winds. Of the 172 foodstuffs listed in the Vienna manuscript of the *Tacuinum*, for instance, 150 contain *gradus* information. The dietetic information on marjoram in the Vienna *Tacuinum* runs as follows:

XIX. Sweet Marjoram (Maiorana)

Nature: Warm and dry in the third degree.

Optimum: The very small and aromatic variety.

Usefulness: It is good for a cold and humid stomach.

Dangers: None

Effects: It purifies the blood. It is good for cold and humid temperaments, for old people, in Winter, in Autumn, and in cold regions.[10]

While Haly Abbas and Ibn Butlan promoted the inclusion of degrees of intensity in the description of foodstuffs, some prominent Arab physicians whose work became equally if not more influential in medieval Europe did not. Following Galen, they applied the system to simple drugs, but did not mention it in their dietaries. Even medical writers who did list *gradus* information never ordered the foodstuffs according to pure and remedial foods, or the basic qualities hot, cold, wet, and dry, and their degrees of intensity. More common was a division of foods into groups such as the following, adapted from Haly Abbas.

Foodstuffs

Food		Drink
from plants	from animals	
grains	four-legged animals	pure drink
bread	birds	medicinal drink
vegetables, legumes	aquatic animals	remedy
fruit (from trees, from plants)	(meat, limbs, "superfluities" [i.e., eggs, milk, dairy products])[11]	
roots		
herbs, spices		

The example of Ibn Butlan's *Tacuinum* has shown that the mere presence of *gradus* information does not yet determine a foodstuff to be remedial, which raises the question of whether it may be the intensity of the basic qualities hot, cold, wet, and dry that lies at the heart of the classification pure foods versus remedial foods. To test this hypothesis, it is instructive to categorize all the foodstuffs included in the Vienna *Tacuinum* according to *gradus* as 1) items with one or two qualities in the fourth degree, 2) items with two qualities in the third degree, 3) items with one quality in the third degree, 4) items with two qualities in the second degree, 5) items with one quality in the second degree, and 6) items with two qualities in the first degree. The lists obtained through such a classification show that the overwhelming majority of foodstuffs have basic qualities in the second and first degree. The higher the degrees of intensity, the shorter the list. Furthermore, third- and fourth-degree items almost all belong to a group that can be described as seasonings, herbs, spices, with the occasional fruit or vegetable thrown in. If we recall that Haly Abbas's examples of remedial foods were lettuce, garlic, and onion, this is an indication that higher degrees of intensity (three to four) describe remedial foods, and lower levels (one to two) pure foods.

Medieval medical writers do not always agree exactly on the degrees of intensity inherent in the basic qualities of a given foodstuff. When there is a difference in intensity, it is usually just by one degree. A downgrading from four to three in intensity does not change the classification of a foodstuff as remedial, but a downgrading from three to two does, thereby making it pure food. This is the case with the description of lettuce in the medieval sources. If we go back to the Greek physician Galen, we find that he describes lettuce in his book on simple drugs as "a moist and cold vegetable, not in the extreme, though, as long as it is not eaten as food, but," he adds, "it has the highest amount of coldness after springwater."[12] With springwater usually being classified as cold and wet in the fourth degree, one would therefore expect lettuce to be somewhat weaker, with intensity levels between three and four. An indication that the qualities of lettuce were downgraded over the centuries is found in the most famous medical text of the Middle Ages, the *Canon medicinae* (Canon of Medicine) by the Arab medical writer Avicenna. In it he writes: "But I say that he who has said that it [lettuce] is cold in the third [degree] has judged it to be of bad and of little nutritional value, since it is not so, it seems that it should be in the second [degree]."[13] Unlike Galen, Avicenna ascribes considerable nutritional value to lettuce and is quite aware of the change in status that a downgrading from three to two entails. For reasons unknown, Avicenna, along with a number of fellow physicians, has turned a previously remedial foodstuff that on account of its coldness was used as an anaphrodisiac, a food item that suppresses rather than incites lust, into a pure foodstuff.

A comparison of the degrees ascribed to the qualities of foodstuffs in Galen and in two Arab writers, Ibn Butlan and Avicenna, for instance, shows a general trend toward downgrading, whereby more and more items move from the classification of simple drug or remedial food to nutritious food, a scientific explanation perhaps of what had been happening over the centuries, namely, that new items were incorporated in a culture first as medicine and gradually made their way into general use in the kitchen. Only rarely are items upgraded, as in the case of aubergines and cherries, to which Ibn Butlan ascribes higher degrees of intensity than Haly Abbas or Avicenna. Leaving aside these minor changes in *gradus* information over time, it is now possible to assemble a list of what was considered remedial food in the Middle Ages: first and foremost it was garlic, onions, mustard, pepper, and rue, followed by the seasonings marjoram, dill, mint, caraway, cinnamon, cumin, mandrake (poisonous southern European plant with narcotic properties, or its root), fennel, old wine, vinegar, parsley, horehound, anise, purslane, vermouth, horseradish, and citrons.

The use of the *gradus* system for the description of foodstuffs and their basic qualities was not generally adhered to in the Arabic texts. When this literature on diet and nutrition written in Arabic reached the medieval West in Latin translation, it was mainly the medical school of Salerno that propagated the system by virtue of the fact that its teaching was based to a large extent on the medical work of Haly Abbas. The rise of Montpellier, in the south of France, as the new center of medical learning put an end to the large-scale application of *gradus* in the field of dietetics. Most foodstuffs belonged to the category pure foods, which meant that the qualities hot, cold, wet, and dry were present in low degrees of intensity only, and this made the information more or less redundant. When *gradus* information is given in nutritional texts compiled in medieval Europe from classical and Arabic sources, it is primarily to identify the remedial foods, garlic, onions, and mustard. In time this information also made its way into medieval and early modern cookbooks, such as the fifteenth-century German *Kochbuch Meister Eberhards* (Cookbook of Master Eberhard), which provides the degrees for garlic and onions, or the sixteenth-century printed edition of the *Koch- vnd Kellermeisterey* (Cook and Cellar Mastery), which tells the reader that mustard is dry and hot in the fourth degree.[14]

The fact that *gradus* information and the ever so hazy distinction between pure and remedial foods had found its way into medieval cookbooks, and that at the same time culinary recipes had found their way into medical texts on nutrition, illustrates how closely connected cooking and medicine were in the Middle Ages. To understand how nutrition fit in the medieval medical system, where it occupied a central position, we must first look at the underlying theory. Influenced by Hippocrates and Galen, medieval Arab medical writers began to organize medicine according to causes of sickness and health that were natural (*res naturales*), non-natural (*res non naturales*), and against nature (*res contra naturam*).[15] The first category included such things as heartbeat and bowel movement that the healthy body performed automatically, the second referred to certain aspects of a person's lifestyle, and the third to external factors than can harm the body, such as being wounded by an arrow, for instance. It is in the second category, the non-natural causes of sickness and health, or "non-naturals" for short, always perceived as six in number, that nutrition is usually discussed, along with the air one breathes (*aer*), exercise and rest (*motus et quies*), sleeping and waking (*somnus et vigilia*), repletion and excretion (*repletio et evacuatio*), and passions and emotions (*accidentia animi*).[16] In other words, for a healthy lifestyle medieval doctors recommended fresh air, moderation in the amount of exercise, food, and sleep, proper hygiene, including sexual hygiene and baths, and finally, a positive attitude toward life.

Beginning with Haly Abbas, the non-naturals have been connected with the number six, and as the expression "causes of sickness and health" indicates, they were thought to require proper management, with the key being moderation. Excessive behavior in these areas, whether in exercise, food, or sex was believed to cause illness. By contrast, when practiced in moderation they supposedly prevented illness. The genre of medical literature that discussed the six non-naturals in the Middle Ages was called *Regimen sanitatis* (Regimen of Health). Food and drink (*cibus et potus*) was normally the biggest chapter of the six, and was either the second or third chapter in a given regimen. When European doctors compiled their own regimens from the Arabic sources, they sometimes included a phlebotomy, that is, a chapter on bloodletting, or a chapter on clysters (enemas). In doing so they went beyond the field of preventive medicine to which the non-naturals originally belonged. Since blood was the most prominent of the four bodily fluids or humors, a whole science developed around the minor surgical procedure of bloodletting, with instructions when to let blood, how much, and from which part of the body, in order to bring a person's blood into line with the other fluids and create a balance.[17]

A less-intrusive way of regulating one's humors was through diet. Typically, a food and drink chapter in a medieval regimen, whether written in Latin or a vernacular language, would start with a set of general guidelines on nutrition, followed by a specific list of foodstuffs divided in groups similar to the one found in Haly Abbas (see diagram). In Germany the Latin regimen most widely known and translated was compiled around 1300 by the physician Konrad von Eichsätt.[18] He begins the general section on nutrition with a discussion of the desire to eat and the right time to do it, which is when the stomach is empty and the person has not felt hunger for too long. In the course of a meal one should not fill the stomach completely, but rather stop eating when one still has a desire to eat. Overeating should be rectified with fasting, becoming hungry again, sleep, exercise, a little clear wine, and reducing the intake of food. More immediate remedies for overeating are vomiting, bloodletting, and drinking warm water. Ideally one should eat one meal a day, or two at the most. Konrad then gives diet recommendations for the four temperaments or complexions, in the order melancholic, choleric, sanguine, and phlegmatic. Given their dominant humors, melancholic persons should eat moist food, choleric ones cold and moist food, sanguine ones delicate (dry) food, and phlegmatic ones delicate and warm food.

The type of food should also change with the season. In winter the recommended food should be warm and fortifying, such as beef, mutton, pork, venison and game; in summer it should be light and cool, such as lettuce, and other potherbs, lamb and goat meat, and young chickens. In the spring dry food in moderate quantities is best, and in the fall warm food eaten in moderation. A discussion of the quantity of food to be eaten during a meal is followed by guidelines for the quality of food. Categories listed are, for instance, hot, cold, watery, acerbic, venomous, humid, dry, unctuous, fat, sweet, bitter, salty, constipating, and acidic foods. Good food includes lamb and kid, veal, hens, capons, partridges, fish with scales, soft-boiled eggs, little birds and birds in general, leavened wheat bread, old wine, and fresh water. Drink in winter should be warm, and pears and cheese should conclude a meal. Food that is too salty and bitter should be counteracted with sweet apples. How to properly start the day, from getting up until the first meal, is discussed, and so is the order of dishes. It is stated that subtle or light food should be eaten first, and strong, hearty food afterward; in other words, courses of chicken and other fowl should be followed by beef, pork, salt meat, and roasts. When it comes to digestion, Konrad warns of eating fish after exercise, of dishes served in the wrong order, or too many dishes eaten at the same time, and explains how the process of initial digestion works. In particular he discusses the digestion of fish combined with raw milk, milk with wine, fruit, salty, and delicate foods.

Konrad's regimen continues with a detailed chapter on the consumption of wine, the most popular drink among the upper and middle classes of late medieval Germany and the rest of Europe. He explains that wine should be drunk after a meal, mixed with water; he warns against drinking wine on an empty stomach; after exercise, bathing, or sex; after hot and sharp food; or at night, and criticizes drunkenness and inebriation. Wine, with its hot quality, should be tempered with water, he writes, and thirst for wine can be suppressed by sleeping. If too much wine was consumed, it helps to vomit, drink a lot of water, take a bath, or sleep. Konrad frowns on frequent drunkenness, but recommends getting drunk once a month to cleanse the system. He also discusses abstinence and things that get one drunk fast, calls old wine a form of medicine (*quasi medicina*), recommends wine that is moderately aged, and specifies the age, color, aroma, and taste of good wine. When consumed in moderation, wine is considered beneficial to a person's health. Among its effects on a person's mood, Konrad lists sadness, fear, and joyfulness. The hot humor of wine and its role in digestion are mentioned, as well as the effect of wine on boys, young men, and older men. Also discussed briefly are beer and mead, red wine, which is especially recommended for older people, white wine, and the relationship between wine and a person's temperament. The author explains that in cold weather and in northern climates the consumption of alcohol is higher because it restores lost heat, which is why Germans supposedly drink more than twice as much as southern Europeans. The section on wine concludes with a look at the connection between inebriation and the sanguine, choleric, phlegmatic, and melancholic temperament or complexion.

Following these general guidelines Konrad provides a dietetic list of foodstuffs, complete with humoral qualities and nutritional information. Starting with bread, the most basic of foodstuffs, he continues with bad and good meat, and the way meat should be prepared, namely boiled, fried, with spices and sauces, or roasted. When he comments on specific animals, he begins with those that were believed to have lighter, more delicate meat and would have been eaten early on in a meal: birds, such as hens, roosters, pullets, and their various parts; partridges, pigeons, and doves, and their young; sparrows, pheasants, starlings, and other birds that eat juniper berries; all little birds, cranes, and ducks. His list of meats from "nonflying" animals, as he calls them, consists of goat and ram, that of their castrated young, ram marrow, veal, beef, mutton, roe deer, and hart meat, hare, hedgehog, the meat of young animals, a meat's fat content, sauces to go with meat, wild boar and the domestic pig, and their feet, snout, and ears. Separately he discusses the animal parts heart, brain, head, skin, liver, spleen, kidneys, and front and hind feet.

The section on fish first provides a general description of what are good and bad fish, and explains the qualities of fresh, salted, and freshly salted fish, processed fish, fried fish, fish in aspic/jelly, fish broth, and crayfish. Konrad then moves on to animal products, the *su-*

Wine making. From *Tacuinum sanitatis in medicina,* 14th century, Cod. Vind. Series Nova 2644, fol. 54v. Courtesy of Österreichische Nationalbibliothek, Vienna (Photo: Bildarchiv, ÖNB Wien).

perfluitates, as they were called in Haly Abbas's work, namely milk, cheese, and eggs. Some general remarks on fresh milk, followed by guidelines on the consumption of milk, lead over to information on the dietetic qualities and benefits of mother's milk, goat milk, sheep's milk, cow's milk, curdled milk, donkey milk, buttermilk, and butter. In the section on cheese he discusses fresh and old cheese, and recommends medium-aged cheese made from good milk of a fatty and buttery consistency that is only moderately salted. Fresh and old cheese should not be consumed often; cheese should be eaten in small quantities at the end of a meal and with bread and pears. In the section on eggs he speaks of chicken eggs, egg yolk and egg white and their qualities, duck eggs, sparrow eggs, soft-boiled eggs and hard-boiled eggs, eggs cooked in vinegar, and goose eggs.

His chapter on the use of fruit is detailed and starts with the fig, in particular the fresh fig, at the time still a rather exotic fruit in Germany. Figs have their proper place at the beginning of a meal, he claims, together with nuts, above all the popular almond. Next are the much less exotic grapes, specifically those that are white, ripe, and sweet, as well as raisins. Unripe grapes were used for the tart food additive known as "verjuice" in the Middle Ages. Sweet and sour apples and apple juice come next, along with pears and pear juice, sweet quinces, peaches, the juice of peach leaves, the prune varieties bullaces and damsons, morellos (cherries), which like figs should be eaten at the beginning of a meal, mulberries, medlars, chestnuts, (wal)nuts, fresh nuts, nuts eaten with figs, hazelnuts, almonds, almond milk, almond oil, and pomegranates. The vegetables he mentions include lettuce, cabbage, leek, chard, spinach, rape, onions, and garlic. The list of legumes that follows contains fava beans, white and black chickpeas, chickpea broth, peas, lentils, rice, millet, spelt, oat, wheat, barley, barley water, and honey, and instructions such as cooking beans and lentils in vinegar, and rice in milk. Konrad concludes his dietetic list of foodstuffs with a chapter on seasonings, starting with the most popular even today, namely salt and pepper, followed by ginger, saffron, cinnamon, mace, cloves, galingale, nutmeg, and vinegar. *Gradus* information is given in the description of pepper, ginger, cloves, and nutmeg only.

Culinary recipes are frequently found in medieval *Regimen sanitatis* literature, usually in the dietetic lists of foodstuffs rather than in the general guidelines on nutrition.[19] Among the Arabic sources, Ibn Butlan's *Tacuinum sanitatis,* which consists almost entirely of a specific list of foodstuffs, contains 12 recipes with three or more ingredients.[20]

Konrad van Eichstätt's section on foodstuffs and their dietetic qualities contains 10 recipes.[21] They include several sauces, recipes for the preparation of meat, salt fish and fish in aspic/jelly, milk, and an almond dish. What Konrad von Eichstätt wrote in his *Regimen sanitatis* was by no means original, but rather a compilation from Arabic sources, primarily Avicenna's *Canon medicinae* and the regimens of two other Arab physicians known in the West as Rhazes and Averroës. In Germany Konrad's was the most popular regimen, copied in Latin and translated into German numerous times. Since it is based on older sources that originated in the Mediterranean, the list of foodstuffs is by no means an adequate reflection of German dietary customs in the thirteenth century. Nevertheless, by recommending certain, often exotic foodstuffs such as figs and almonds, it influenced German cuisine and taste. Physicians like Konrad were often employed at the courts of high-ranking individuals in Germany and abroad, among them kings, lords, dukes, archbishops and the like, whom they served not just as healers but also as nutritionists. They worked closely with the cook, to whom they gave dietary advice that ultimately played a role in his decision what to cook, how to prepare it, and in what order and combination with other dishes to serve it. That physicians were quite knowledgeable when it came to cooking can be seen from the recipes they included in their dietetic lists of foodstuffs. The vast majority of regimens, including Konrad's, were written with the healthy adult diner in mind. When needed, a physician would also design customized diets for members of his master's household who suffered from a particular illness. These regimens were known as *consilia* (counsels). Cooks, who usually could read and sometimes also write, if only in their vernacular language and not in Latin, were familiar with the basic principles of humoral theory, and, we can assume, had a general idea of the humoral qualities of foodstuffs, the effects processing and cooking had on them, and the humoral disposition of the average diner for whom they cooked.

By the thirteenth century two texts began to circulate in Europe that eventually brought bits and pieces of this dietary and dietetic information to the broader public. They were known as the *Secretum secretorum* (Secret of Secrets), and the *Regimen sanitatis Salernitanum* (Salernitan Regimen of Health).[22] The *Secretum* was a collection of letters Aristotle supposedly wrote to his famous pupil Alexander the Great, but was more likely put together in the Arab world in the tenth century. As a reference text for kings, it addresses such diverse areas as governing a country, warfare, personal conduct, physiognomy (that is, the way to tell a person's character from how he or she looks), alchemy, and health care. Twenty-seven chapters deal with the non-naturals, and 21 of them contain dietetic information on food similar to the general guidelines on nutrition contained in Konrad's regimen. In Europe the Latin *Secretum* was a bestseller, translated into at least 10 vernacular languages ranging from Spanish, Castilian, Anglo-Norman, English, Provençal, and French, to Dutch, German, Italian, and Hebrew.

In some way even more successful, because easier to memorize than the *Secretum,* was the *Regimen sanitatis Salernitanum.* Although it bears the name of the famous Italian medical school, it is not clear whether the text actually originated there. What we do know is that from the thirteenth to the nineteenth century the regimen grew from a modest 364 hexameter verses to 3,526. In its early form the regimen dealt mainly with the six non-naturals, the humors, and temperaments or complexions, some diseases, and a phlebotomy (information on bloodletting). Like the *Secretum secretorum* it was copied all over Europe and translated from Latin into various vernacular languages, among them Irish, Bohemian, Provençal, Hebrew, German, French, and Italian. The invention of the printing press in the fifteenth century dramatically increased the spread of these two texts. The following is an example of some verses from the *Regimen sanitatis Salernitanum* in an English translation from 1608:[23]

> 94.
>
> The choice of meat to health doth much avail,
> First Veal is wholesome meat, and breeds good blood,
> So Capon, Hen, and Chicken, Partridge, Quail,
> The Pheasant, Woodcock, Lark and Thrush be good,
> The Heath-cock wholesome is, the Dove, the Rail,
> And all that do not much delight in mud.

If the right diet was so important for healthy adults, it was even more so for the sick, for those who wanted to ward off disease, for those who changed their natural environment (through travel, for instance), for the rich and poor, and for those whom medieval medicine considered to be in a "neutral state" between sickness and health. This group included pregnant women, children, the elderly, and convalescents whose bodies, though not exactly sick, still had special dietary requirements that differed from those of the healthy (male) body in its prime.

The survival of the self and the survival of the species are two of the most powerful drives in humans; in the pregnant woman, food is the key element that ensures both. Little wonder then that for thousands of years the diet of pregnant women has been of concern to people.[24] In analogy to the *Regimen sanitatis* for healthy adults, which used the six non-naturals as its ordering principle, regimens for pregnant women evolved as a genre of medical writing in Byzantium and the Arab world in the early Middle Ages. They built on the medical knowledge found in Hippocrates and Galen but also may have been influenced by Hindu medicine. A lot of the information contained in such pregnancy regimens revolves around three areas: morning sickness, strange cravings known as *cittosis* or *pica,* and the optimal diet for the developing fetus. Hindu medicine warned women against sharp and hot food; too much or too little food; and an addiction to sweet, sour, pungent, bitter, and astringent foods (salt, wine, pork, and fish, among others), which could keep women from becoming pregnant. If the woman was pregnant already, consumption of these foods could lead to an abortion or a sickly child. Hindu medical texts even go so far as to map out the diet of a pregnant woman according to each month of pregnancy.

Greek, Arabic, and Western medical texts never provided such minute, monthly diet plans, usually just some general guidelines on what to eat and what to avoid. What captured their attention more, it seems, were women's strange cravings during pregnancy and the phenomenon of morning sickness. Hippocrates already warns of the consequences if women's cravings for eating earth or coal are met, namely that the baby to be born will bear the signs of these things on its head. Galen attempts an explanation of such cravings on the basis of humoral pathology and claims that women who display the symptom have an excess of a bad humor, or bodily fluid. According to him, women crave sour, very bitter, or acrid things, along with earth, shells, coals, and other strange substances. He sees a progression from the strange cravings early on in the pregnancy to morning sickness in the fourth month that manifests itself in vomiting and nausea. Medical writers in Byzantium were among the first in Europe to devise corrective dietary regimens for pregnant women suffering from disorders such as vomiting, overeating, increased secretion of saliva, heartburn, and nausea. Exercise and savory food that is neither too bitter nor too sweet (in particular, poultry, bread, starch, and fragrant wine, all to be consumed in moderation) are often recommended. Occasionally, even acrid food like mustard or cold food like lettuce is recommended.

The famous Arab physicians Rhazes, Haly Abbas, and Avicenna also comment on the diet of pregnant women in their respective regimens. Rhazes warns against acrid and bitter foodstuffs—capers, lupines, and unripe olives in particular—and foodstuffs such as chickpeas, green beans, and rue that provoke urine and menstruation, that is, induce an abortion. Rue had been known and used in antiquity as a means of birth control. What Rhazes recommends is delicate food, in particular, chicken, partridge, and kid, all eaten in several small meals a day, and moderate quantities of fragrant wine that has been diluted slightly with water. Onions, mustard, pomegranates, sour apples, and limes, he claims, help restore lost appetite. Haly Abbas's pregnancy regimen gives much the same advice. Avicenna, who pays special attention to corrective nutrition, expands on the information his predecessors provide. He tells which type of bread pregnant women should eat, the acrid and bitter foods they should avoid, the beverages that enhance a woman's fertility, and the type of food a woman should eat during the second month of her pregnancy, namely raisins, sweet quinces, pears, apples, and pomegranates.

As with the general regimens for healthy adults compiled in Latin by European physicians, regimens for pregnant women followed those of the Arab medical authorities. Here and there other material is included, such as the warning that too much salt in the mother's diet results in babies being born without nails, a warning already voiced by the Roman writer Pliny. But by and large they continue to recommend wholesome food that in Haly Abbas's classification would belong to the category "pure food," above all chicken, partridge, kid, and some wine.

Mortality was high throughout the Middle Ages, but it reached crisis proportions in the mid-fourteenth century when the plague reached Europe and within a few years decimated its population by more than a third. With the survival of mankind in question, many of the Latin pregnancy regimens were translated into the vernacular languages of Europe by physicians and clerics for the purpose of making the information accessible to a wider audience. In the early fifteenth century one of these translators was the cleric Heinrich Laufenberg from Freiburg in southern Germany.[25] His pregnancy regimen recommends food in moderation and nutritious foods such as veal, kid, chicken, partridge, small birds, game, and soft-boiled eggs. Coarse and harmful foods are to be avoided, such as foods that cause diarrhea and constipation, and medicinal potions. Hot milk and mush are recommended for the parturient woman.[26]

Laufenberg also pays great attention to the food of the newborn, the selection of a wet nurse, and to weaning and putting the child on a diet of solid food.[27] He recommends feeding the baby milk until teething sets in. However, the milk produced by the mother immediately after she has given birth is considered harmful to the newborn, which is why the baby initially should be fed by another woman until the mother's breast has settled. From then on the best milk, according to Laufenberg, is that of the mother, an opinion not shared by all medieval doctors. Especially in the aristocracy, where producing an heir was often a primary concern, newborns were frequently handed over to a wet nurse shortly after birth. That way the mother would stop lactating and potentially become pregnant sooner than if she breast-fed the child herself for a year or two. Laufenberg, whose audience is middle class, considers continuity in the diet as more important. The newborn should be fed the food it has already grown used to in the womb, and the mother is advised to continue eating the food she ate during her pregnancy. The baby should be breast-fed two to three times a day and be given a little honey before feeding starts. In the morning the mother is told to remove the "coarse" milk before feeding the baby. By invoking an unnamed medical authority referred to as a "great master," Laufenberg informs the reader of the belief that the baby should be given some wine along with the mother's milk, an opinion that would probably raise some eyebrows in the medical community today. That Laufenberg himself was not too sure about this recommendation can be seen from the fact that he returns to the subject at the end of the section and stresses that if a baby would like to drink wine, it should be only a very small quantity that has been diluted in water.

Once the child starts teething, the gums should be rubbed with butter, chicken fat, olive oil, the brain of a hare, or herbs. The gums and throat also may be anointed with violet oil and the head washed with a chamomile infusion. The child should be fed light, delicate food, neither too hot nor too cold, a little soft and well-boiled piece of meat, and nuts and bread chewed first by the mother. Bread crumbs soaked in honey water or wine water in small quantities are also recommended. When the child begins to speak, the tongue should be rubbed with salt. Honey, incense, and licorice are also described as useful in inducing the child to speak.

Even if Laufenberg himself did not think highly of wet-nursing, it was still a widely held practice in Europe, often out of necessity if the mother had died in childbirth or did not produce enough milk, or if the infant was abandoned at birth. Laufenberg recognizes this and includes a detailed section on wet nurses. According to medieval humoral theory, the milk an infant was fed was not only nutrition for the body, but it also influenced the child's character and intelligence. This meant that careful consideration had to go into the selection of a wet nurse. Among the criteria mentioned are that she should be between 25 and 35 (the ages when women were thought to produce the best milk), have rosy cheeks and strong, big breasts of medium firmness, not be too close to having given birth herself, not be sick, have kind eyes, be of medium weight, chaste, and have good manners. The latter qualities are important, he says, because they affect the temperament or complexion of the child.

The ideal breast milk for an infant is described as white, sweet, and neither too thick nor too thin. Green milk and red milk are considered harmful. Like the mother, the wet nurse has to be careful with her own diet, which should contain plenty of white bread with meat, almonds, hazelnuts, rice, and lettuce. She should drink good white wine. Another regimen from Italy recommends good food in moderate quantity such as lamb, capon, hen, chicken, partridge, pheasant, veal, and a mixture of egg yolk, goat milk, and sugar.[28] To increase her milk production, the wet nurse should eat chickpeas, beans, and gruel. Laufenberg warns of onions, garlic, all sour food prepared with pepper, and all food seasoned with too much salt or too much vinegar. His final comments hint at some problems connected with wet-nursing. If the wet nurse has sex too often and becomes pregnant, the milk she produces is unhealthy for the child. The Hospitale degli Innocenti, a foundling hospital in Florence that had no other choice than to send infants out to wet nurses in the countryside, repeatedly had to deal with wet nurses who became pregnant. When an infant in their care died, the hospital was not always informed right away because often both the women and their families depended on the income from wet-nursing.[29]

When the child has reached the age of two, Laufenberg recommends weaning with easily digestible food dipped lightly in sugar. Coarse food when fed too early was thought to give the child colic and cramps. Weaning on hot summer days he finds not advisable. If the child insists on sucking the mother's breast, myrrh and mint pounded together and applied to the breast will serve as a dissuasion, he claims, on account of the bitter taste. Children who by the age of four drink too much wine should be given wine mixed with water, or the wine should be replaced altogether with water at the end of the meal. Between the ages of 6 and 10 the child is finally old enough to be given the coarser food of grown-ups.

As the body aged, it was thought to lose some of its inherent heat and humidity and eventually become cold and dry.[30] To counteract this development, old people were advised to eat food that had the prime qualities of hot and humid. In addition, their food was to be easily digestible, nourishing, eaten in small quantities, and reheated often. The elderly were to avoid food that supposedly generated phlegm and melancholy and food that had a drying effect on the body. Recommended foods included goat milk and foods that easily descended to the stomach, such as well-leavened bread; little fish; chicks; the meat of goats, sheep, geese, and ducks; and runny eggs. The consumption of beef, viscous fish, and unleavened bread, as well as hard and coarse things, was discouraged. Equally problematic were foods that made the body hot and dry, such as onions and garlic; phlegmatic, such as mushrooms; or melancholic, such as lentils and cabbage. Old people were also told to stay away from vegetables and fruits, with the exception of figs, grapes, dates, prunes, and the like.

Not just pregnancy, childhood, and old age were regarded by Arab physicians as the neutral state between sickness and health that required a diet of pure nourishing food, but also convalescence. People who had overcome an illness were still weak and needed food that would strengthen their bodies and provide sustenance, food, in other words, that the physician Haly Abbas classified as "pure food." As we have seen in the dietary recommendations for the other special groups, foodstuffs with high degrees of intensity (third or fourth *gradus*) such as onion and garlic are largely excluded. This is also the case with food for invalids, an area clearly of primary concern to physicians and cooks alike. Dietetic lists of foodstuffs often contain information on ingredients and dishes suitable for the sick, the sickly, and the convalescent. Some cookbooks also provide a separate section of recipes for dishes for the sick. Barley soup is such a dish, and in Ibn Butlan's *Tacuinum sanitatis* we find under barley an illustration showing this creamy soup being served to an invalid.[31] A Neapolitan cookbook from the late Middle Ages lists as a dish for the sick barley-porridge made with almond milk and chicken broth.[32] The *Viandier* (The Provisioner) of Taillevent, a well-known French cookbook from the fourteenth century, contains seven dishes for the sick.[33] The recipes include chicken bouillon, pink water of capon or hen, Flemish caudle, a gruel of husked barley, perch bouillon, and a white dish of capon. The ingredients that figure prominently are poultry, sugar, saffron, egg yolks, white wine, barley, almonds and almond milk, salt, perch, and pomegranate seed. Verjuice is mentioned once together with the qualifier "very little." In Ibn Butlan's list of food-stuffs, nearly all of these items belong to the category "two qualities in the second degree" or lower. The two exceptions are verjuice, which is to be used sparingly, and salt, which, incidentally, Avicenna classifies as hot and dry in the second degree. No remedial foodstuffs of the highest levels of intensity are represented in the recipes. This strongly suggests that medieval cooks were fully aware of the distinction be-tween pure foods and remedial foods.

Another French cookbook by the master cook to the duke of Savoy contains 17 recipes for dishes for the sick, which is more than 20 per-cent of the total number of recipes. According to the modern editor of the cookbook, these recipes fall into "four general categories: those that are based on certain cereal grains or legumes, those that are based on almonds, those that are based on fruits, and those that are based on chicken."[34] If money is no object, a dish to restore one's health, such as the restorative "restaurant" in Chiquart's cookbook, can have the most amazing ingredients. Boiled capon flesh is cooked in a sealed container with rose water liqueur, gold coins, pearls, and a host of pre-cious and semiprecious stones from diamonds, rubies, sapphires, turquoises, emeralds, coral, and amber, to sardonyx, chrysolite, beryl, topaz, chrysoprase, and amethyst. Gold in food preparation had more than the decorative function of gilding, it was also a preferred medi-cine for the rich.[35]

Slightly less costly than the above gem of a dish for the sick were the various white dishes known as *blanc manger* in the Middle Ages. They were both the hallmark of an international upper-class cuisine and a dish for invalids. And this is no coincidence. Many members of the ar-istocracy and high clergy had sedentary lifestyles and digestive systems considered by the medical community as more delicate than that of manual laborers. One food historian has recently referred to the ety-mological connection between the words "dignity" and "dainty" to il-lustrate the point.[36] The rich with their fastidious digestive system had to be given dainty food because that was all their stomachs could han-dle; they were, in other words, sickly even at the best of times. This meant, of course, that the work of the court physician/nutritionist and the cook who were put in charge of managing the dietary needs of these delicate creatures was of utmost importance.

If maintaining one's health as a member of the nobility or high clergy was a challenge in normal times, how much more so was this the case in times of epidemics? When the plague reached Europe in the mid-fourteenth century, the social elite stood to lose a lot more than the lower classes by the calamity. Estates, territories, and whole kingdoms were threatened if the bloodline died out. Needless to say, physicians from the most famous medical schools scrambled to come up with explanations for the contagious disease that ravaged Europe and regimens to help people avoid falling victim to it. In the spring of 1348, shortly after the plague had reached Italy, a medical doctor from Perugia wrote one of the earliest regimens, called *Tractatus de pestilentia* (Treatise on Pestilence). In October of the same year the medical faculty at the famous University of Paris compiled a regimen at the request of the king of France, called the *Compendium de epydimia* (Compendium on Epidemic).[37] Both works attribute the disease to corrupt vapors in the air, which were thought to enter a person's body through the pores of the skin and then travel to the heart, liver, and brain. This came to be known as "miasma theory."[38] The Paris plague treatise contains three theoretical and six prophylactic chapters dealing with the causes of the epidemic, prognostication and signs of the disease, and the non-naturals air, food and drink, sleeping and waking, repletion and excretion, and emotions in times of epidemic. It concludes with a variety of preventive measures, natural remedies, and antidotes. In keeping with the advice for people belonging to the neutral state between sickness and health, the sick, the sickly, and convalescent, the dietary guidelines in times of epidemic advocate light food that is easily digested, such as wheat bread and the meat of lamb, kid, roe-deer, rabbit, chicken, hen, and partridge. Roasting is recommended over boiling to prepare the meat and is mandatory for preparing fish. Great emphasis is put on the use of sauces made from cloves, cubebs, cardamom, galingale, saffron, and cinnamon mixed with vinegar or verjuice. Beef, pork, goat, stag and other coarse meat, dairy products, and fruits were regarded as harmful. The beverages recommended by the Paris physicians include wine, water boiled with vinegar, and barley water. People who suffer from too much humidity in the body are advised to have blood taken from their bodies (bloodletting) and purge the body with diuretics. Simple and composite drugs to ward off the plague include vinegar, garlic, theriac, rose water, and pills made from aloe, myrrh, and saffron.

Gentile da Foligno in his plague regimen recommends castrated animals, lactating animals, fowl, veal, pork, bread, and wine consumed in moderation, as well as bloodletting and purgation to combat excess humidity. He deals extensively with theriac, a compound drug used against poisons of various kinds, and its application. Susceptible not just to the plight of the nobility but to that of the masses who could not afford the foodstuffs and drugs listed by the Paris physicians, da Foligno also provides a poor man's substitute for theriac in the form of garden herbs cooked and drunk with wine, vinegar, or water. Pomanders, which are containers held in the hand and filled with aromatic drugs mixed with resin or amber (called *Pomum ambre* in Latin), were popular with the wealthy, but da Foligno lists two cheaper versions for the poor as well. The *Regimen sanitatis Salernitunum,* which reached wider circles of society than just the rich, contains the following information on poison-fighting agents the average medieval European could afford:

> 86.
>
> Six things, that here in order shall ensue,
>
> Against all poisons have a secret power,
>
> Pear, Garlic, Radish-roots, Nuts, Rape, and Rue,
>
> But Garlic chief; for they that it devour,
>
> May drink, and care not who their drink do brew:
>
> May walk in airs infected every hour.
>
> Sith Garlic then hath powers to save from death,
>
> Bear with it though it make unsavory breath:
>
> And scorn not garlic, like to some that think
>
> It only makes men wink, and drink, and stink.[39]

The degree to which the plague was a concern for physicians and cooks alike can be seen in a manuscript from the mid-fifteenth century that combines a French cookbook known as the *Vivendier* (A Provisioner), and a plague regimen attributed to Master Jacques Despars, whose credentials included chief physician to the king of France and rector of the University of Paris.[40] His guidelines relating to food state that salt, heavily salted meat, strong spices, sauces with onions, leeks, mustard, strong wines, *claret, hippocras,* and all other things that warm the blood should be avoided; likewise all constipating foods, such as unleavened bread, beans, cabbage, pork, beef, stag meat, tripe, sausages, chitterlings, fish, lemon, must (unfermented grape juice), and opaque beverages. He, too, recommends clean light foods, such as good wheaten bread, chicken broth with verjuice and a little saffron, veal broth, pea puree, almond white dish, and purees of beet greens or borage. He further approves of chicken and hen, capon, partridge, pheasant, woodcock, plover, lark, kid, rabbit, mutton, veal, fresh, uncooked eggs, sole, red mullet, pike, perch, dace, crayfish, and currants. Meat and fish should be eaten with a mash of old verjuice grapes and a little vinegar, and cooked in a third of a goblet of the same. The preferred drink should be a little French white wine or *claret*, much diluted with boiled water.[41]

With the vast majority of nutritional advice geared toward the thin upper crust of medieval society, it was not until the Renaissance that doctors turned their attention to the health care and nutritional needs of the poor. In the mid-sixteenth century the Montpellier physician Jacques Dubois, also known as Sylvius, published several regimens for the poor and for plague and famine victims. Dubois follows medieval medical doctrine with his statement that people engaged in heavy physical labor have different dietary needs from those with a more sedentary lifestyle, in which category he counts the nobility and intellectuals. Coarse food is recommended for day laborers, peasants, artisans, and journeymen, and easily digestible delicate food for the rich, for bureaucrats and scholars.[42]

In accordance with humoral pathology, the leisure class is advised to stay away from cold, humid food such as dairy foods, cheese, fish, and various fruits and vegetables. Food that heats and dries the body is equally bad, and so are leeks, onions, garlic, chives, mustard, salt, and smoked meat, dry vegetables, lentils, peas, and beans. Pork is preferable to beef. Other recommended foods are white bread, the meat of birds, veal that is fried rather than boiled, fresh eggs, and tangy fruits such as oranges, lemons, cherries, quinces, and black currants. Clear wine and not beer should be the beverage of choice.

For the poor, of course, it is not a question of choice. They have to eat whatever they can find to stay alive. And the foods Dubois lists were generally regarded as heavy and coarse, which, of course, medieval physicians had recommended for laborers in the first place. The cookery of the poor, according to the sixteenth-century author, consists mainly of gruel, soups, and ragouts whose main ingredient is bread. Cheaper types of bread included barley, rye, and oat breads, and in times of famine, breads from ground rice, beans, millet, chestnuts, bran, or any other edible plant. The bread is cooked in water with butter, stock, cow's milk, cider, cabbage, or beer. Dubois does recommend some herbs, especially those cultivated in Europe, such as rosemary, sage, hyssop, savory, thyme, marjoram, and the leaves and seeds of the laurel tree. They are to be used ground and in spice mixes.

Soups or potages are made with herbs, squash, cucumbers, onions, leeks, turnips, and other common tubers, as well as lard, beef, tripe, and cheap inner organs like liver, kidney, spleen, and heart. Tough pieces are pounded and put in water mixed with vinegar, powdered spices, and bread. Dubois maintains that this is good food for hardworking people. Furthermore, cartilage, soft bones, tendons, and nerves, pounded and well cut are acceptable ingredients. Thick and sticky ragouts with ingredients such as testicles, milk, sour milk, or bread soaked in milk are also for the lower classes. All the animals and birds peasants and townspeople can catch are edible, he claims, among them dogs, cats, rats, foxes, donkeys, crows, barn owls, magpies, kites, starlings, and any other birds that are young and supple. Tough birds, such as ringdoves, are to be parboiled in water, then cooked with herbs or cabbage. Also listed as edible foods by Dubois are snails, earthworms, ring snakes, and frogs. The latter are to be cleaned, washed, and fried in butter or oil with a little bread or flour. For lean days he recommends herring, fresh cod, squid, oysters (for instance, cooked in salted butter), and salted salmon. When it comes to drink, he concedes that wine is too expensive and therefore advises the poor to drink other fermented drinks, such as beer, cider, pear must, apple juice, pear juice, other juices made from wild berries, or water boiled and flavored with a little honey, sugar, grapes, licorice, vinegar, or bran, yeast, bread, or an assortment of herbs and spices, beer, cider, or pear must, or water mixed with tartar (acid sediment deposited during fermentation) of good strong wine.

Regarding poor intellectuals, medieval and Renaissance medicine faced a dilemma. On the one hand, their bodies were considered incapable of digesting the coarse food of the hardworking peasants due to their sedentary lifestyle, but on the other their modest incomes made it impossible for these individuals to indulge in the fine foods of the leisure class. Dubois suggests starting the day with gruel made from rye bread, wheat bread if possible, or cereals such as barley, oats, rice, or millet prepared with a little fat, lard, butter, or oil. Water mixed with a little vinegar, cow's milk, or beer makes for a cheap beverage. In cold weather spices can be mixed in whose humor adds heat to the beverage. Gruel with cheese, and the veins of liver are to be avoided. Starving students can appease their hunger with vegetable soup, or with cod or other cheap fish that can be smoked for flavor. Fresh eggs are a good staple, and for dessert Dubois lists boiled or roasted chestnuts, almonds, hazelnuts, prunes, raisins, dry figs, or fruits fried in butter. Pastries are too expensive and unhealthy anyway, he maintains. Moderately priced light wine is the ideal drink, but fermented drinks like those recommended for the poor in general are also acceptable. Compared to the peasants and urban poor, intellectuals such as students, underpaid or underemployed solicitors, notaries, and even professors and physicians had much less choice in their diet if they wanted to follow the medical advice of the time, since their bodies required dainty luxury foods that were largely incompatible with their financial situation.

NOTES

1. For information on the medieval medical system, see Nancy G. Siraisi, *Medieval and Early Renaissance Medicine: An Introduction to Knowledge and Practice* (Chicago: University of Chicago Press, 1990).

2. The following brief overview of the development of the theory of the four humors is based on Melitta Weiss Adamson, *Medieval Dietetics: Food and Drink in Regimen Sanitatis Literature from 800 to 1100* (Frankfurt am Main: Peter Lang, 1995), 10–15; more detailed studies on the humoral system are, for instance, Erich Schöner, *Das Viererschema in der antiken Humoralpathologie* (Wiesbaden: Franz Steiner, 1964); and Klaus Schönfeldt, "Die Temperamentenlehre in deutschsprachigen Handschriften des 15. Jahrhunderts" (diss., University of Heidelberg, 1962).

3. See Adamson, *Medieval Dietetics,* 16–18; and the in-depth study by Georg Harig, *Bestimmung der Intensität im medizinischen System Galens* (Berlin: Akademie-Verlag, 1975).

4. For an English translation of the latter see Mark Grant, *Galen on Food and Diet* (London: Routledge, 2000).

5. The English translation of the passage in Haly Abbas is contained in Manfred Ullmann, *Islamic Medicine* (Edinburgh: Edinburgh University Press, 1978), 100.

6. See Melitta Weiss Adamson, "The Greco-Roman World," in *Regional Cuisines of Medieval Europe: A Book of Essays,* ed. Melitta Weiss Adamson (New York: Routledge, 2002), 5.

7. For information on the history and contents of the *Liber pantegni* see Adamson, *Medieval Dietetics,* 42–49.

8. J. Berendes, trans., *Des Pedanios Dioskorides aus Anazarbos Arzneimittellehre in fünf Büchern* (Stuttgart: Ferdinand Enke, 1902; repr. Wiesbaden: Martin Sändig, 1970).

9. Adamson, *Medieval Dietetics,* 83–91; Louisa Cogliati Arano, ed., *The Medieval Health Handbook: Tacuinum Sanitatis,* trans. Oscar Ratti and Adele Westbrook (New York: George Braziller, 1976); and Franz Unterkircher, ed. and trans., *Das Hausbuch der Cerruti: Nach der Handschrift in der Österreichischen Nationalbibliothek* (Dortmund: Harenberg Kommunikation, 1979).

10. Arano, *Tacuinum Sanitatis,* 67; the *Tacuinum* together with illustrations can be found on the Internet; see http://www.godecookery.com/tacuin/tacuin.htm.

11. For the diagram in Latin see Adamson, *Medieval Dietetics,* 196; the English translation is my own.

12. C. G. Kühn, ed., *Galienus: Opera Omnia* (=*Medicorum Graecorum Opera quae exstant,* vols. l–20), vol. 11 (Leipzig 1821–33; repr. Hildesheim: Olms, 1964–65), 887; the English translation is my own.

13. Avicenna, *Liber Canonis* (Venice 1507; repr. Hildesheim: Olms, 1966), Liber II, *lactuca,* 131rb–131va.

14. Anita Feyl, "Das Kochbuch Meister Eberhards: Ein Beitrag zur altdeutschen Fachliteratur" (diss., Freiburg im Breisgau, 1963) 93; and Julius Arndt, ed., *Meister Sebastian: Koch und Kellermeisterey* (Frankfurt am Main: Sigmund Feyrabend, 1581; facsimile repr., Stuttgart: Steingrüben, 1964), fol. 44r.

15. Wolfram Schmitt, "Theorie der Gesundheit und 'Regimen sanitatis' im Mittelalter" (Habilitationsschrift, Heidelberg, 1973).

16. For a brief history of the six non-naturals see Adamson, *Medieval Dietetics,* 18–21.

17. The contents of 23 medieval Latin and German *Regimen sanitutis* texts can be found in Adamson, *Medieval Dietetics,* 39–190.

18. Ibid., 142–50; for a study and edition of Konrad's Latin regimen and later versions in Latin and German see Christa Hagenmeyer, *Das Regimen Sanitutis Konrads van Eichstätt: Quellen-Texte-Wirkungsgeschichte* (Stuttgart: Franz Steiner, 1995). The following is a brief summary of the information on food and drink in Konrad's popular regimen.

19. Adamson, *Medieval Dietetics,* 196f. et passim.

20. Ibid., 89f.

21. The total number of recipes is 11, but 1 is repeated; see Adamson, *Medieval Dietetics,* 147f.

22. For a brief history of the *Secretum secretorum,* see Adamson, *Medieval Dietetics,* 50–56, and of the *Regimen sanitatis Salernitunum,* ibid., 97–102.

23. The complete translation is available on the Internet; see http://user.icx.net/~richmond/rsr/ajax/harington.html.

24. For the following see Melitta Weiss-Amer [Adamson], "Medieval Women's Guides to Food During Pregnancy: Origins, Texts, and Traditions." *Canadian Bulletin of Medical History* 10 (1993): 5–23.

25. Heinz H. Menge, ed., *Das 'Regimen' Heinrich Laufenbergs: Textologische Untersuchung und Edition* (Göppingen: Kümmerle, 1976); and Melitta Weiss-Amer [Adamson], "Dietetics of Pregnancy: A Fifteenth-Century Perspective," *Fifteenth-Century Studies* 19 (1992): 301–18.

26. Menge, *Das 'Regimen' Heinrich Laufenbergs,* 364–70.

27. The following is a brief summary of Laufenberg's food recommendations in ibid., 377–91; see also Melitta Weiss Adamson, "Baby-Food in the

Middle Ages," in *Nurture: Proceedings of the 2003 Oxford Symposium on Food & Cookery* (2004, forthcoming).

28. See Wolfram Schmitt, "Bartholomäus Scherrenmüllers Gesundheitsregimen (1493) für Graf Eberhard im Bart" (Med. diss., University of Heidelberg, 1970), 53.

29. Philipp Gavitt, *Charity and Children in Renaissance Florence: the Ospidale degli Innocenti 1410–1536* (Ann Arbor: University of Michigan Press, 1990).

30. The following dietary advice is contained in a regimen for old people (*De regimine senum*) written by an Italian physician of the fifteenth century and based on the writings of Avicenna; see Luigi Belloni, ed., *Antonii Benivienii De Regimine Sanitatis Ad Laurentium Medicem* (Turin: Publicazione della Società Italiana di Patologia in occasione del II. Congresso, 8–10 Giugno, 1951), 49f.

31. See fol. 44v of the Vienna manuscript of the *Tacuinum* in Unterkircher, *Das Hausbuch der Cerruti,* 87; Arano, *Tacuinum Sanitatis,* 77.

32. Terence Scully, *The Art of Cookery in the Middle Ages* (Woodbridge, U.K.: Boydell Press, 1995), 188.

33. Terence Scully, ed., *The Viandier of Taillevent: An Edition of All Extant Manuscripts* (Ottawa: University of Ottawa Press, 1988), 290f.

34. Scully, *The Art of Cookery,* 193; for an English translation of the cookbook, see Terence Scully, trans., *Chiquart's "On Cookery": A Fifteenth-Century Savoyard Culinary Treatise* (New York: Peter Lang, 1986).

35. See Scully, *The Art of Cookery,* 194.

36. Ibid., 191f.

37. For the following information on plague treatises, see Melitta Weiss Adamson, "Preventive Medicine in Fourteenth-Century Würzburg: The Evidence in Michael de Leone's *Hausbuch,*" in *Ir sult sprechen willekomen: Festschrift für Helmut Birkhan zum 60. Geburtstag,* eds. Christa Tuczay, Ulrike Hirhager, and Karin Lichtblau (Frankfurt am Main: Peter Lang, 1998), 511–14.

38. For miasma theory see Fielding H. Garrison, *An Introduction to the History of Medicine,* 4th edition (Philadelphia: Saunders, 1929), 189.

39. The text is found on the Internet; see http://user.icx.net/~richmond/rsr/ajax/harington.html.

40. Terence Scully, ed., *The Vivendier: A Critical Edition with English Translation* (Totnes, U.K.: Prospect Books, 1997); 12.

41. For the above guidelines on nutrition see ibid., 123.

42. The following is based on Jean Dupebe, "La diététique et l'alimentation des pauvres selon Sylvius," in *Pratiques et Discours Alimentaires à la Renaissance: Actes du colloque de Tours de mars 1979, Centre d'études supérieures de la Renaissance,* eds. Jean-Claude Margolin and Robert Sauzet (Paris: G.-P. Maisonneuve et Larose, 1982), 40–56, esp. 41–50.

CONCLUSION

Medieval food culture, like medieval society, was hierarchical in nature. The limited resources of the peasants meant that their main cooking facility was the stewpot over the fire, and this in turn meant that soups and potages were their regular fare. The higher up the social ladder, the more sophisticated the kitchen equipment, the more specialized the staff, and the more diversified the menu became. At the medieval banquet the political power structure was transferred directly to the table. Status determined where one was seated, how new the tablecloth was and how far away the salt was, how many people one had to share one's food with, how many dishes one partook in, how big one's overall food intake was, and whether one was allowed to taste the most luxurious food creations or just to marvel at them. The poor, standing on the sidelines and watching the spectacle (if they were lucky), had to make do with the leftovers handed to them by the almoner, the official dispenser of alms. Not just a seat at the table separated the haves from the have-nots, the cultured from the boors, but the all-important mastery of table manners.

Christianity was the main religion in medieval Europe, and this meant that the year was divided into meat days, lean days, and the occasional feast day such as Christmas or Easter when rich and poor tried to splurge. Judging from the upper-class cookbooks and menus that we have, it was substantially more pleasant to endure the food deprivations during Lent as an aristocrat or bishop than as a peasant or monk. In fact, with the various imitation meat dishes the cooks of the nobility invented, one could almost convince oneself it was not Lent at all. It was in the big medieval cities, such as Paris, London, Venice, and Florence, that cookshops first catered to the needs of the busy urban dweller. Pies, roasted birds, standard sauces, waffles, and confections were all available to the discerning consumer planning a fancy meal. Taverns and alehouses, too, often served more than liquid refreshments to the patrons.

When we look at the way food was prepared in the later Middle Ages, what stands out is a predilection for color, spices, shapes, fine texture, a sweet-and-sour taste, and drama, lots of drama. If medieval cooks had had access to our modern food processors, they would have had a field day. Instead, kitchen staff spent hours and hours pounding ingredients in a mortar, or straining them through a sieve cloth to achieve the desired fineness that allowed for the perfect coloring or shaping of a dish. Spices, the more exotic and costly the better, were used extensively, both for their taste and their colors, and so were sugar and almonds, the two main ingredients in marzipan, a sweetmeat already popular in medieval times. To counteract the sweetness of a dish, wine, vinegar, or that tart juice of unripe fruits known as "verjuice" were frequently added. This seems to suggest that sweet-and-sour was the preferred taste in food. And then there were the food theatrics, peacocks, swans, and pheasants cooked and redressed in their plumage and made to breathe fire, pies filled with live birds, or boar's head colored in green and gold, to name just a few. Playing with food, far from being discouraged, was elevated to an art in aristocratic circles. So popular were these surprise dishes, they even had their own set place in the sequence of a fancy meal: after the fruits, potages, and roasts, and before dessert, cheese, and breath mints in France, for example.

Italy was already fond of pasta then and managed to export this fondness all the way to Britain, from whence comes the oldest surviving recipe for ravioli. By far the biggest innovations in medieval cookery came from contacts with the Arab world. A whole host of foodstuffs, from spinach to eggplants and oranges, they introduced to Europe, along with a variety of cooking techniques, dishes, and dish names. If there is one thing broad-based studies on the culture of food make clear, it is that internationalization is not a modern concept. Since time immemorial food has traveled. Some plants and animals not indigenous to Europe had already arrived in prehistoric times, while others were introduced by Alexander the Great and his army, or by the Romans as their empire expanded westward. And when the Arab influence on European food and cookery began to wane in the later Middle Ages, Columbus set out in search of spices and accidentally discovered the New World. What he initiated was a two-way transfer of plants and animals so grand that historians even gave it a name: the "Columbian exchange." It added tomato sauce to Italian pasta, potatoes to Irish stew, and helped transform medieval food into our food of today.

GLOSSARY

adafina   traditional Hispano-Jewish and Arab dish cooked overnight

blanc manger   white dish usually made from the meat of chicken or fish, rice, almond milk, and sugar

boutehors   piced wine and spiced sweetmeats to aid digestion, served after dinner in another room

cameline   a camel-colored sauce made with cinnamon

claret   spiced and strained wine

codignac   a quince paste

comfits   sugar-coated seeds of anise, fennel, caraway, etc., eaten at the end of a meal

dais   raised platform in the great hall for the lord and special guests

entremets   French term for surprise dish (*sotelty*) served between courses; in the fifteenth century also for nonedible dinner entertainment

escabèche   spicy marinade used to season and preserve fried fish

frumenty   a dish made from hulled wheat, milk, sugar, and spices

GLOSSARY

galentine jelly

hippocras spiced wine drunk at the end of a meal

humors the four bodily fluids, blood, yellow bile, black bile, and phlegm

malmsey a strong, sweet wine named after the Greek port of Monemvasia

mazer shallow wooden drinking vessel

messe a serving of food, a course of dishes

nef a saltcellar in the shape of a ship

pasty a meat pie baked without a dish

porrey stewed vegetables

potage thick, often creamy, soup

regimen sanitatis health book outlining a healthy lifestyle with regard to air, food and drink, sleep, exercise, excretions, and emotional well-being

sops pieces of bread dunked in wine or other liquid

sotelty a surprise dish

stockfish halved and dried cod

theriac compound drug containing dozens of ingredients that were pulverized and mixed with honey; used as an antidote against poison and the plague

torte a pie made from edible shortcrust pastry

trencher a piece of bread used as an edible plate

Turk's Head a dessert of Arab ancestry in the shape of a human head

voider vessel for collecting table scraps

SUGGESTED FURTHER READINGS

CHAPTER 1

Arano, Luisa Cogliati. *The Medieval Health Handbook (Tacuinum Sanitatis)*. Translated and adapted by Oscar Ratti and Adele Westbrook. New York: George Braziller, 1976.

Bennett, Judith M. *Ale, Beer and Brewsters in England: A Women's Work in a Changing World, 1300–1600*. New York: Oxford University Press, 1996.

Dalby, Andrew. *Siren Feasts: A History of Food and Gastronomy in Greece*. London: Routledge, 1996.

———. *Dangerous Tastes: The Story of Spices*. Berkeley and Los Angeles: University of California Press, 2000.

Davidson, Alan. *The Oxford Companion to Food*. Oxford, U.K.: Oxford University Press, 1999.

Flandrin, Jean-Louis, and Massimo Montanari, eds. *Food: A Culinary History from Antiquity to the Present*. Translated by Albert Sonnenfeld. New York: Penguin Books, 2000.

Flower, Barbara, and Elisabeth Rosenbaum, trans. *The Roman Cookery Book: A Critical Translation of "The Art of Cooking" by Apicius for Use in the Study and the Kitchen*. London: George G. Harrap, 1958.

Freeman, Margaret B. *Herbs for the Medieval Household: For Cooking, Healing and Divers Uses*. New York: Metropolitan Museum of Art, 1943.

Gies, Francis and Joseph. *Cathedral, Forge, and Waterwheel: Technology and Invention in the Middle Ages*. New York: HarperCollins, 1994.

Katz, Solomon H., ed. *Encyclopedia of Food and Culture*. New York: Scribner, 2003.

Kiple, Kenneth F., and Kriemhild Coneè Ornelas. *The Cambridge World History of Food*. Cambridge, U.K.: Cambridge University Press, 2000.

Larousse Gastronomique. New York: Clarkson Potter, 2001.

The Oxford English Dictionary. 2nd edition. Prepared by J.A. Simpson and E.S.C. Weiner. 20 vols. Oxford, U.K.: Clarendon Press, 1989.

Stuckey, Maggie. *The Complete Spice Book*. New York: St. Martin's Griffin, 1999.

Throop, Priscilla, trans. *Hildegard von Bingen's Physica: The Complete English Translation of Her Classic Work on Health and Healing*. Rochester, Vt.: Healing Arts Press, 1998.

Toussaint-Samat, Maguelonne. *A History of Food*. Translated by Anthea Bell. Cambridge, Mass.: Blackwell, 1992.

Trager, James. *The Food Chronology: A Food Lover's Compendium of Events and Anecdotes, from Prehistory to the Present*. New York: Henry Holt, 1995.

White, Eileen. *Feeding a City: York. The Provision of Food from Roman Times to the Beginning of the Twentieth Century*. Totnes, U.K.: Prospect Books, 2000.

CHAPTER 2

Adamson, Melitta Weiss. *Food in the Middle Ages: A Book of Essays*. New York: Garland, 1995.

Black, Maggie. *The Medieval Cookbook*. London: British Museum Press, 1996.

Brears, Peter, Maggie Black, Gill Corbishley, Jane Renfrew, and Jennifer Stead, eds. *A Taste of Britain: 10,000 Years of Food in Britain*. London: English Heritage in association with British Museum Press, 1993.

Gies, Joseph and Frances. *Life in a Medieval Castle*. New York: Harper & Row, 1979.

———. *Life in a Medieval City*. New York: Harper & Row, 1981.

———. *Life in a Medieval Village*. New York: HarperPerennial, 1991.

Hammond, P.W. *Food and Feast in Medieval England*. Stroud, U.K.: Alan Sutton, 1993.

Henisch, Bridget Ann. *Fast and Feast: Food in Medieval Society*. University Park: Pennsylvania State University Press, 1976.

Montanari, Massimo. *The Culture of Food*. Translated by Carl Ipsen. Oxford, U.K.: Blackwell, 1994.

Scully, Terence. *The Art of Cookery in the Middle Ages*. Woodbridge, U.K.: Boydell Press, 1995.

Wheaton, Barbara Ketcham. *Savoring the Past: French Kitchen and Table from 1300 to 1789*. Philadelphia: University of Pennsylvania Press, 1983.

Wilson, C. Anne, ed. *'The Appetite and the Eye': Visual Aspects of Food and Its Presentation within Their Historic Context*. Edinburgh: Edinburgh University Press, 1991.

CHAPTER 3

Adamson, Melitta Weiss. *Daz buoch von guoter spise (The Book of Good Food): A Study, Edition, and English Translation of the Oldest German Cookbook.* Sonderband 9. Krems, Austria: *Medium Aevum Quotidianum,* 2000.

———, ed. *Regional Cuisines of Medieval Europe: A Book of Essays.* New York: Routledge, 2002.

Arberry, A. J., trans. "A Baghdad Cookery Book," *Islamic Culture* 13 (1939): 21–47 and 189–214.

Bayard, Tania, trans. and ed. *A Medieval Home Companion: Housekeeping in the Fourteenth Century.* New York: HarperCollins, 1991.

Dembińska, Maria. *Food and Drink in Medieval Poland: Rediscovering a Cuisine of the Past.* Translated by Magdalena Thomas. Revised and adapted by William Woys Weaver. Philadelphia: University of Pennsylvania Press, 1999.

Flandrin, Jean-Louis, and Carole Lambert. *Fêtes Gourmandes au Moyen Âge.* Paris: Imprimerie nationale éditions, 1998.

Grewe, Rudolf, ed. *Libre de Sent Soví: Receptari de cuina.* Barcelona: Editorial Barcino, 1979.

Grewe, Rudolf, and Constance B. Hieatt, eds. and trans. *Libellus de arte coquinaria: An Early Northern Cookery Book.* Tempe: Arizona Center for Medieval and Renaissance Studies, 2001.

Hagen, Ann. *A Handbook of Anglo-Saxon Food: Processing and Consumption.* Pinner, Middlesex: Anglo-Saxon Books, 1992.

———. *A Second Handbook of Anglo-Saxon Food and Drink: Production and Distribution.* Pinner, Middlesex: Anglo-Saxon Books, 1995.

Hieatt, Constance B. *An Ordinance of Pottage: An Edition of the Fifteenth Century Recipes in Yale University's MS Beinecke 163.* London: Prospect Books, 1988.

Hieatt, Constance B., and Sharon Butler, eds. *Curye on Inglysch: English Culinary Manuscripts of the Fourteenth Century (Including the Forme of Cury).* Early English Text Society, S. S. 8. London: Oxford University Press, 1985.

Hieatt, Constance B., Brenda Hosington, and Sharon Butler. *Pleyn Delit: Medieval Cookery for Modern Cooks.* 2nd edition Toronto: University of Toronto Press, 1996.

Lambert, Carole, ed. *Du manuscrit à la table: Essais sur la cuisine au Moyen Âge et répertoire des manuscrits médiévaux contenant des recettes culinaires.* Montréal: Presses de l'Université de Montréal, 1992.

Laszlovsky, József. *Tender Meat under the Saddle: Customs of Eating, Drinking and Hospitality among Conquering Hungarians and Nomadic People. In memoriam Guyla Lázló (1910–1998).* Sonderband 7. Krems, Austria: *Medium Aevum Quotidianum,* 1998.

Leimgruber, Veronika, ed. *Mestre Robert, Libre del Coch: Tractat de cuina medieval.* Barcelona: Curial Catalanes, 1977.

Milham, Mary Ella, ed. and trans. *Platina: On Right Pleasure and Good Health: A Critical Edition and Translation of De honesta voluptate et valetudine.* Tempe, Ariz.: Medieval and Renaissance Texts and Studies, 1998.

Perry, Charles, ed. *Medieval Arab Cookery.* Totnes, U.K.: Prospect Books, 2001.

Power, Eileen, trans. *The Goodman of Paris (Le Ménagier de Paris): A Treatise on Moral and Domestic Economy by a Citizen of Paris (c. 1393).* London: G. Routledge, 1928.

Redon, Odile, Françoise Sabban, and Silvano Serventi. *The Medieval Kitchen: Recipes from France and Italy.* Translated by Edward Schneider. Chicago: University of Chicago Press, 1998.

Santich, Barbara. *The Original Mediterranean Cuisine: Medieval Recipes for Today.* Kent Town, Australia: Wakefield Press, 1997.

Sass, Lorna J. *To the King's Taste: Richard II's Book of Feasts and Recipes Adapted for Modern Cooking.* New York: Metropolitan Museum of Art, 1975.

Scully, D. Eleanor, and Terence Scully. *Early French Cookery: Sources, History, Original Recipes and Modern Adaptations.* Ann Arbor: University of Michigan Press, 1996.

Scully, Terence, ed. *The Viandier of Taillevent: An Edition of All Extant Manuscripts.* Ottawa: University of Ottawa Press, 1988.

———, ed. *The Vivendier: A Critical Edition with English Translation.* Totnes, U.K.: Prospect Books, 1997.

———, ed. *The Neapolitan Recipe Collection: Cuoco Napoletano.* Ann Arbor: University of Michigan Press, 2000.

———, trans. *Chiquart's 'On Cookery': A Fifteenth-Century Savoyard Culinary Treatise.* New York: Peter Lang, 1986.

Serventi, Silvano, and Françoise Sabban. *Pasta: The Story of a Universal Food.* Translated by Antony Shugaar. New York: Columbia University Press, 2002.

CHAPTER 4

Bober, Phyllis Pray. *Art, Culture, and Cuisine: Ancient and Medieval Gastronomy.* Chicago: University of Chicago Press, 1999.

Brett, Gerard. *Dinner Is Served: A Study in Manners.* Hamden, Conn.: Archon Books, 1969.

Camporesi, Piero. *Bread of Dreams: Food and Fantasy in Early Modern Europe.* Translated by David Gentilcore. Chicago: University of Chicago Press, 1989.

Carlin, Martha, and Joel T. Rosenthal. *Food and Eating in Medieval Europe.* London: Hambledon Press, 1998.

Cosman, Madeleine Pelner. *Fabulous Feasts: Medieval Cookery and Ceremony.* New York: George Braziller, 1976.

Elias, Norbert. *The Civilizing Process: The Development of Manners: Changes in the Code of Conduct and Feeling in Early Modern Times.* Translated by Edmund Jephcott. New York: Urizen Books, 1982.

Furnivall, Frederick James, ed. *Early English meals and manners: John Russell's Boke of nurture, Wynkyn de Worde's Boke of keruynge, The boke of curtasye, R. Weste's Booke of demeanor, Seager's Schoole of vertue, The babees book, Aristotle's A B C, Urbanitatis, Stans puer ad mensam, The lytille childrenes lytil boke, for to serve a lord, Old Symon, The birched school-boy, &c. &c.: with some forewords on education in early England.* London: N. Trübner, 1868; repr. Detroit: Singing Tree Press, 1969.

Mollat, Michel. *The Poor in the Middle Ages: An Essay in Social History.* Translated by Arthur Goldhammer. New Haven, Conn.: Yale University Press, 1986.

Paston-Williams, Sara. *The Art of Dining.* London: National Trust, 1993.

Pleij, Herman. *Dreaming of Cockaigne: Medieval Fantasies of the Perfect Life.* Translated by Diane Webb. New York: Columbia University Press, 2001.

Rickert, Edith, and N. J. Naylor. *The Babees' Book: Medieval Manners for the Young, done into modern English from Dr. Furnivall's texts.* New York: Cooper Square, 1966.

Tannahill, Reay. *Food in History.* New York: Crown, 1988.

Wilson, C. Anne. *'Banquetting Stuffe': The Fare and Social Background of the Tudor and Stuart Banquet. Papers from the First Leeds Symposium on Food History and Traditions. April 1986.* Edinburgh: Edinburgh University Press, 1991.

CHAPTER 5

Beardsworth, Alan, and Teresa Keil. *Sociology on the Menu: An Invitation to the Study of Food and Society.* London: Routledge, 1997.

Bell, Rudolph M. *Holy Anorexia.* Chicago: University of Chicago Press, 1985.

Bloomfield, Morton W. *The Seven Deadly Sins: An Introduction to the History of a Religious Concept, with Special Reference to Medieval English Literature.* East Lansing: Michigan State College Press, 1952.

Bynum, Caroline Walker. *Holy Feast and Holy Fast: The Religious Significance of Food to Medieval Women.* Berkeley and Los Angeles: University of California Press, 1987.

Cosman, Madeleine Pelner. *Medieval Holidays and Festivals: A Calendar of Celebrations.* New York: Scribner, 1981.

Douglas, Mary. *Purity and Danger: An Analysis of Concepts of Pollution and Danger.* New York: Praeger Publishers, 1966.

————. *Implicit Meanings: Essays in Anthropology*. Boston: Routledge and Kegan Paul, 1975.

————. *Food in the Social Order: Studies of Food and Festivities in Three American Communities*. New York: Russell Sage Foundation, 1984.

Fernández-Armesto, Ernesto. *Food: A History*. London: Macmillan, 2001.

Fiddes, Nick. *Meat: A Natural Symbol*. London: Routledge, 1991.

Henisch, Bridget Ann. *The Medieval Calendar Year*. University Park: Pennsylvania State University Press, 1999.

Lévi-Strauss, Claude. *The Raw and the Cooked*. Translated by John and Doreen Weightman. London: Cape, 1970.

Magennis, Hugh. *Anglo-Saxon Appetites: Food and Drink and Their Consumption in Old English and Related Literature*. Dublin: Four Courts Press, 1999.

Mintz, Sidney W. *Tasting Food, Tasting Freedom: Excursions into Eating, Culture, and the Past*. Boston: Beacon Press, 1996.

Roden, Claudia. *The Book of Jewish Food: An Odyssey from Samarkand to New York*. New York: Alfred A. Knopf, 1998.

Soler, Jean. "The Semiotics of Food in the Bible." In Robert Forster and Orest Ranum, *Food and Drink in History: Selections from the Annales–Economies, Sociétés, Civilisations*. Vol. 5. Translated by Elborg Forster and Patricia M. Ranum. Baltimore: Johns Hopkins University Press, 1979, 126–38.

Spencer, Colin. *The Heretic's Feast: A History of Vegetarianism*. London: Fourth Estate, 1993.

CHAPTER 6

Adamson, Melitta Weiss. *Medieval Dietetics: Food and Drink in Regimen Sanitatis Literature from 800 to 1400*. Frankfurt am Main: Peter Lang, 1995.

Albala, Ken. *Eating Right in the Renaissance*. Berkeley and Los Angeles: University of California Press, 2002.

Copland, Robert, trans. *Aristotle: Secretum secretorum. English*. Amsterdam: Theatrum Orbis Terrarum, 1970.

Fieldhouse, Paul. *Food and Nutrition: Customs and Culture*. 2nd edition London: Chapman & Hall, 1995.

Harington, Sir John. *The School of Salernum: Regimen Sanitatis Salerni, The English Version*. Salerno: Ente Provinciale Per Il Turismo, 1959.

Siraisi, Nancy G. *Medieval and Early Renaissance Medicine: An Introduction to Knowledge and Practice*. Chicago: University of Chicago Press, 1990.

Ullmann, Manfred. *Islamic Medicine*. Edinburgh: Edinburgh University Press, 1978.

SUBJECT INDEX

RECIPE INDEX

About the Author

MELITTA WEISS ADAMSON is Professor of Modern Languages and Literatures at the University of Western Ontario.